JANE AND MICHAEL STERN

LYONS PRESS
Guilford, Connecticut

An imprint of Globe Pequot Press

Lyons Press is an imprint of Globe Pequot Press.

Project editor: David Legere
Text design: Sheryl P. Kober
Layout artist: Melissa Evarts

Photos by Michael Stern unless otherwise noted.

Library of Congress Cataloging-in-Publication Data is available on file.

ISBN 978-0-7627-6094-7

Printed in the United States of America

10 9 8 7 6 5 4 3 2 1

ACKNOWLEDGMENTS

Our deepest thanks go to the restaurateurs, waiters and waitresses, cooks and chefs, pit-masters, pie bakers, pastrami slicers, chocolatiers, and chili wizards who uphold American culinary tradition. Without these people, and without the adventurous eaters eager to support and savor their efforts, America could be a land of nothing but soul-killing Happy (NOT) Meals.

Over a decade ago when Stephen Rushmore conceived Roadfood.com, we never imagined it would become such a lively community of food lovers and a source of endless inspiration for us as we continue to explore the American food landscape. We are grateful to Stephen, to Roadfood team members Bruce Bilmes and Sue Boyle, Chris Ayers and Amy Briesch, Tony Baldamenti, Marc Bruno, and of course Big Steve Rushmore, as well as to all the good-food tipsters, restaurant reviewers, trip reporters, eat-n-greet organizers, and opinionated foodies who make Roadfood.com a daily unfolding adventure.

One of the most enjoyable ways we communicate our cross-country food adventures is to report about them weekly on Public Radio's "The Splendid Table." There is nobody more delicious to chat with than host Lynne Rossetto Kasper; and thanks to Sally Swift and Jen and Jen, the conversation flows like soft butter on a hot biscuit.

We've been writing long enough to say with assurance that book publishing has pretty much gone to hell in a hand basket. But there are some wonderful exceptions to its meanness; and we are fortunate enough to have worked with them as we created this lexicon. Our agent, Doe Coover, remains a steady hand who is always helpful, encouraging, and focused. Our editor, Mary Norris, and the folks at Globe Pequot Press demonstrate daily that creating a book still can be a process where intelligence, dignity, and kindness prevail.

INTRODUCTION

American food, like the population that eats it, is wildly diverse. From crab cakes to cupcakes and from whoopie pie to chicken booyah, our cuisine is brash, irreverent, and always changing. Its energy comes from wave after wave of immigrants, as well as from a spirit of reckless creativity that can be as corporate as the Massachusetts fluffernutter or as down-home as Kentucky burgoo. Mutable as it is, the country's culinary hall of fame is also enamored of tradition. Consider styles of barbecue indigenous to Texas and the Carolinas or shrimp De Jonghe in Chicago or date shakes around the Salton Sea: All are dishes from decades past, unaffected by fashion or whimsy.

Since we started researching the first edition of *Roadfood* in the early 1970s, we have polished off tens of thousands of meals alongside all sorts of citizens, from stockbrokers in pinstripes to stock brokers in overalls (the stock being cattle), in restaurants that range from lace-doily tearooms to lumberjack mess halls. In that time, we have learned a thing or two about real American food. To be clear, by "real American" we do not mean some pure and inviolable cuisine that is this nation's alone. We are happy to report that there is no such thing.

Travel from Frenchville, Maine, to Calexico, California, and you'll find almost nothing to eat that is unadulterated American, except for such obscure native dishes as Navajo nok-qui-vi (mutton stew) in Monument Valley and jonnycakes (griddle-cooked corn bread) around Narragansett Bay. American cuisine is made up of hundreds of different cuisines. Cooks feel free to borrow ingredients and techniques from all over the world and to invent dishes with no precedent anywhere. If you doubt that, consider the recent popularity of Korean tacos in Los Angeles or the all-American chili dog: a wiener (originally German) topped with Greek-accented Tex-Mex chili and frequently called a *Coney Island,* except in upstate New York, where it is inexplicably named a *Michigan,* and in Rhode Island, where it is called a *New York System.* In West Virginia, expect your chili dog to be topped with coleslaw; in Tucson, it comes wrapped in bacon.

Whether you see the national diet as a melting pot or a smorgasbord, as something to be celebrated for its cultural diversity or fretted over for its worrisome homogenization, the fact is that ours is a cuisine that has always been happy to hyphenate with the rest of the world. Ergo chop suey, cioppino, and chimichangas. Consider pizza, once an exotic Italian flatbread and now as mainstream as a cheeseburger. The simple Neapolitan tomato pies that appeared in Northeastern cities' Italian neighborhoods early in the twentieth century have been recast in all kinds of ways, some pretty silly (dessert pizza, anyone?). But visit New Haven for a white clam pizza strewn with tiny, tender littlenecks and a hailstorm of garlic—a 1950s innovation—and it seems ludicrous to contend that culinary miscegenation is a bad thing.

The American food described herein is democratic, not elitist. Rarified meals created by ambitious chefs who earn important critics' benediction can be a taste-buds thrill; they may honor local produce and customs, and in the case of molecular gastronomy, they are fun to look at. But they are no more reflective of the nation's soul than is an atonal avant-garde symphony. Food that is the creation of a uniquely gifted artist/chef, yummy though it may be, seldom means anything other than you will pay a lot of money to eat it. On the other hand, food that is part of everyday life is as fascinating as life itself (and probably a good bargain, too). The real American food of which we write is not a sui generis symphony. It is more like folk music—accessible to all, expressing the personality of the cultures and subcultures that created it more than the talent of an individual creator. America's colloquial cooks may disrespect the rules, but neither are they interested in being cutting-edge.

Our goal is to honor dishes that are part of the fabric of people's lives and are enjoyed at leisure and for celebration meals by friends, families, and communities. Some are relative newcomers, such as the banh mi, aka Saigon sub, and the juicy Lucy of Minneapolis; on the other hand, clambakes and pig pickin's are older than the United States. Some of the entries in this lexicon describe local favorites as obscure as Springfield's unique take on cashew chicken (a Dixie/Chinese/Midwest fusion) and Buffalo's Charlie Chaplin candy. For widely appreciated specialties that don't need a from-scratch definition (like the hamburger) and culinary rituals with which we're all familiar (the salad bar), we have tried to find their origins, enumerate their variations, and highlight their meaning in America's food firmament.

We aim to describe, not to prescribe or to anoint bests. The Platonic ideal for our approach is the inclusive spirit with which H. L. Mencken looked at *The American Language*. We see the nation's diet very much like its language:

sometimes vexing for its vulgarity and its disdain of high-minded principles, but endlessly, endearingly exuberant. Just as our guidebook *Roadfood* celebrates eateries that for so long remained under the radar of the food establishment (though loved by millions), we hope this lexicon encourages a fuller appreciation of our country's irrepressible foodways.

AMERICAN CHOP SUEY

New England great-grandparents might remember **American chop suey** as school lunch or supper at home the day before payday. It is a frugal, homely, hopelessly nerdy dish, completely unlike the region's small repertoire of exotic fare, including fiddlehead ferns, glass eels, and cherrystone ceviche. It is too mundane to ever become trendy, especially considering its dubious genealogy as the penurious cook's knock-off of a discredited pseudo-Chinese dish.

We have seen a recipe in a 1930s cookbook that calls for it to be made with rice, which would explain its Asian moniker, but traditional ingredients are elbow macaroni, ground beef, and tomato sauce: generally, lots of sauce and noodles and just enough beef that the eater doesn't feel too deprived. It is more likely that the name was appropriated because it is a fanciful way to describe a dish of higgledy-piggledy, small-size ingredients. Unlike the déclassé names of such similar mystery meals as slumgullion, cannibal stew, **sloppy joe,** and **garbage plate,** "American chop suey" adds a faintly exotic twist to its plebian ingredients.

It is so ignoble that even hidebound Yankee **diners** and small-town cafes specializing in cheap eats rarely put it on the menu anymore. But you can count on it every Monday at the Wayside Restaurant, between Barre and Montpelier, where it is listed as the "Vermont Special."

Deluxe American Chop Suey

Now, there's an oxymoron for you. By its nature, American chop suey is not deluxe. It is spare and stingy. But several years ago, when we wrote our book *Chili Nation,* we augmented the basic formula with the likes of grated cheese and chow mein noodles and came up with a big bowl of comfort— maybe not quite deluxe, but presentable in polite company. True to the soul of the dish, it is no trouble to make and is easy on the pocketbook.

American chop suey is fusion cuisine: Italian sauce and elbow macaroni, a Chinese name, and Yankee ingenuity.

2 tablespoons cooking oil
⅔ cup diced onion
1 cup diced celery (about 2 ribs)
1 pound lean ground chuck
2 10-ounce cans Ro-Tel Diced Tomatoes and Green Chilies
1 teaspoon ground cumin
1 tablespoon chili powder
1 teaspoon salt
8 ounces elbow macaroni
1 cup grated sharp Cheddar cheese
Chow mein noodles, for garnish

1. Heat the oil in a heavy saucepan, and then sauté the onion and celery until soft. Stir in the beef and cook until brown, breaking it up for a pebbly consistency. Add the Ro-Tel tomatoes and chilies, cumin, chili powder, and salt. Simmer vigorously for 15 minutes or so to reduce the liquid.

2. While the chili simmers, cook the elbow macaroni in boiling salted water until tooth-tender. Drain. Stir the noodles into the beef mixture.

3. Divide chop suey among four bowls and serve piping hot with grated cheese melting on top and chow mein noodles sprinkled atop the cheese.

4 SERVINGS

ANDOUILLE

A coarsely ground, highly spiced, and extremely smoked sausage made by butchers in French-accented Louisiana, **andouille** is a popular ingredient in **gumbo** and **jambalaya**. It is intense enough that it is frequently combined with blander elements: cheese grits or red beans and rice, for example. The Andouille Capital of the World is LaPlace, in St. John the Baptist Parish, just west of New Orleans. The official slogan of LaPlace's annual October andouille festival is "A Smokin' Good Time!"

APIZZA

On the signs of **pizza** parlors throughout southern New England, you will see the word **apizza** where it seems like *pizza* is what's meant. Starting in the 1930s, when bakeries in Italian neighborhoods began to turn their attention to pizza, the *a* was added at the beginning of the word to give it a Neapolitan flavor when spoken. To pronounce it correctly, do not simply add an *a* to the start of the word pizza. The last *a* is always silent and the *p* is treated like a *b*. With a slow-rolling halt at the first syllable and a downward spike on the second, the word is properly pronounced "uh-BEETZ." If you want to get an apizza the way virtually every Connecticut pizzeria made it in the early days, and the way purists still demand it, ask for a tomato-only pie, with perhaps a sprinkling of grated hard cheese. Those in the know call out, "*Uhbeetz, hold the mutz,*" "mutz" being shorthand for mozzarella cheese (known to pizzaioli—pizza makers—as cream cheese in American pizza's early days because of its consistency).

Derby, Connecticut: Roseland Apizza, named for the ballroom in New York, opened in 1935.

Wooster Street, New Haven, Connecticut. Sal Consiglio, cousin of Frank Pepe, opened his own place in 1938.

APPLE PAN DOWDY

Different takes on apple pie abound in Northeastern cookery. One of the oldest is **apple pan dowdy**. Made with the ingredients of apple pie plus molasses, it traditionally is baked in a square pan with crust at the top and bottom. Speculation about the origin of its name runs in two directions: It is *dowdy* meaning "homely," or its crust is *dowdied* (broken into pieces) before it is served. It was pretty well forgotten by the mid-twentieth century in all but the most hidebound kitchens until singer Dinah Shore topped the music charts in 1946 with a novelty song about Pennsylvania Dutch cooking called "**Shoo-Fly Pie and Apple Pan Dowdy**," about which she sang, "Makes your eyes light up and your stomach say howdy." Today virtually any time one sees the recipe in print, its name contains the modifier *old-fashioned*.

BAKERY PIZZA

Less a particular style of **pizza** than a way of serving it, **bakery pizza,** as its name suggests, is pizza served in bakeries. Found mostly in the Northeast and areas of the Midwest, it always is part of a large kitchen repertoire that, of course, includes breads and rolls but usually sweet pastries, too. With rare exceptions, it is rectangular, served by the slice at room temperature, and minimally adorned, with sauce and cheese or sometimes sauce alone. The crust can be either medium or thick (extended shelf tenure makes thin's requisite crispness impossible). Most business is take-out; there is no table service, but many bakeries offer tables at which to sit and eat. A whole bakery pizza is known as a *tray*.

Fall River, Massachusetts: Bakery pizza.

BANH MI

Like the Creole **muffaletta,** the **banh mi** is named after the bread it uses—in this case, a Vietnamese baguette that includes rice flour and sports an especially crisp, fragile crust. To Americans living in places with significant Vietnamese populations, such as Minneapolis, the "Saigon sub," which first was noticed by foodies in the early 1990s, has become increasingly prevalent among available street-food cheap-eats sandwiches. Unlike the muffaletta, it comes in as many diverse configurations as the **hero,** ranging from egg banh mi for breakfast to the classic combo of cold cuts (frequently a version of **pork roll**), pâté, pickled carrot and radish slices, cilantro, and mayonnaise. Hot banh mi include pork, shrimp, or even meatballs.

BARBECUE

Pigs are a prominent motif on barbecue signs throughout the South and Southwest.

Although the casual meaning of the word *barbecue* is to cook anything over an open fire, probably outdoors, serious barbecue aficionados hold the term to a higher standard: cooking by indirect heat. Real barbecue is made in a pit, which simply is a way to contain smoldering coals in one area, with a chimney somewhere else for the smoke to escape and a grate to hold the meat between the two. Hours of basking in hot smoke as it travels from the source to the smokestack turns even tough cuts tender.

Barbecue is also a noun with myriad meanings, including:

♦ A specific food produced by the pit. ("For dinner, we shall eat barbecue, Tater Tots, and beans.")

- ♦ The whole meal. ("Let's go to Bubba's for barbecue.")

- ♦ The place where the meal is served. ("Quick, name your five favorite barbecues in eastern North Carolina.")

- ♦ A party. ("Let's have a barbecue!")

- ♦ A ham sandwich. In eastern Pennsylvania, around Scranton, restaurants serving barbecue, such as Victory Pig in the town of Wyoming, use the term to refer to shaved ham fried in butter, served with sweet relish on a potato-flour bun. Up into New York state, barbecue means ham, turkey, or pork that is sliced and bunned, then topped with sauce. No smoke is involved.

- ♦ **Sloppy joe.** In much of the Midwest, ground beef in sweet tomato sauce is called barbecue.

Hickory wood at Stamey's in Greensboro, North Carolina, before being burnt down to coals that get shoveled into one of twelve huge pits.

Few food words have so many different definitions and no word, except perhaps *chili*, causes partisans to get their shorts twisted into so tight a knot. If you doubt that, just tell a barbecue cognoscente that you have a Hibachi grill on your patio where you like to barbecue the occasional hot dog. He'll have a stroke explaining to you that cooking over direct heat is not only not barbecue but a veritable crime against protein.

The word itself most likely originally was Spanish, from the *barbacoa* grills seventeenth-century explorers encountered in the Caribbean. That word is believed to have come from the Arawak Indian word for a wood frame erected over a fire used to cook or dry meat: *barbicu*. The Spaniards took the term to mean any sort of above-the-ground rack, referring to the sleeping platforms they used to avoid snakebite as *borbecus*. But there are also more colorful tales to explain the source of the word, among them:

- *BBQ* began as shorthand to describe Southern beer parlors with pool tables that had neon signs advertising Bar, Beer, and Ques.

- French explorers described the Caribbean natives' technique of cooking whole hogs as "beard to tail," which in French is *barbe à queue.*

- The Texas cattle rancher Barnaby Quinn was well-known for serving his neighbors meals of cattle cooked over fire pits. Quinn's brand was a straight line above his initials: the Bar B Q brand.

Devoted aficionados say that barbecue is like DNA: No two examples are precisely alike, and each plate contains markers that indicate its exact origin. Beef or pork? Sauced or not? What kind of sauce? Hushpuppies or fries, creamy coleslaw or vinegar slaw?

Geography is a good way to diagram the diversity. Traditional styles reflect specific regions, although as barbecue has become a national passion, that kind of parochial perspective has stopped working so well. It is not at all uncommon to find Texas-style barbecue in New York, Carolina barbecue in Wisconsin, or a Memphis pig sandwich in Miami. Pitmasters move and take their techniques with them, blurring the lines of who eats what where. Most barbecue in the cities of the North and much on the West Coast is Southern or Southwestern style, brought by African Americans who came with recipes from their homes in the South or were inspired by them.

A variety of pit-smoked meat from the great Louie Mueller of Taylor, Texas.

One illustrious example is the late **Arthur Bryant,** the Zeus of Kansas City barbecue. He learned to smoke meat in Texas, thus explaining the goodness of the beef brisket at the legendary Missouri restaurant he and his brother took

The indoor smoke pit at Smitty's in Lockhart, Texas, fills the air with smoke-meat perfume.

over from Henry Perry (originally a Tennessean) in 1940. The much-loved Reo's of Portland, Oregon, still makes hot sauce from peppers retrieved from a particular kind of tree back in ancestral Mississippi. Likewise, one of the great barbecues in West Virginia, Hocutt's Carolina Barbecue, offers pulled pork and hush puppies made from recipes that proprietor Travis Hocutt learned from his Tarheel parents.

The most basic geographic picture is based on meat. Not that these lines aren't blurred, too, but the rule is beef in Texas and the Southwest, pork throughout the South, and mutton in western Kentucky. You'll find plenty of ham and chicken in Arkansas; and true California barbecue is, by definition, beef.

Significant subcategories exist in the Carolinas. Central South Carolina barbecue frequently is flavored with a mustard sauce. North Carolina barbecue comes in at least three significant styles: eastern, where the whole hog gets minimally seasoned with vinegar and pepper spice; Lexington-style, in which shoulders are the cut of choice and sauce tends to be somewhat more important; and western, in the mountains, where thicker, tomato-based sauce becomes significant. And even these subcategories can be further divided, sometimes county by county and town by town.

In a nutshell, America's barbecue is hugely diverse, but it can be divided into five major categories (not counting **ribs,** which are a subject unto themselves). Each has many variations.

1. PULLED PORK

The ultimate way to turn a hunk of Boston butt into a plate of edible ecstasy is to pull the meat apart by hand, carefully separating out any gristle or fat. The result is a hodgepodge of shreds, nuggets, and chunks, those from the inside butter-soft, those from the outside chewy or even a bit crunchy. The method presupposes that the piece of meat in question is tender enough to yield at a gentle tug of the fingers. Depending on the region, pulled pork may be subtly haloed by a vinegar-pepper sauce or bathed in a sweet/hot tomato-based sauce. It tends to be succulent enough that it can come sauceless, giving that option to the eater.

Pulled pork on the table of the Loveless Cafe, Nashville, Tennessee.

2. WHOLE HOG

To go "whole hog" is to do something to the max, no holds barred, no bets hedged. So it is with whole hog barbecue, which is an arduous, time-honored ritual that few modern restaurants continue to perform. There are so many easier ways of doing things. But to the classicist, whole hog is the only way. The process commences late in the afternoon, when the pitmaster starts burning oak logs until they turn to charcoal. The coals are pushed from the chimney where they burned into an adjoining pit, where halved hogs are arrayed on a grate above the heat. At midnight, then again at dawn, more coals are moved to the pit. At the Skylight Inn of Ayden, North Carolina, where Sam Jones continues a family hog-cooking tradition that dates back to 1830, no thermometers are used to check the temperature of the pit or of the meat. Doneness is determined by feel. At daylight, the meat is almost ready. "But it is still tough at the bone," Mr. Jones told us. "It has to be that way because we need to flip the hog. If it was too soft, it would fall apart." By 9 a.m., the meat is fully tender and ready to be chopped.

One of the most alluring aspects of whole hog barbecue in the Carolinas is its sound. When you enter a restaurant that does it this way, you will hear the thump of heavy cleavers hacking up large sections of cooked meat on a hard-rock maple butcher block. The beat might emanate from a back kitchen or be done in an open space where customers can watch. (It's hypnotic!) The

Skylight Inn does its chopping right behind the counter which, like an altar in a church, is a hallowed space. Congregants come to place their orders and receive them. Here stands cleaver-master James Howell, just behind a large pass-through window, working at the cutting block, a cleaver in each hand, whacking at the meat. This chopping table is the sanctum sanctorum, where cooked pig becomes North Carolina's signature smokehouse meal. Periodically, Mr. Howell puts the blades down and reaches back for a bottle of vinegar or Texas hot sauce to splash onto the pork. He shakes on salt and pepper straight from the carton. Nothing is measured out and there are no secret ingredients. When he's got a moist, steaming heap of five pounds, chopped to the texture of coarse hash, he uses both cleavers to shovel it forward through the window, onto an adjoining butcher block in the preparation area toward the counter. Here servers assemble trays and sandwiches. Sandwiches, which include cole-slaw, are wrapped in wax paper. Trays full of meat are topped with a square of dense corn bread.

Sandwiches are a twentieth-century addition, but the combination of barbecue and corn bread goes back to 1830, when Skilton M. Dennis, who cooked whole hogs in pits dug in the ground, took some of the meat to sell at a nearby Baptist convention. "As far as we know, that was the first time barbecue was served to the public in North Carolina," says Sam Jones, who is Dennis's seventh-generation descendant. Jones is fully aware that he is upholding a longstanding culinary tradition, and if you doubt his passion, just bring up the subject of barbecue sauce. "Sauce has absolutely nothing to do with making good barbecue!" Samuel intones, quoting his grandfather Pete. And if you wonder how devoted the Skylight Inn is to whole hog barbecue, have a look at the menu. Nothing else is offered.

3. KENTUCKY MUTTON

Following the barbecue trail west of Louisville along the Ohio River and south toward the Land Between the Lakes, you will find an open-pit culture unlike anywhere else and radically diverse from county to county. While there is plenty of good pork down around Marion—indeed, in virtually every barbecue restaurant in the area—the primary pit meat is mutton. Mature lamb makes for some big-flavored barbecue very unlike the aristocratic smoke-laced pork that is more typically southern; and while its sharp sheep tang is undeniable, hours of smoke make its wallop as soft as a prize-fighter's glove. Mutton can be found elsewhere—it's on the menu at Arthur Bryant's in Kansas City and available in some places in Texas—but nowhere else does it get the respect given it by Western Kentucky pitmasters.

As is true of pork in North Carolina, each chef and town in the mutton belt gives its meat a special twist. In Owensboro (self-proclaimed barbecue capital of the world), every restaurant also serves **burgoo,** the mulligan stew that foodlore says was traditionally made of whatever small critters you could catch, and which now always contains barbecue. You won't find burgoo in the mutton parlors of nearby Henderson (which happens to be the Stern-proclaimed fried chicken capital of the solar system). The subtleties of local nomenclature and service are dizzying. Owensboro restaurants offer mutton chopped, sliced, and as ribs, but twenty-five miles west in Henderson, another presentation appears on menus: **chipped.** Chipped is like chopped, but extreme, yielding a fine hash that is moist and mellow. Chipped mutton is generally offered already sauced, but no one in this region calls it "sauce." It is known as *dip,* and it is the consistency of natural gravy in the north and more like traditional tomato sauce as you head south. Mutton served without any sauce is labeled "off the pit." A chipped *tray* includes meat, pickle, onion, and bread; a chipped *platter* adds barbecue beans and coleslaw. Alternatively, you can have a chipped *sandwich,* which is always offered on white or rye, the latter resembling Wonder Bread with a slight tan.

4. TEXAS BEEF

In the barbecue belt of central Texas, a wedge of prairie east of I-35 and north of I-10, brisket, prime rib, and beef sausage are cooked in a haze of oak smoke, slow enough that they baste themselves. Not much fat drips out: The fire is low enough that it cooks in. The fibers of the meat absorb all its flavor, giving the beef tremendous heft. Even the dark-crusted rim of brisket fairly drips with protein potency and the outer, less pink circumference of a slice of prime rib radiates the earthy perfume of burning wood.

The word *primitive* does not do justice to the elemental nature of dining in one of the great barbecue parlors of this region. Originally evolved early in the twentieth century, when butchers decided to smoke unsold and unwanted cuts of beef and serve them at makeshift tables in the back rooms of their meat markets, Texas barbecues are secret-seeming places where amenities are minimal. Order meat by the pound. It is cut, weighed, and slapped down onto a sheet of pink butcher paper along with a stack of soft white bread. Plates are extraneous, as are forks. As for side dishes beyond bread or saltines, don't expect more than onion, pickle, and jalapeños, maybe beans. Sandwiches are unheard of. Barbecue sauce? Some places have it, some don't; in the best of them, sauce is inconsequential. Meat is all that matters, and this meat doesn't need it.

5. SANTA MARIA (CALIFORNIA) BARBECUE

Anchored by the heft of fire-charred red meat, **Santa Maria barbecue** is more than a distinct style of grilling or an especially tasty cut of meat. It is a feast that evokes the bygone spirit of California cattle country as surely as the sight of a cowboy in a silver saddle. It was the vaqueros' round-up meal—time to celebrate a job well done by indulging in the bounty of the cows they herded.

Tri-tips bask over live oak flames in California cattle country.

Beyond beef, the correct complement of side dishes is paramount. They must include pinquito beans (also known as *poquitos*), which are pink pillows half the size of red beans, cooked long and slow, seasoned with pork, pepper, garlic, and onion. After four or five hours in the bean pot, the silk-soft little pods develop serious snap that mingles brilliantly with juices from adjacent beef. Lengths of buttery garlic toast are important for mopping the plate. Another crucial element is salsa, which can be used on everything: dolloped on the beans, spread on bread, and as relish for the meat. It is usually a mild salsa, mostly tomatoes, flavored with onion and perhaps a dash of horseradish, and laced with droopy bits of soft green chiles, known to one and all by their supermarket brand name, Ortegas.

Unlike barbecue in the South and Southwest, where meat is cooked for many hours by indirect heat in closed pits over smoldering wood, Santa Maria beef is done in the open on a grate over a lively fire of oak logs. Almost any good cut can be prepared this way. Eat your way through Guadalupe, Casmalia, Nipomo, and Los Alamos, and you will encounter oak-cooked prime rib, filet mignon, top sirloin, and rib eye. The most popular cut is tri-tip. Although it will never be as supple as filet mignon or as succulent as densely marbled prime rib, properly barbecued (and perhaps marinated) tri-tip is sheer pleasure to eat—packed with resounding flavor and robust character that sing of California's frontier days.

Santa Maria barbecue is a party/picnic/celebration meal, rare in restaurants (with the conspicuous exceptions of the Hitching Post in Casmalia, Jocko's in Nipomo, and the Far Western Tavern in Guadalupe), but it's easy to find all around Santa Maria, especially on weekends. It is then served alfresco from stands and wagons in parking lots and on street corners. Money made by the barbecuists is usually destined for charity.

BARBECUE SALAD

Barbecue salad, pre-sauce, at Coletta's Italian Restaurant, Memphis, Tennessee.

A sign at the old Shady Rest in Owensboro, Kentucky, used to read, IF IT FITS THE PIT, WE WILL BARBE-CUE IT. Almost anything tastes good after a long day enveloped in hickory smoke. But salad? No, the lettuce and tomatoes are not pit cooked. **Barbecue salad,** as found in and around Memphis and especially into Arkansas, is a pretty regular array of cool greens, tomatoes, maybe radishes, onions, and cucumbers that are served with a crown of room-temperature pulled pork. Most restaurants offer an eater's choice of salad dressing or barbecue sauce, the former creating a piggy chef's salad and the latter demoting traditional salad fixin's to glorfied garnishes for pit-cooked meat. A small barbecue salad may be an hors d'oeuvre; a large one will have enough substance to be a main course.

Barbecue Salad

Think of barbecue salad as a chef's salad, but in this case the chef is a pitmaster. Pulled pork is the most common meat, but shreds of beef or chicken also work. The recipe is totally forgiving in all respects except one: Iceberg lettuce is essential. It is the only variety crisp enough to hold up under the weight of meat and sauce.

½ head iceberg lettuce, washed and torn into pieces
1 large tomato, cut into eighths
½ red onion, sliced thin
½ green pepper, diced
10 slices cucumber
Radish slices to taste
¼ pound barbecued pork—preferably pulled, although chopped is OK—at room temperature
Tomato-based barbecue sauce at room temperature and/or gloppy salad dressing to taste

Arrange lettuce on two broad plates with the other vegetables on top. Add the barbecued meat, then top with sauce and/or dressing.

2 SALADS

BARBECUE SPAGHETTI

Cooks in Memphis, Tennessee, like to transform all kinds of food into **barbecue,** not just **ribs,** Cornish hens, and bologna, but also shrimp, **pizza,** wings, and—among side dishes on a majority of the city's smoke-pit eateries—spaghetti. It makes culinary sense. Sharply spiced smoky meat is best appreciated in concert with gently flavored carbs; that is why the bread that traditionally accompanies almost all barbecue is supposed to be bland and uninteresting. An artisan loaf would encroach upon barbecue's star power. Similarly, you never will find barbecue capellini, tagliatelle, or even linguine, and imported noodles are anathema. It always is spaghetti—thick, commercial-quality product cooked significantly beyond al dente. The quality of **barbecue spaghetti** has nothing to do with the noodles and everything to do with the sauce. Memphis is a sauce-centric city, which is why barbecue spaghetti thrives—as another handy way to get that sauce from plate to mouth.

Barbecue Spaghetti

Why not? If the barbecue sauce you love isn't too sweet or too pepper-hot, it just might make the perfect partner for a plate of soft-cooked spaghetti noodles. That's the way they do it in Memphis, where barbecue spaghetti is as common a side dish as hushpuppies in the Carolinas.

1 pound spaghetti, cooked and drained
1 pint of your favorite barbecue sauce, heated
Shreds of pulled pork shoulder, heated (optional)

Combine ingredients.

SERVES 4–6

BARBERTON CHICKEN

Fried in lard, **Barberton chicken** is distinguished by a brittle red-gold crust that encloses juice-laden meat. It also differs from familiar fried chicken because the available pieces include not only wings, breasts, legs, drumettes, and thighs, but also backs—the result of an arcane technique of maximizing the amount of meat that one bird can offer. In the restaurants of Barberton (at the edge of Akron, Ohio), it is the anchor of a ritual feast that also includes a timbale of tart coleslaw, French fries, and a bowl of spicy tomato-rice hot sauce. Dinners come large, medium, or small, with whatever pieces the customer specifies. Recipes for the hot sauce have been batted around in newspaper food columns for decades.

Barberton chicken came to the New World from Serbia when the Topalsky family immigrated to the farmland of Ohio at the beginning of the twentieth century. (Cognates with similar genealogy can be found on **Chicken Dinner Road** in Kansas as well as in northern Indiana, at a **boned and buttered perch** restaurant called Teibel's.) During the Depression, when the family dairy farm failed, Mike and Smilka Topalsky opened a restaurant called Belgrade Gardens in Mike's father's house. It had a normal repertoire of steaks and chops, but the Topalskys served their special fried chicken to the staff. Word got out, and soon customers began asking for chicken and hot sauce. Once it was put on the menu, Barberton chicken became such a sensation that three more restaurants opened offering the very same thing. Like Belgrade Gardens, the White House, DeVore's Hopocan Gardens, and Milich's Village Inn continue to thrive. The White House now has a number of locations in the area and is looking to franchise nationally.

BEAN DOG

Hot dogs and beans are a familiar combo almost everywhere. The **bean dog,** which combines the two in a hot dog bun, is a specialty of weenie shops in and around Fall River, Massachusetts. Bean dogs frequently are topped with the same hot cheddar cheese used in the region's **hot cheese sandwich,** and most places that sell them offer chouriço (Portuguese) sausage in place of the dog as well as a sandwich that is just beans in a bun. The latter works best when the beans are very porky and onion laced, but most beans on bean dogs are more spartan: just beans, sweet and starchy enough to balance a fatty little frank.

The Fall River bean dog: frank and beans in a bun.

JAMES BEARD

Food's big breakthrough on television, and the initial successful coupling of gourmet cookery with the medium,
was the appearance of **James Beard.** After some success
doing cooking demonstrations on NBC television's *Radio
City Matinee* and a show called *For You and Yours* in
the mid-forties, Beard got his own regular segment on
a Borden Dairy Company variety and talk show called
Elsie Presents in 1946. The show began with Harriet
Van Horne at a desk giving viewers shopping tips, gossip,
and theater criticism. Then a giant puppet of the sponsor's mascot, Elsie the Cow, appeared and announced,
"Elsie presents James Beard in '*I Love to Eat*'!" and
Beard spent the last half of the show (fifteen minutes)
showing viewers how to cook something. The program
was a success because Beard formulated a charming

James Beard, the dean of American cookery,
at home with his beloved pug, Percy.

blend of instruction and fun—the pattern for nearly every successful TV chef
who came after him. Prior to Beard, no one knew quite how to make a television cooking show entertaining, so recipes were swapped and read aloud and
prepared step-by-step, as they had been on the radio, and home economists
in pince-nez glasses told housewives how to conserve leftover bacon fat. Beard
was no recipe-swapper or home economist. He was a performer: His first career
goal had been to be an opera singer; when that failed on the West Coast, he
came to New York in 1937 and gained fame not as an actor, but as a caterer,
at Hors d'Oeuvre, Inc. He remembered coming back to New York after the war
and being offered a food show job by NBC: "At last—a chance to cook and act
at the same time."

For Beard, serving good food was always more than a matter of sustenance
or proper nutrition; it was a performance. "Put on a fine show!" he goads readers of his autobiography *Delights and Prejudices.* "Like the theater, offering
food and hospitality is a matter of showmanship, and no matter how simple
the performance, unless you do it well, with love and originality, you have a
flop on your hands." As a cooking teacher, Beard put on that kind of show
when he gave lessons in his Greenwich Village townhouse (now home of the
James Beard Foundation)—sharing wine with students, eating the mistakes
as well as the successes, encouraging them to be original, to not be afraid of

trying something new and crazy. "I think if I have done nothing else," he once told us, "I have taught people to enjoy making food." That attitude made him terrific on television, where even the most daunting recipes were transformed into enjoyable romps with pots and pans and acres of garlic. Beard loved to be outrageous, once making the rounds of prime-time variety programs with a specially made skillet, six feet long and three feet wide, and cooking crepes in it with a blowtorch.

He was America's best-known chef throughout the fifties and into the sixties, not only because of his own television appearances but also because he was popularized by the food industry, which found there were profits to be made by associating products with the James Beard brio. He endorsed innumerable foodstuffs, wines, and utensils, and he served as company figurehead in advertisements for Omaha Steaks, Camp Maple Syrup, the French National Association of Cognac Producers, and the Taylor Wine Company. Beard never seemed shy about putting his imprimatur on sponsor's products, which was another reason he fit so well on television (which, after all, exists to sell products). In the post-Nader years of the 1970s, he took plenty of guff from anti-business critics for being too cozy with big food companies. Some worried that he had become more of a pitchman than a pure-souled culinary artiste, but his relationships with products rarely bothered him. After all, they helped feed his enormous appetites, and he enjoyed the position of authority they conferred. Although there were some endorsements he came to regret privately, Beard always liked being in the spotlight they provided.

More important, Beard's television persona as willing and eager spokesman for various foods never seemed to bother the millions of home cooks who respected him and learned from him. In fact, the opposite is true. Until the 1960s, most Americans generally liked and trusted big companies, especially big food companies, which had supplied decades' worth of recipes, free cooking brochures, reassurances from spotless test kitchens, and loveable mythical product mascots (from Elsie and Betty Crocker to California Raisins and cutesy-poo M&Ms) and were proud sponsors of favorite television programs. Traditionally, Americans have also respected elected spokesmen for multimillion-dollar food corporations. Because of his lifetime alliance with such a wide variety of people's favorite things to eat, Beard earned a position that to many consumers and cooks seemed far more important than mere epicure. He became a pop culture icon, the ultimate product pitchman, and, in the eyes of many Americans, the definitive chef.

BEEF ON WECK

One of several major roadfood specialties from Buffalo, New York (see also **sponge candy, Charlie Chaplin, loganberry juice,** and, of course, **Buffalo wings**), **beef on weck** in its proper form always will remain parochial. That is because *proper form* requires that a roast be expertly hand-carved for every sandwich. Ray Schwabl, whose family tavern may have been the first place to serve beef on weck, well over a hundred years ago, explained that no slicing machine can navigate through the subtle topography of a roast's fibers with the finesse of a master carver with a good knife. "Beef on weck will never experience the same popularity as Buffalo chicken wings," he said when we interviewed him about ten years ago. "I could teach a chimp to make wings in twenty minutes, but it takes me a year to train a man to slice roast beef."

Beyond perfectly cooked and expertly sliced beef, the weck part of the equation cannot be streamlined. From the German word *Kummel,* meaning "caraway seed," a *kummelweck,* or simply *weck,* looks vaguely like an ordinary hard roll spangled with caraway seeds and coarse salt. But it is not ordinary. A correct weck is delicate, its freshness evanescent. Lightness is crucial because the roll cushions, but must not compete with, the extreme delicacy of the sliced beef. On the other hand, it cannot be too fragile, for the customary way of assembling the sandwich is to immerse the top half in pan juice, just long enough for it to start to soften, before setting it atop the beef.

"It is surprisingly difficult to maintain the kummelweck," says Dale Eckl of Eckl's Beef & Weck Restaurant. "You can't ship them or store them because they stale so fast and the salt crust will break down if it is exposed to humidity."

The salt and caraway seeds on a kummelweck roll are a beautiful match for rare roast beef and its juices.

According to Charlie Roesch, proprietor of Charlie the Butcher's Kitchen and third-generation Buffalo butcher, it was beer that inspired the invention of beef on weck. He believes that, sometime in the 1880s, a now-forgotten local tavern owner (*perhaps* a Schwabl) decided to offer a sandwich that would induce a powerful thirst in his patrons. He had plenty of coarse salt on hand for the pretzels he served, so he painted a mixture of the salt and caraway seeds atop some hard rolls, cooked a roast and sliced it thin, and piled the meat inside the rolls. As a condiment, he served hot horseradish. To slake the thirst these sandwiches induced, beer sales soared. And Buffalo's passion for beef on weck—served with fiery fresh horseradish and accompanied by schooners of cold beer—was born.

BEIGNET

New Orleans's favorite morning pastry comes blanketed with a blizzard of powdered sugar.

As much an edible symbol of New Orleans as **gumbo** and a **po'boy** sandwich, the **beignet** ("bean-yay") is a rectangular, hole-less donut with a bit of crunch to its crust and creamy insides. Sugared fritters are found in most cuisines—Italian *zeppoli*, Mexican *buñuelos*, Portuguese **malasadas,** etc.—but the presentation of beignets is unique. Always served piping hot from the fry kettle, they come covered with so much confectioners' sugar that they are impossible to eat without clouds of the white powder covering fingers, hands, face, and clothes. The customary companion is café au lait, a smooth half-and-half mix of milk and chicory coffee. The time-honored place to eat beignets is in the old French Market at Cafe du Monde, a brash, alfresco commissary open 24/7/365. If you want them with espresso and strong coffee, visit Cafe Beignet on Royal Street in the French Quarter.

BENEDICTINE CHEESE

Jennie Benedict was a native of Louisville, Kentucky, who studied with Fannie Farmer in Boston and helped start the Louisville Businesswoman's Club in 1897. Miss Jennie opened a tearoom and soda fountain and was a successful caterer as well as a beloved community volunteer (serving at the King's Daughters Home for Incurables). She died in 1928, but her name lives on in the mid-South, thanks mostly to the cheese she invented. **Benedictine** isn't really a unique kind of cheese. It's simply cream cheese mixed with chopped green onions, mayonnaise, and—Miss Jennie's stroke of genius—green food coloring. Usually lots of it, enough that the finished product looks like something the family Frankenstein might offer as an hors d'oeuvre. It is a hostess food, rarely found on restaurant menus but frequently used in dainty crustless sandwiches or, in a much heartier configuration, as costar in a Benedictine and bacon sandwich.

BIEROCK

In and around Lincoln, Nebraska, there is a fast food chain found nowhere else: Runza Drive-Ins. Trademarked in 1949, the term *Runza* was originally used by nineteenth-century heartland settlers known as Volga Germans. To avoid religious persecution, the Germans fled their homes some two centuries ago and settled around the Volga River in Russia; when the Communists seized power in Russia, they fled again for the United States. They brought with them recipes for a baked yeast-dough bread pocket filled with onions and beef, cabbage, or sauerkraut. These portable meals (similar to the Upper Midwest's **pasties**) were a favorite lunch among farm workers; today they are served at church suppers and fund-raisers throughout Nebraska and Kansas. The settlers called them *runzas, runzies,* or **bierocks,** and they still are popular in community cookbooks. Beyond the Runza chain, which owns that particular name, the dish is rarely found on independent restaurant menus. A common appellation throughout Nebraska is *cabbage burger,* a food that can be found not only at lunch in town cafes but in bakeries as well—sold either warm for dashboard dining or ready to take home and heat for supper.

BILOXI BACON

Smoked mullet, a specialty of the Gulf Coast from Louisiana's Lake Borgne to Tampa Bay, got the name **Biloxi bacon** because it was the people's meat when real bacon was scarce. The term likely goes back as far as the Civil War, when the Union blockade couldn't make the population submit because people were able to survive on fish they caught: "You can't starve us into submission unless you put a blockade on the mullet," said a Biloxi native. In subsequent lean times, such as the Great Depression, when buying bacon was out of the question, mullet was once again a lifesaver. Netted in shallow-draft boats, mullet is a dense-fleshed fish that is almost always served smoked. A long spell over red oak coals saturates the meat with savory oils and makes it truly as rich as bacon.

BISCOCHITOS

The **biscochito,** which New Mexico's legislature declared the state's official cookie in 1989 (although they spelled it "bizcochito"), is a crisp, tan disc or diamond of fragile shortbread that is cinnamon and anise-flavored and dusted with sugar. It is brittle, so luxuriously rich that it melts in the mouth, and it frequently packs an eye-opening licorice buzz. While it is possible to make biscochitos with butter or shortening, tradition calls for lard, which creates the lightest, most savory cookies. Because they are only slightly sweet, biscochitos are as good a companion for dessert wine as they are for coffee. While suitable as snack or dessert any time, they are almost always on the table at weddings, birthdays, and religious holidays.

BOILED DINNER

Boiled dinner is the only-in-New-England version of the Irish-American dish corned beef and cabbage. Everything in the meal, except for corn bread, is prepared by boiling, usually all in the same pot: corned beef and cabbage plus any combination of potatoes, carrots, parsnips, turnips, and rutabagas. Beets are also frequently included, but they are cooked separately so as not to dye everything else red. Never fancied up with gravy or upscale cuts of meat, boiled dinner is a quintessential square meal that has become an emblem of the Yankee kitchen's forthrightness. Leftovers are the ingredient list for **red flannel hash.**

Meat and potatoes. And carrots, cabbage, parsnips, and beets: the classic New England boiled dinner.

BOILED PEANUT

If you like roasted peanuts, if you love their brittle body and toasty crunch, chances are you will be stunned when you first encounter a **boiled peanut.** The shell doesn't crack. It gets peeled away, revealing little legumes that are as soft as boiled Fordhooks. (Some boiled peanuts, made from very young pickin's, are eaten shell and all.) Colloquially known as goober peas, boiled peanuts were once available only from spring through autumn, sold warm and ready to eat at roadside stands throughout the Carolinas and much of the Deep South. While ad hoc sellers continue to offer a seasonal snack opportunity for motorists, boiled peanuts have become a year-round *amuse-bouche* in Southern-themed restaurants and are often found as free snacks in bars. They usually are eaten standing up, sitting in a rocking chair on a porch, or while driving. Alternatively, they can be threaded through the neck of a full bottle of Dr Pepper, where they mix with the syrupy sweet soft drink.

Visitors are welcome to tag Timbo's boiled peanut Airstream with their handle or an appropriate sentiment.

BONED AND BUTTERED PERCH

Boned and buttered perch does not only describe a way of serving fish. It defines a whole meal that has been popular along the southern shore of Lake Michigan for a century. The small panfish are cooked the way fishermen used to prepare them when South Chicago and Gary, Indiana, still were a kind of fisherman's paradise. The fillets are lightly breaded in seasoned flour and fried in a skillet. Restaurants used to give diners a choice: whole or boned, plain from the skillet or drizzled with melted butter. Nowadays, the few places that continue to serve them do it only boned and almost always buttered, offering them either by the plate (up to ten) or on an all-you-can-eat plan. The flesh of perch is firm and compact, flaking into tiny sections when prodded with a fork; the meat seems to draw melting butter deep into its crevices, creating unspeakable luxury.

The proper collective noun for multiple perch fillets is mess. Bruce Bilmes photographed this mess in northern Indiana.

The joy of eating boned and buttered perch includes not only the sublime taste of the fish itself but also the traditional five-relish array at the beginning of the meal—cottage cheese, pickled beets, potato salad, coleslaw, and kidney bean salad—along with such old-school highballs as neat martinis with olives, sweet Manhattans with maraschino cherries, Tom Collinses, and Rob Roys. Every menu that features perch also offers frog legs—another delicacy once appreciated by local fishermen but now more a culinary anachronism.

BOOMERANG FORMICA

No motif evokes mid-twentieth-century **diner** culture more fully than **boomerang Formica,** a material and pattern still found—usually very well worn—on counters and tables in hash houses that never gentrified . . . or those seeking a retro look. The design was created in 1950 and predates other such quaintly dated images of modernity as the automobile tailfin and the atomic molecule motif.

Formica itself goes back to 1913, when it was created and named because its heat-resistant properties made it a good substitute for mica, which was used as insulation in electric motors. In 1950, as Americans were poised to move to the suburbs and sur-

Boomerang Formica's formal name is Skylark.

round themselves with convenient, modern kitchens, Brooks Stevens Associates designed the Skylark pattern—a series of similar-but-not-identical thin-lined boomerang-shaped outlines in one, two, or three colors, overlapping one another on a plain Formica surface. The design was finessed four years later by Nettie Hart of Raymond Loewy Associates, and the result was a then-ultra-stylish pattern suggesting supersonic airplane wings.

The boomerang pattern on anything was considered as modern as tomorrow; on Formica, the manmade miracle plastic, it was an epiphany of jet-age design. The truly inspired thing about Skylark Formica is that it was not made to look like artificial wood or stone or even linoleum. It was Formica, and darn proud of it! The dancing boomerangs signify a triumph of manmade plastic over such archaic materials as wood or marble. That ingenuous faith in better living through science is why Skylark pattern Formica today has become an amusing emblem of a time when one-upping nature was a virtue.

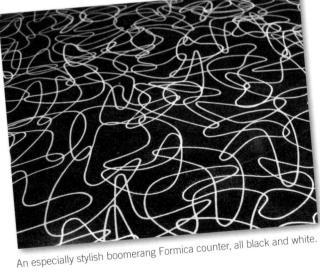
An especially stylish boomerang Formica counter, all black and white.

BOSTON CREAM PIE

Boston cream pie was invented at the Parker House Hotel in Boston in 1855, when the French chef put a thick ribbon of custard between two layers of sponge cake and topped them with a chocolate glaze. It originally was known as *Parker House chocolate pie,* and it was in fact a variation on a dessert called *pudding cake,* which dates back to Colonial times. No one can say with certainty how it got to be called a pie—it is most definitely a cake—but a logical explanation would be that it almost always is cut into triangular wedges like pie. In 1996, Boston cream pie was named Massachusetts's official dessert.

BOUDIN

West of New Orleans, from Baton Rouge to St. Charles, and from the swamps of Avery Island to the prairies of Evangeline Parish, hundreds of establishments sell **boudin** sausage. It is served on plates in some restaurants, but locals buy it by the link from groceries and quick-stop stores where it is made. It comes hot from a steam box and ready to eat—either at home, on a picnic table, or off the hood of one's car in the butcher shop parking lot. There is no big-name brand. Each source sells its own, and Cajuns' opinions about which is best are more fervent than New Orleanians' about **po'boys** and **Sazeracs.** For a taste of the passion, visit www.boudinlink.com, a website devoted exclusively to rating boudin sausage.

One needn't specify *boudin blanc* in Cajun country (as opposed to the blood sausage known as *boudin noir*). Unless otherwise noted, *boudin* means boudin blanc: a mix of cooked pork (with varying amounts of liver), rice, onions, and spice fed into a casing that ranges from crisp to chewy. Boudin is not a firm tube steak. Unlike a Texas **hot link** or chorizo sausage, once it is cut, it spills, tumbles, or gets squeezed out, depending on the link's consistency. It comes in shades of beige, hot ones tinged pepper red, some speckled with a confetti of green and yellow onion. Differences among them can be subtle. Are the rice grains firm or soft? Is the pork pulverized or rough-hewn? Does it glisten? Does it have a sweet, fresh smell? Does the filling drip unctuously or is it dry?

An alternative to the sloppiness of a boudin link, which demands a fork and lots of napkins, is the boudin ball, an egg-size sphere scooped from the link and deep-fried. A good boudin ball will crunch when bitten, the crisp surface cracking apart to offer two or three bites of moist sausage.

BREADED STEAK

The least known of Chicago's old-time street food specialties, and increasingly the scarcest, **breaded steak** is the South Side version of Italian steak Milanese, central European Wiener schnitzel, Cuban *bistec empanizado,* and Texan **chicken-fried steak.** For this sandwich, a broad, pounded-tender sheet of beef gets breaded and fried, and then it is rolled hot with mozzarella cheese (which melts instantly), spicy tomato sauce, and, optionally, hot giardiniera relish or roasted peppers. The awesome lode, stuffed into a length of chewy Italian bread, is barely pickupable, but rarely is it served with utensils. Made by neighborhood grocery stores and a few vintage restaurants, breaded steak customarily is presented well-wrapped in butcher paper that can be unfolded as a makeshift tablecloth for a laminate counter or automobile dashboard. In Kansas City, a very similar sandwich is known as *Italian steak.*

Breaded Steak

Of all the messy sandwiches that theoretically can be picked up in two hands, Chicago's breaded steak is the messiest. It therefore demands a rugged bread. International cooks will note that the steak itself is something like Milanese, but by the time the sandwich is constructed, all resemblance is lost.

> Flour
> 1 flank steak, 8–10 ounces
> 1 egg
> 1 tablespoon water
> ½ cup seasoned bread crumbs
> 1 tablespoon grated Parmesan cheese
> ¼ teaspoon salt
> ¼ teaspoon pepper
> Oil for frying
> 1 10- to 12-inch length of sturdy Italian bread, sliced horizontally

¼ cup shredded mozzarella cheese (optional)
⅓ cup warm marinara sauce (sometimes known as gravy)
Sweet peppers, giardiniera, or hot peppers to taste

1. Sprinkle a bit of flour on a smooth, clean surface, flip the steak on it a couple of times so it has some flour on both sides, and then use a meat pounder to pound it to less than ¼ inch thick and nearly a foot square.

2. Mix together the egg and water in a broad, shallow dish. In a separate broad, shallow dish, combine the bread crumbs, Parmesan cheese, salt, and pepper.

3. Heat cooking oil in a broad skillet to 360°F.

4. Dip the steak in the egg mixture, turning and folding until it is fully moistened, then dredge it in the seasoned crumbs and cheese, trying to coat it thoroughly. Slide the steak into the hot oil and cook until light brown, about 4 minutes. Do not let the steak cook until dark.

5. Remove the steak from the pan onto paper towels and instantly roll it up so it will fit inside the bread. Immediately place it in the loaf and top it with the shredded mozzarella. Pour on the marinara and add condiments as desired.

6. Do not be concerned if you are now staring at a plate of food that scarcely bears any resemblance to a portable sandwich. This is the way a breaded steak should look.

1 SANDWICH

BROASTING

A portmanteau of *broiling* and *roasting*, **broasting**—almost always applied to chicken—in fact is neither. To broast a chicken is to deep-fry it in a pressure cooker. The technique and equipment were devised in the 1950s by L. A. M. Phelan, who already had made a name for himself as the founder of Zesto **drive-ins,** a franchise that eventually became a small group of independently owned eat shops known for their **frozen custard.** In 1954 the Broaster company trademarked the term and began selling pressure-fryers and seasoning to foodservice operations around the country. Among the advantages of broaster-made chicken, other than juiciness that verges on viscous, is that cooking time is much less than old-fashioned pan-frying.

Although the Broaster company boasts that its fried product contains a mere fraction of the fat, carbs, and calories of KFC chicken, it did recently introduce a Bro-Tisserie, which cooks whole chickens in a rotisserie oven, bypassing the deep fat altogether.

BROWNIES

Sweet chocolate brownies are universal. Savory **brownies** are a specialty of Kansas City barbecue parlors. Known also as *burnt ends,* brownies are analogous to Creole **debris**—the shreds, nuggets, strips, and chunks of meat that fall off the barbecued brisket (or ham) as it is sliced and chopped. Most are outside pieces with crusty-crunchy areas and thick ribbons of melt-in-the-mouth fat. They are to pit-cooked meat what clotted cream is to milk—the distilled essence—and they are flush with wood smoke and oozy protein satisfaction. Brownies come on a plate or in a sandwich, but because they are so bold flavored, a straight brownie meal can fatigue the brain's pleasure center to a point of ravished meltdown. Therefore, novitiates are advised to make their Kansas City barbecue experience at least a half-and-half affair, if not a trio: brownies sided by chopped pork, sliced brisket, or spare ribs, all three of which seem positively ascetic by comparison.

29

Brownies, aka burnt ends, garnish chili at the Woodyard in Kansas City.

Brownies to go, sopped with sauce.

As barbecue's star has risen in the last decade or so, brownies have appeared on menus beyond Kansas City, usually listed as *burnt ends*. Because they are so alluring to smoke-pit aficionados, many restaurants mass produce them by slicing off outside chunks of a brisket and cutting them into cubes. While such strategies may yield extremely succulent mouthfuls, they bypass the variegated texture and raid-the-kitchen mischief that make cutting-board brownies always seem like such a special treat.

BRUNSWICK STEW

Likely named for either Brunswick, Georgia, or Brunswick County in southernmost Virginia (both of which claim it), **Brunswick stew** historically was a hunter's potluck of whatever critters could be bagged along with whatever vegetables were ripe and ready. Now that the government forbids serving game that its agencies have not inspected, Brunswick stew is made with shreds of barbecued pork or chicken that gives it a smoky punch. It is thick stuff, easily eaten with a fork, and stout enough to be a meal (along with some corn bread),

but it almost always appears as a companion to barbecued meats. Recipes vary tremendously: Tomatoes always are part of the mix; lima beans and corn kernels are common; okra sometimes is added. Brunswick stew is rarely encountered outside of Virginia, North Carolina, and Georgia.

Brunswick Stew

True to its role on menus in Virginia, North Carolina, and Georgia, this Brunswick stew serves either as a hearty companion to barbecue (pork, preferably) or a meal by itself, with perhaps some corn bread on the side. If you're going to serve it as a main course, leave the chicken pieces whole, as in the following recipe. If it's a side dish, remove the meat from the bones, hack it fine, and return it to the stew. Shreds of barbecued pork can also be included.

2 large onions, sliced
2 tablespoons bacon fat
1 2- to 2½-pound frying chicken, cut up
Salt and pepper
3 cups water
3 tomatoes, peeled and cut in eighths, or 1 14-ounce can diced tomatoes, drained
½ cup sherry
1 teaspoon Worcestershire sauce
1 pound fresh lima beans or 1 10-ounce package frozen lima beans
1 cup fresh or frozen corn kernels
½ cup seasoned bread crumbs
2 tablespoons butter, melted

1. In a large frying pan, brown the onion slices in the bacon fat until they are limp. Remove them with a slotted spoon to a heavy 4-quart saucepan.

2. Sprinkle the chicken with salt and pepper. Add it to the frying pan. Cook over medium-high heat for 6–8 minutes per side, turning frequently.

3. Use a slotted spoon to place the chicken parts in the saucepan. Add water, tomatoes, sherry, and Worcestershire sauce. Bring to a simmer and cook, partially covered, for 30 minutes. Add the lima beans and corn. Continue to simmer, partially covered, for 15–20 minutes. (Debone the chicken and return it to the pot at this point, if desired.) Sprinkle on bread crumbs and drizzle on the butter. Continue cooking, uncovered, for 15–20 more minutes.

SERVES 4–6

ARTHUR BRYANT

No one was more surprised than **Arthur Bryant** in 1974 when journalist Calvin Trillin named Bryant's restaurant the best in the world. No question, Trillin loved the place; but especially in 1974, at a peak of gastronomic pretense and pomp in America, to anoint a bare-tabled **barbecue** as a culinary superstar was *épater le bourgeois* in spades. Bryant himself frequently referred to the place as a "grease house," and during his reign, the tile floor was famously slippery. But the slow-smoked meats were magnificent and Bryant's sauce was liquid sorcery.

Arthur Bryant, photographed in the kitchen of his barbecue restaurant in 1978.

The restaurant was started by brother Charlie Bryant, who learned the barbecue trade from Henry Perry, a Tennessean who came to Kansas City in 1908 and began smoking beef—as well as opossum and raccoon—over oak and hickory and selling it at a stand in the garment district. When Perry died in 1940, Charlie Bryant took over the business. Charlie sold it to Arthur, who is said to have taken some of the bite out of Perry's peppery sauce, and who moved the restaurant to its current location in 1958. In addition to the good taste of the food, the new address was instrumental in Bryant's gaining national renown. Just a few blocks from Municipal Stadium, the humble eatery was frequented by ballplayers, sports journalists, and fans, who all spread the word.

Arthur Bryant never was spoiled by all the attention. When we met him in 1980, two years before his death, he was busy behind the counter, on the phone alternately taking orders and chewing out suppliers. When we finally had a chance to sit down and talk, we did so around a bowl of sauce and a half loaf of white bread. As we interviewed the Master, he occasionally folded up a slice of bread and dipped it in the sauce, enjoying the simple combo with no meat whatsoever.

BUFFALO WINGS

Chickens always have had wings, and it is reasonable to assume that since humans discovered that chickens taste good, their wings were on the menu. But the chicken wing as we know it was invented in 1964 by Teressa Bellissimo. Mrs. Bellissimo, who ran Buffalo's Anchor Bar with her husband, Frank, cut wings in half, creating drumettes and bows, pan-fried them, and served them bathed in buttery hot sauce along with blue cheese dressing and celery sticks to offset the sauce's heat. Exactly what inspired her is a subject snack-food historians have tossed around for decades. Did she have no other chicken parts on hand to feed her son's hungry friends? Was it a Friday treat for Catholic customers who wouldn't eat red meat? Was it simply thrift—a way to make use of chicken pieces destined for the stockpot or garbage can? Or is it possible that an entirely different Buffalonian, named John Young, invented them in the mid-1960s and the Bellissimos somehow got the credit?

As is the case with the contested genesis of **fried clams, hamburgers, and chimichangas,** the true story likely never will be known, but who cares? Pan-fry chicken pieces that already boast maximum subcutaneous fat, put a butter-enriched hot-sauce exclamation point on them, balance that with rich blue cheese dressing, and you have a winning harmony of flavors that goes way beyond an inspired bar snack. The term *Buffalo* is now applied to countless different chicken dishes (and even nonchicken dishes) that are flavored in a similar hot-creamy way. It is safe to say that many people who ask for **Buffalo wings** by name have never thought of their connection with the Nickel City, where Buffalo wings are known as *chicken wings* or simply *wings*.

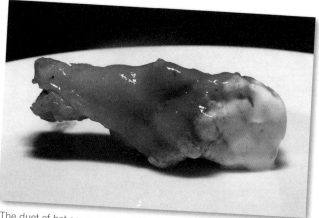

The duet of hot sauce and cool blue cheese dressing has made wings America's favorite bar snack.

BURGOO

Western Kentucky's burgoo is fork-thick and vividly spiced.

Almost every place that serves **barbecue** in and around Owensboro, Kentucky (which has proclaimed itself "BBQ Capital of the World"), also offers the fork-thick vegetable soup/stew known as **burgoo.** Supposedly named when a Civil War cook with a speech impediment tried to say "bird stew," burgoo traditionally contained meat from whatever small game the cook could get, usually including squirrel. Modern burgoo, a staple on Derby Day along with the **mint julep,** is made with barbecued mutton (the smoke-pit meat of choice in Western Kentucky) and also possibly chicken, pork, or beef. Its thick and hearty character is similar to **Brunswick stew,** but it tends to be significantly spicier, verging into Creole **gumbo** territory.

BUTTER BEANS

Big, fresh **butter beans** have a fleshy opulence that forces serious reconsideration of legumes in the hierarchy of edible luxuries. "They're like eating steak!"

Butter beans laced with ham at the Old Post Office restaurant on Edisto Island, South Carolina.

rhapsodized Lowcountry chef Philip Bardin, explaining that the big Fordhooks he serves in his Old Post Office restaurant on Edisto Island, South Carolina, are thick and supple enough to absorb vast amounts of the pig meat with which they are cooked. A frequent choice on **meat and three** menus throughout the South, butter beans can be the most unvegetarian vegetable imaginable, as lavish as bacon. Unlike ordinary baby limas, which are small, dense, and bright-colored, these large celadon sachets are hefty enough to cut with a knife.

BUTTER BURGER

Wisconsin, which used to boast that it was "America's Dairyland" on license plates, banned sales of margarine in 1925. Although the law was repealed two years later, Wisconsin remained the last state in the Union to maintain strict rules designed to make sure no one mistook margarine for the real thing. Among these restrictions was a color ban that forbade the sale of margarine in any way tinted to disguise its chemical white hue. Well into the mid-twentieth century, Wisconsinites who craved margarine that looked edible had to sneak over the Illinois border and smuggle it in. Either that or buy the white stuff and mix in food coloring until it resembled butter.

There is no better demonstration of the state's passion than the **butter burger,** which is so popular that many restaurants where it is served don't even bother to call it that. Order a hamburger and it automatically comes soaked with melted butter. Not margarine, not flavored oil: pure, dairy-rich butter. Words cannot describe the wanton opulence of hoisting one of these big boys from plate to mouth and feeling commingled butter and beef juices running hot rivers down one's chin, fingers, and wrist. Similarly, most of the charcoal-cooked **brats** served in Wisconsin sandwiches come glistening not only with their own fat, but with that of a few melting butter pats as well.

35

A Dairy State double butter burger with cheese.

CALIFORNIA DIP

When **California dip** was concocted by a housewife in the 1950s, Lipton named it for her home state to suggest the casual panache that West Coast living once embodied. Nothing could be easier to make: Simply zip open a packet of dehydrated onion soup, pop a pint of sour cream, and stir them together. The result was an hors d'oeuvre requiring no utensils, plates, or napkins. Guests could hold a highball in one hand and shovel up a gob of dip with the other, needing only a sturdy corrugated **potato chip** as an edible implement. Here was a snack made for mid-twentieth-century America's style of informal entertaining on the patio or in the family room.

The big beneficiary of California dip's success was sour cream, which had been a rare ingredient in early twentieth-century cookbooks. Even *Sour Cream Cookery*, published in 1947, denigrates its star ingredient as a member of "the fermented milk tribe," but it says that it is good to use anyway because it is healthful, exotic, and a thrifty way to use up spoiled cream. The idea of it being chic was then preposterous: Like yogurt, sour cream was considered quite odd, nutty, ethnic, possibly subversive. California dip made it a staple of suburban cookery, paving the way for America's home epicures to embrace beef stroganoff, sour cream Jell-O molds, and sour cream cheesecake.

CARNE ADOVADA

Carne adovada: Intense chile puree tenderizes pork chunks even before they are baked.

Carne adovada, which means marinated meat, is hugely popular in New Mexico, where it is pork chunks or chops sopped in a puree of red chile and baked slowly enough to become dramatically tender—and, in serious chile-growing country, even more dramatically hot. Served at all levels of restaurant, it can be a substantial and quite elegant main dish (as at La Posta de Mesilla in Las Cruces) or it can be the companion for truck-stop eggs.

CARNE SECA

Literally "dried meat," **carne seca** is beef squared. Served in bite-size strips, it is glistening mahogany and fairly dripping flavor, dry and yet wildly succulent, rugged and pure pleasure to chew. A specialty of Sonoran Desert country and product of a time when refrigeration was unavailable, it traditionally is marinated then air-dried, after which it is shredded, spiced, and sautéed. In concert with grilled onions, chopped tomatoes, and hot chile, it is an echt-Southwest dish. In Mexico and on Mexican restaurant menus, it often goes by the name *machaca*, and it is a very close cousin to *beef jerky*.

Tacos are a natural home for carne seca, as is Tucson's awe-inspiring **topopo salad**, in which the verdurous flavor of lettuce and vegetables offers profound contrast to the chewy shreds of dark beef. It also is a natural topping for a *tostada grande*, aka "**Mexican pizza**," which is a crisp foot-and-a-half-wide tortilla blanketed with molten cheese and strewn with green chiles, guacamole, and refritos. With scrambled eggs, it is a breakfast of champions.

CASHEW CHICKEN, SPRINGFIELD-STYLE

Stir-fried cashew chicken is common on Chinese-American restaurant menus all around the country. But deep-fried **cashew chicken** is so much the signature dish of Springfield, Missouri, that acolytes know it as *Springfield chicken*. Introduced in 1963 by restaurateur David Leong, who was seeking a way to attract fried-chicken-loving Missourians to his Cantonese tearoom, it is a happy mix of breaded and crisp-fried chicken pieces dolloped with brown oyster sauce and decorated with halved cashews and chopped scallions. The *Springfield News-Leader* labeled it "an example of 'fusion' cooking before the term became a justification for $30 entrees"; and in fact its jejune taste and economical nature have made it a favorite not just in Chinese restaurants but in local **diners** and school cafeterias. The *News-Leader* reported that fifty Springfield restaurants serve it and that it has earned fans in Arkansas and as far away as South Lake Tahoe, California.

CAT HEAD BISCUIT

Most biscuits are small, flat-topped, and circular, the dough rolled out and cut with a floured glass. A **cat head biscuit,** which in the old days was a special-occasions treat and could be the focus of a meal rather than just an accompanying breadstuff, by contrast, is knobby-topped and asymmetrical, closer in size and shape to a cat's noggin than to a smooth hockey puck. Like a **drop biscuit,** a cat head is not rolled or cut; it is formed from dough using a spoon or bare hands. And the dough, like that for all good Southern biscuits, is made from soft flour. (White Lily or Martha White is the Dixie cook's preferred brand.) While they generally are cooked in open formation on a baking sheet, it is not uncommon for cats to be crowded into an iron skillet, where they bake together as they rise, resulting in a large, pull-apart megabiscuit.

CHARLIE CHAPLIN

You won't find Charlie Chaplin candy anywhere other than at the chocolatiers of Buffalo, New York.

Charlie Chaplin is unheard of outside the candy stores of Buffalo, New York (which happens to have some of the finest chocolatiers in the country). Buffalonians with a sweet tooth are crazy for it. Every bit as addictive as the Nickel City's distinctive **sponge candy,** this unique confection is a chocolate cluster studded with hunks of cashew nut and laced with shreds of toasted coconut around a mooshy marshmallow filling. Charlie Chaplin is sheer hedonistic opulence as its marshmallow and chocolate melt into a soft sea of sweetness around the butter-rich cashews and tropical luxury of coconut. Legend says it was named for the silent film comedian because he once convinced a Buffalo chocolatier to combine his favorite ingredients into one candy. Exactly when this happened, as well as why and the identity of the chocolatier, remains a mystery.

CHEESE CURDS

Cheese curds, bite-size nuggets of fresh cheese known for the squeak they make when teeth bite into them, started as a byproduct of cheesemaking (they're the leftover pieces when the whey is drained). They have become such a popular snack in dairy farm country that they are a more significant product than the cheese itself in many small creameries.

Freshness is the key to excellence, for within hours of their manufacture the squeak diminishes along with the bright freshness of the curd. Even deep-fried cheese curds are best when they start with absolutely fresh product, which yields the creamiest insides. But in bars throughout Wisconsin and Minnesota, such nicety is of secondary consideration compared to their goodness as a pop-in-the-mouth snack food to go with beer. Fried curds also are hugely popular at fairs and festivals, where the subtle savor of freshness isn't nearly as important as the fundamental pleasure of eating hot, salty, fried fat.

CHEESE STEAK

Not that anyone needs a definition of a **cheese steak.** The sandwich of shaved beef and molten cheese on a sturdy Italian roll, once uniquely Philadelphian, is known pretty much everywhere. But exactly how to order one remains an art that is little known or poorly practiced elsewhere. As posted near the order window at Pat's (where the sandwich was invented by Pat and Harry Olivieri in 1930), this is how to do it:

1. Say "wit" or "wit'out," referring to onions.

2. Specify your cheese: provolone, American, or **Cheez Whiz.** Or tell the order taker you want a **pizza** steak, which adds red sauce to the sandwich.

3. Have your money ready: "Do all of your borrowing in line."

4. Practice all of the above while waiting in line.

A few annotations are in order. While Cheez Whiz is by far the current most popular topping for a cheese steak, molten cheese in a jar was not introduced until after World War II. The earliest steak sandwiches sold by the Olivieris from their hot dog cart in the Italian market had no cheese on them at all, the presumption being that the essence of cheesesteakhood is not in the cheese but in the right combination of beef and bread. When cheese was introduced sometime in the 1930s, it no doubt was provolone.

While most cheese steak connoisseurs are fairly liberal vis-à-vis provolone vs. Whiz and even American, ordering any other cheese is an awful faux pas. In 2003, when Senator John F. Kerry was campaigning in Philadelphia for the Democratic Party nomination for president, he tried to show he was an ordinary Joe by ordering a cheese steak at Pat's. His handlers had not done their research, however, and the abashed Kerry was caught by reporters ordering his steak *with Swiss cheese*—sacrilege!—and was then photographed nibbling daintily at the corner of the mammoth sandwich—marking Kerry as a street food weenie or, even worse, a cultural snob out of touch with the people's way of chowing down. Craig LaBan, food critic for the *Philadelphia Inquirer,* said flat-out, "It will doom his candidacy in Philadelphia," explaining that to get Swiss cheese on a steak in Philly was "an alternative lifestyle."

Finally, a note about the meat itself. There are two fundamental styles. The classic way, as done at Pat's, Steve's, and Geno's, is to grill very thin slices of steak and leave them fairly intact, folding them into the roll separately from the onions. The second method, practiced at Mama's and Lorenzo's, is to use a spatula to hack up the beef as it sizzles. The latter technique allows the onions to be blended with the beef on the griddle. Mama's even adds the cheese before piling the whole load into the bread's jaws.

CHEEZ WHIZ

Although it is a brand name, **Cheez Whiz** also is an unavoidable regional passion in Philadelphia, where it graces many of the finest **cheese steaks.** It was invented in the early 1950s by Kraft scientists whose goal was to design a stable cheese for the rarebit trade (a popular luncheon dish of beer, bread, and cheese quickly grilled), but their creation was far greater than they intended. In the tradition of Velveeta, which Kraft had introduced in the 1930s as better than plain cheese (because "nutritive value" was added by scientists), Whiz was marketed as nothing short of a miracle. It has a near eternal shelf life; it melts on contact with hot food, thus eliminating the need for grating; and, unlike so many cheeses, it doesn't clump or curdle—it is as smooth as a baby's bottom. Instead of being just one monotonous kind of cheese, it is "cheese food," containing American, mozzarella, Muenster, and Gouda, as well as the tastes of mustard, salt, and Worcestershire sauce, the preservative powers of sorbic acid, and the distinctive school-bus orange hue of food dye #A001M.

When it was test-marketed in 1952, housewives reported 1304 uses for Cheez Whiz, including spooning it into hot macaroni, mixing it with vegetables (as a way of getting children to eat broccoli), dolloping it warm on frankfurters, and spreading it on crackers. They even praised the glass jar it came in (eight- or sixteen-ounce size), which could be reused for jelly or even as an emergency drinking glass. The dissemination of microwave ovens in the 1960s gave Cheez Whiz a whole new life. Bombarded by electromagnetic energy, the claylike stuff in the jar slackens into fluid custard usable as hot cheese sauce or five-layer Mexican dip without a single pot or pan getting soiled.

CHESS PIE

In an era when overexcited food reporters swoon over desserts that are decadent or sinful, **chess pie** is probably too virtuous for the spotlight. But to the educated pastry devotee, it is a study in the sort of cookery that exalts simple goodness over strained excess. No doubt, there are relatively fancy chess pies—chocolate chess, amaretto chess, even caramel chess—but the essence of this pie is purity. Eggs, butter, sugar, and a bit of cornmeal are the only necessary ingredients, and sometimes the only ingredients at all. A dash of vanilla or lemon zest gives it a nice twist, and some Old South cooks add a teaspoon of vinegar that adds twang to its mighty sweet nature.

A great chess pie is unambiguous: Flaky crust holds a ribbon of sunny yellow curd, its top perhaps faintly browned, its interior an adult pabulum of unspeakable tenderness. Chess pies sometimes are crowned with meringue or whipped topping, which is fine for flavor but does detract from any texture the top of the filling may have.

Rarely found outside the South, where it is a staple on cafe menus, at fried chicken restaurants, and even in some barbecues, chess pie's name is a favorite puzzler among food etymologists, whose speculations range from it being a bastardization of English *cheese pie* to a cook who, queried about what kind of pie he had made, answered, "Nothing special. Jes' pie." Or because it keeps well in a pie chest, it might originally have been named *chest pie.*

CHICAGO MIX

A **Chicago mix,** or simply *mix,* is a bag filled half-and-half with caramel corn and cheese corn. Originated by the small Chicago-based chain of Garrett Popcorn Shops, which has branded its toasty, butter-rich caramel corn Caramel-Crisp, Chicago mix pairs the very crisp caramel corn with bright orange, well salted cheese corn, which is more tender than crunchy, creating a one-two punch that that satisfies both sweet and savory cravings simultaneously and also leaves a semipermanent stain of orange cheese on the eater's fingers.

CHICKEN BOOYAH

Don't expect to come across **chicken booyah** as the daily special in a restaurant; and we doubt if many families have it at home for a quiet supper. It is a northeast Wisconsin community dish made in large quantities for church picnics and town rallies, always by a number of cooks around 50-gallon pots over wood fires. Similar to such gallimaufries as **Brunswick stew, jambalaya,** and **burgoo,** it contains chicken, beef, pork, and vegetables, and it can take a couple of days to prepare. Explanations of the name are that it is a bastardization of *bouillon* or *bouillabaisse* or that it descends from the Walloon word *bouyu,* meaning "boil." Credence to that last explanation can be found in the fact that many north country folks for whom chicken booyah is the fundamental celebration dish still refer to it as "Belgian penicillin." The word refers not only to what is served, but to the event itself: At a booyah, booyah is the main course.

CHICKEN DINNER ROAD

Deep in farmland northeast of Pittsburg, Kansas, on a country lane formally named 600th Avenue but known to adventurous foodies as **Chicken Dinner Road,** two big restaurants just a few hundred yards apart serve big, nearly identical dinners. The nexus of good eats began during the Depression, when Ann Pichler's husband, Charley, got hurt and could no longer work in the local coal mine. Starting in 1934, Ann made ends meet by serving meals out of her home, which soon became known as Chicken Annie's. About ten years later, when Mary Zerngast's husband, Joe, developed a heart condition that precluded his going down into the mines, Mary—seeing Annie's success—opened her own chicken dinner restaurant. She was from then on known as Chicken Mary. Although goofball television has tried to position the two restaurants' proximity as a food war, they have thrived for over half a century with little evidence of feuding.

The draw at both is deep-fried chicken that arrives at the table glistening with grease and girdled with chewy, fat-rich skin of unspeakable opulence. You can have whatever parts of the bird you like in whatever quantity: dark meat, white meat, wings, and backs, even an appetizer of livers, gizzards, and hearts. Customary side dishes are German potato salad and German coleslaw.

Similar large-scale chicken dinners are served nearby at Gebhardt's Chicken and Dinners in Mulberry (opened in 1946) and Barto's Idle Hour in Frontenac (opened in the early 1950s).

CHICKEN-FRIED STEAK

It seems logical that the Lone Star State's favorite comfort food, **chicken-fried steak,** traces its heritage back to the many Central European immigrant cooks who found themselves in Texas but without the fixin's for a fine, tender cut of veal to make Wiener schnitzel. Instead, they took a hunk of cow and beat the chaw out of it (with an old glass Coke bottle, according to legend), then fried it up like Southern-style chicken and served it with pan-dripping peppered milk gravy and mashed potatoes. This genealogical speculation is supported by the fact that the Hill Country, with its preponderance of German great-grandmas, is home to so many excellent chicken-fried steaks. In so many other places throughout the Southwest, CFS means **diner** grub at its worst.

CHICKEN VESUVIO

Chicken Vesuvio is served nowhere outside of Chicago, and even many new Chicagoans are unaware of it. An aromatic, intoxicatingly garlicked dish of sautéed and baked, bone-in, skin-on parts of chicken and wedges of potato saturated with white wine and presented as a mountain on the plate, it most likely was named after a pre–World War II downtown restaurant named Vesuvio's. One culinary urban legend has long held that it was named because it looks like a huge volcano when plated. Only a handful of restaurants continue to serve it, among them steak houses Harry Caray's and Gene and Georgetti, as well as such Italian bastions as Il Vicinato Ristorante and Francesco's Hole in the Wall in the suburb of Northbrook.

Chicken Vesuvio

½ cup flour
½ teaspoon pepper
½ teaspoon salt
½ teaspoon dried thyme
½ teaspoon dried rosemary
1 teaspoon dried oregano
Olive oil for frying
1 cut-up frying chicken, rinsed and patted dry
4 baking potatoes, cut lengthwise into eighths, soaked in ice water
4–8 cloves garlic, minced (to taste)
1 cup dry white wine
⅓ cup chopped fresh parsley
1 cup cooked green peas

1. Mix together the flour, pepper, salt, thyme, rosemary, and oregano. Lightly dredge the chicken in the flour mixture.

2. Heat about ½ inch olive oil in a large, heavy, ovenproof skillet to 360°F. Fry the chicken pieces a few at a time (don't crowd the pan) until well-browned, turning once or twice and allowing 15–18 minutes per piece. Drain the chicken on paper towels.

3. Pat the potatoes dry, then add them to the skillet of hot oil. Cook until golden brown all over. Remove and drain on paper towels.

4. Heat oven to 350°F. Leave about ¼ inch of fat in the skillet, but drain off the rest. Return the chicken parts and the potatoes to the skillet, crowding them in as necessary. Sprinkle with minced garlic and pour on the wine. Sprinkle with parsley. Bake uncovered 20–25 minutes, until potatoes are tender and chicken is fall-apart soft. Serve drizzled with pan juices and scattered with peas.

4 SERVINGS

JULIA CHILD

No one revolutionized home cooking more than **Julia Child,** who is such a pop culture icon that even people who never read *Mastering the Art of French Cooking* or saw her on TV know who she is. And nearly everybody loved her. Unlike boob-tube product pitchmen before her, when Julia first appeared on PBS, the noncommercial network, she was selling nothing other than the glory of French cuisine. Beginning in 1962 and airing for a decade (then followed by *Julia Child & Company*), *The French Chef,* as the show and she were called, was a revelation. Here was serious cooking that was nonetheless casual, carefree, and sometimes flat-out hilarious. The chef herself could be hypnotically butterfingered and frequently seemed unpolished and unprofessional—which made her appear all the more true-to-life and made the recipes she demonstrated seem within reach of anyone with the will to try them. What a character she was! A jovial clown with an upper-crust whinny who acted looped (but was only loopy) as she hooted her way through recipes that worked or didn't (it hardly mattered) and lurched through her TV kitchen and made a big mess of it just as we all do at home.

Like so many cultured people in the early days of television, she looked down her nose at the very medium itself, revealing in her introduction to *The French Chef Cookbook* (1968) that she kept her own ugly little television set hidden away in an unused fireplace in her Cambridge house. Still, no chef was ever so naturally telegenic, so charming in her awkwardness, and so farcically irrepressible. Like *The Continental* ten years before her, the video personality Julia Child projected was so original that she became a Dan Ackroyd character on *Saturday Night Live,* in a legendary sketch where she winds up lying on the floor in a pool of her own blood (having hacked off her thumb) but nonetheless unflappable and crying out her trademark salutation, "Bon appétit!"

Although many viewers tuned in only to enjoy her antics (and discovered good food as a fringe benefit of the fun), Julia Child was an inspiring television teacher and a major force behind ambitious home cooks' infatuation with French food in the sixties. Americans have always had a fondness for didactic self-improvement schemes, from *How to Win Friends and Influence People* to the Dummies guide series, and *The French Chef* was the culinary version: a fast, workmanlike instructional half-hour without a trace of one-upmanship or snobbery. As in her book, every single step of the cooking process was documented and demonstrated so that even a completely inexperienced cook could try to follow along. And to help the detailed instruction go down easy, the soundtrack pulsated with the breathlessly buoyant, reassuring voice of Julia herself (nearly every viewer felt familiar enough to call her by her first name) crooning over the beauty of a poaching egg or the aroma of onions sizzling in butter, laughing off her mistakes, slamming a big old fish around the counter or dropping it on the floor, and gaily extolling the results as the program rushed to its conclusion. Thanks to *The French Chef,* amiably eccentric cooking teachers became a staple of the television airwaves.

CHILE

Forgive us, chili-lovers. There is no separate entry in this lexicon for *chili*, nor for *chilli* or *chili con carne*. We have put these under the heading of **chile** because the *e* at the end signifies the plant on which all are based, no matter what the spelling. Whether the subject is botanical or gastronomical, New Mexicans like to use the *e* spelling out of respect for the co-state vegetable (along with the pinto bean).

Is it a vegetable? The chile is an ambiguous critter, a berry of the nightshade family (like the tomato) that agronomists know as a fruit but is so intensely green-flavored that it tastes like the ultimate vegetable. Its most famous characteristic is heat, but there is so much more. Recently Dr. Paul Bosland of New Mexico State University's Chile Pepper Institute devised a useful method of taste taxonomy that goes beyond describing a chile as hot or not. Unlike oenophilic poesy, his *Five Characteristics* are specific measures that assist eater, writer, or cook in describing peppers' diversity:

1. What is the heat profile? Does it come on quick (like a jalapeño) or is the punch delayed (like an habañero)? The speed of the feeling depends on the balance of capsaicinoids, of which there are twenty-two.

2. Where does the heat develop? You feel jalapeños at the front of the tongue; New Mexican pods work mid-palate; habañeros ignite nearest the throat.

3. Is the heat sharp or broad? Most Asian chiles have a pinprick feel. (There is one with a name that translates as "claws of the eagle.") New Mexico chiles paint the tongue like a broad brush.

4. How fast does the chile's feel dissipate? Some are hit and run. A scotch bonnet's heat can linger for hours.

5. How intense is it? This is measured by the Scoville scale. Pimientos are zero, as are bell peppers. A jalapeño registers 5000. Habañeros can approach 500,000. The world's hottest pepper, the Bhut Jolokia of India, scores a raging 1,000,000+.

This happy trio of musical chiles was spotted on a wall in San Antonio, Texas.

Chili with an *i* always refers to a dish, not the plant, and when most people hear the word *chili,* it is chili con carne that they think of. Literally meaning *chili* (er, *chile*) *with meat,* that is just about all it is in its purest, true-Texas form: beef that is chunked or coarsely ground saturated with the flavor of chile (either in the form of pureed roasted pods or chile powder) and a liquid medium. Some spices, such as cumin, salt, and pepper, are welcome in the Lone Star paradigm, known as a "bowl of red," but beans are taboo.

Chili con carne's beginnings predate the Republic of Texas. Historians speculate that Mexican families living on both sides of the Rio Grande stewed beef with peppers not only to stretch the quantity, but, in the same way other cultures use curry spices, to disguise the taste of less-than-fresh provisions. After the Civil War, chili became identified with the "chili queens" of San Antonio's *mercado,* an anything-goes outdoor bazaar where Texans dined on **tamales,** enchiladas, and fiery chili con carne. The queens who served it were colorful women in festively embroidered peasant blouses, and most contemporary accounts make a point of their virtue, despite a reputation for flirting with customers. Still, by the time the chili queens and their wares were banished for propriety's sake in 1943, Texas-style chili had developed an enduring reputation as a red-hot meal at the edge of dining respectability.

Throughout most of the rest of the country, it is common for chili con carne to also include tomatoes, bell peppers, and, of course, beans, and to be topped with grated cheese and/or sour cream. Up the Rio Grande towards New Mexico's Mesilla Valley, restaurants may offer a choice of red chili or green chili, the latter very unlike the familiar bright red stew and actually more of a soup, containing potatoes and onions and very likely pork instead of beef. Amend your order with the word "Christmas" and it will come topped with both red and green chili.

Despite its high status in the state, you are unlikely to see chile as a stand-alone dish on the menu of a New Mexican restaurant. But chile surely will come with any native-foods meal, probably as a sauce of seasoned, pureed pods suitable for dipping tortillas or ladling on stuffed chiles (**chile rellenos**). Chile is most common in New Mexico as the primary agent in other dishes, such as **carne adovada** or enchiladas.

According to the Illinois State Legislature, the correct spelling of the word is with two *l*'s, and the Chilli Capital of the World is the city of Springfield. Texans (and many other Americans) might not recognize Springfield chilli as chili. It is a forceful combo of "chili meat" (seasoned ground beef) and beans topped with a slick layer of oil that ranges from quite hot to thermonuclear. Oyster crackers always are served alongside.

Also see: **chili mac, Cincinnati chili, Green Bay chili, green chile cheeseburger, Minorcan chowder.**

Texas Chili

When we began hunting roadfood, one of the best books that guided us was Frank X. Tolbert's *A Bowl of Red,* which was about all sorts of good Texas eats, but especially chili. In its description of the early 1970s Terlingua chili wars (godfather to virtually all modern cook-offs and contests), Tolbert noted that Tigua Indian tribal chief Jose Sierra began his chili by filling a huge pot one-third full with hot peppers.

So you can imagine that, years ago, when we stopped to have lunch at the urban reservation of the Tiguas (say "Tee-wa"), we were thrilled to run into Mr. Sierra himself. Pegging us as out-of-towners, he kindly suggested that we would be wise not to order the chili. He thought it would be too hot for our Anglo palates. Being proud and ignorant, we took his warning as a cry to arms and ordered two big bowls. As we ate them with tears streaming out our eyes and beads of sweat popping on our foreheads, we came to understand that it is not wise to play macho games with a Texas chilihead. You will lose.

After the heat on our tongues subsided enough for us to regain the power of speech, we begged Mr. Sierra for the recipe. Here it is, but toned down to mid-level hot. If you want to goose it up to tear-wrenching standards, double the jalapeño pepper powder, include other fiery peppers of your choice, or add ½ stick dynamite.

1 cup chopped onion
2 cloves garlic, minced
2 tablespoons vegetable oil
2 pounds beef round, cut into ½-inch cubes
1½ teaspoons salt
1 tablespoon sugar
1½ teaspoons coarse ground pepper
1½ teaspoons oregano
1 tablespoon ground cumin
5 tablespoons chili powder
1½ teaspoons ground jalapeño powder
1 15-ounce can tomato sauce
1½ cups water
1 tablespoon masa harina, dissolved in ½ cup water

1. Sauté onion and garlic in oil until soft. Add beef and cook until it is browned. Add salt, sugar, pepper, oregano, cumin, chili powder, jalapeño powder, tomato sauce, and water. Stir well. Bring to a boil. Reduce heat to a low boil and simmer, partially covered, for 70 minutes. Remove from heat. Add masa harina dissolved in water to chili. Place the chili over low heat for 5 minutes, stirring occasionally.

2. Serve with beans, rice, or bread on the side: All are useful for muffling the heat.

6 SERVINGS

Topeka Chili

Porubsky's Grocery of Topeka, Kansas, has been a chili landmark for generations. Its version is Midwestern style, meaning the beef is ground, beans are included, and the spice level is moderate. When we inquired, not one of the Porubsky family was able to write down the recipe—for the simple reason that there is no recipe. It is an uncomplicated dish made by taste, feel, and experience: a little of this, a jot of that, a dash more of something else. We spent a morning watching Charlie Jr. prepare a day's worth, so here is our educated version of Porubsky's pride. Its heat level can be adjusted by using hot or mild chili powder and by adding more or less hot sauce.

1 cup chopped onion
2 cloves garlic, minced
2 tablespoons vegetable oil
2 pounds coarsely ground chuck
1½ teaspoons salt
3 tablespoons chili powder
1 tablespoon ground cumin
2 teaspoons Worcestershire sauce
1 tablespoon sugar
3 cups tomato sauce
2 cups water
2 16-ounce cans red kidney beans, drained
Tabasco sauce, to taste (we use 10 drops for a faint heat)
Saltine crackers
Dill pickles, thickly sliced and halved into bite-size nuggets

1. In a heavy saucepan, sauté the onions and garlic in oil over medium heat until they are soft. Add beef and salt. Cook until the beef is browned throughout, breaking it up with a fork as it cooks. Drain off any excess fat. Add chili powder, cumin, Worcestershire, sugar, tomato sauce, and water. Bring the pot to a low boil and simmer 30 minutes, stirring occasionally. Add the beans and simmer 15 minutes more. Add Tabasco sauce to taste, and more salt if desired.

2. Serve with saltines crumbled on top of each portion and dill pickle pieces as a garnish.

6 SERVINGS

CHILE RELLENO

Like **chicken-fried steaks, chile rellenos** range from hideous to glorious. At their best, made from freshly roasted chiles that still have muscular vegetable walls, stuffed with cream-rich molten queso, and haloed in a coat of feather-weight batter fried to a fragile crisp, they are food of the gods. Nearly all of those encountered in the Southwest are made from mild pods—Anaheims, Big Jims, or poblanos—so the chile experience is far more about their sunshiny flavor than about any kind of ferocious heat. Rellenos usually are served decorated with sauce or salsa cruda, and while cheese is the classic filling, some are stuffed also with beef brisket, picadillo (beef hash), or shredded chicken.

In 1992, the term *jalapeño popper* was trademarked by a Wisconsin food company, recognizing the immense popularity of cheese-stuffed, deep-fried jalapeño peppers. These pint-size, three-alarm variations of chile rellenos are an ideal bar snack.

53

CHILI MAC

The combination of chili-seasoned ground beef, spaghetti or elbow noodles, and beans—usually topped with a crown of shredded orange cheese—is popular throughout the Midwest and beyond. In **Cincinnati chili,** the ingredients are layered. To the west, around Lake Michigan, you're more likely to encounter chili-spiced meat and cooked elbow macaroni mixed together in a skillet on the stove. That version, possibly amended by beans, onions, and cheese, is known as **chili mac.**

For years, chili mac was a staple in neighborhood taverns, **diners,** and town cafes around Chicagoland, but it has virtually disappeared in recent years. In fact, the last time we found some in a restaurant was at Mike's Chili Parlor in Seattle, Washington. Chili mac also remains available in a handful of St. Louis diners, where chili meat and noodles topped with fried eggs is known as *chili mac a la mode.*

Chili Mac

Nachos and wings have eclipsed chili mac as a preferred bar food in the Midwest, but on a cold winter's day at home, when settling down for an afternoon of reading, TV viewing, or just hanging around the house, nothing induces a feeling of security and comfort better than the come-hither aroma of an honest pot of chili mac keeping warm on the stove.

1 pound lean ground chuck
2 tablespoons cooking oil
1 28-ounce can diced tomatoes with juice
1 cup chopped onion
3 cloves garlic, minced
1 teaspoon salt
1 tablespoon Worcestershire sauce
2 tablespoons chili powder
1 teaspoon ground cumin
1 teaspoon dried marjoram
½ teaspoon pepper
2 tablespoons sugar
1 bay leaf
1–2 cups tomato sauce
2 16-ounce cans red kidney beans, drained and rinsed
1 pound elbow macaroni or spaghetti
Butter
Tabasco or other hot pepper sauce of choice, to taste
Grated cheese (optional)
Oyster crackers

1. Brown the beef in oil in a Dutch oven, stirring to separate it. Drain excess fat. Add tomatoes, onion, garlic, salt, Worcestershire, chili powder, cumin, marjoram, pepper, sugar, bay leaf, and 1 cup of tomato sauce. Partially cover and simmer 25 minutes, stirring occasionally and adding more tomato sauce to keep the chili nice and moist but not too soupy. Add the kidney beans. Cook 10 minutes more (as you prepare the macaroni). Add hot sauce to taste.

2. Cook the noodles al dente. Drain and lightly butter. Combine the hot noodles with the chili and serve in bowls, topped with grated cheese if desired, with oyster crackers on the side.

6–8 SERVINGS

CHIMICHANGA

Chicago chef Rick Bayless, of Frontera Grill and author of *Authentic Mexican,* believes the **chimichanga** originated in Baja, where it was known as a *chivechanga,* but the history of El Charro restaurant in Tucson says that one day, many decades ago, founder Monica Flinn accidentally dropped a stuffed burrito into a vat of sizzling oil, christening what came out of the fry kettle a *chimichanga,* meaning "thingamajig." However it came to be, the chimi is now one of the most popular items on Mexican-American menus all around the country—basically a deep-fried burro that looks like a gigantic egg roll. Like burritos, chimichangas can be filled all sorts of ways: with **carne seca,** shredded chicken, pork, or only vegetables, including beans.

CHIPPED (BARBECUE)

In the barbecue parlors of western Kentucky, customers can have their meat sliced, chopped, or **chipped,** the last one meaning shredded into hash. That treatment does away with whatever textural excitement may be found in hunks of smoke-cooked mutton, pork, beef, or ham, but it can intensify the flavor, especially if the chipped barbecue is combined with the robust mix of drippin's and spice known as **dip.**

In western Kentucky, chipped barbecue is even more hacked up than chopped.

CHITLINS

Chitlins are offal. Pig intestines, to be precise. When eating swine from the rooter to the tooter, they are as low on the hog as you can go. They joined the American diet as African slaves' food, while masters ate hams and pork chops from high on the hog. Unlike many other once lowly dishes that have gradually been elevated to culinary stars (lobster, barbecue, bread made from coarse-ground flour), chitlins, formally known as *chitterlings,* remain uncouth. They are savored by few, prized by some proud poor whites as well as blacks because they are so symbolic of culinary humility, but they are a taste that many who did not grow up with them find very difficult to acquire. There are a number of well-attended chitlin festivals around the country (the foremost being in Salley, South Carolina), at which the in-your-face food is honored with the same mischievous pride found at festivals that celebrate such love-it-or-hate-it fare as ramps, pickled eggs, and fried testicles.

Particularly malodorous when being cooked, chitlins frequently are deep-fried, a process that tends to mask their intestinal essence. Through a wide swath of southernmost Virginia, however, they are steamed in vinegar, the tang of the liquid serving as a kind of palate cleanser. Needless to say, given chitlins' point of origin, they are a food that must be cleaned extremely well before being cooked and eaten.

CHOWDER

Chowder is a bowlful of comfort thick with crackers or flour and milk and flavored with salt pork. Usually it stars seafood, although a *farmhouse chowder* can be made with the likes of corn and potatoes, and Illinois has a chowder all its own (see **downstate chowder**). In New England, *chowder* is different from *stew,* the latter meaning warm milk or cream seasoned with salt and pepper, pooled with melted butter, and containing nothing but large morsels of fish or lobster, clams, or oysters: no potatoes or vegetables of any kind. Chowder, no matter how it's made, always contains potatoes. There are several basic varieties.

The Maine Diner consistently wins blue ribbons for its mighty seafood chowder.

MANHATTAN CHOWDER

Red like minestrone and thick with many kinds of chopped-up vegetables, in addition to clams.

NEW ENGLAND CHOWDER

Milk or cream-based, enriched with the flavor of salt pork, and thick with potatoes. Clams are the customary ingredient, although it can be made with pieces of flatfish, shrimp, oysters, or scallops.

Boston's Durgin-Park is a bastion of traditional Yankee cooking, including chowder.

RHODE ISLAND CHOWDER

A creamy bisque with just enough tomatoes to turn it blushing pink. Traditionally served with fried **clam cakes** on the side.

SOUTHERN NEW ENGLAND CHOWDER

Found only along the Connecticut shore and into Rhode Island. Made without milk or cream and no vegetables other than potatoes and onion, it is minced clams and their nectar: a bracing, steel-gray broth made to pique the appetite before a full-bore **shore dinner.**

OREGON CHOWDER

Featuring clams and nuggets of potato, Oregon chowder ranges from rib-sticking to elegant and usually is flavored with smoked bacon or salt pork. It is thick enough that when it is served with a pat of butter on top, the butter forms a pool that does not blend until it is stirred in.

Oregon chowder: thick enough to float a butter pat.

Southern New England Clear Broth Clam Chowder

"The trouble with most people's chowder is they cook it too long," said Flo Klewin of Kitchen Little in Mystic, Connecticut. "It gets too strong. Take it off the heat fast if you want it to be nice." The result is a gentle-flavored broth that tastes as much of the ocean as of clams.

8 slices thick bacon (about ½ pound)
2 cups chopped onion
2½ cups diced redskin potatoes, skin on
3 cups clam broth
1 8–20 large, hard-shell clams, shucked and drained, and their liquor
Pepper
¼ cup chopped fresh basil

1. Cut the bacon into 1-inch pieces. Fry in a large pot until crisp. Remove the bacon pieces and save them to put in omelets the next morning. Add onion to the rendered bacon fat and sauté until soft. Add potatoes, clam broth, and enough water to fully cover the potatoes (at least 1 cup). Bring to a boil, cover, and simmer 12 minutes or until the potatoes are tender.

2. Coarsely cut the clams (do not mince or use a food processor). You should have about 3 cups of clam meat. Strain the clam liquor through a double-layer of cheesecloth to remove impurities, or boil it and skim off the foam that rises to the top. Add the clams and clam liquor to the chowder pot. Bring it back to a boil. Simmer 3 minutes. Remove from heat and add pepper to taste. Sprinkle on basil; serve with crackers.

6–8 SERVINGS

CHOW MEIN SANDWICH

The **chow mein sandwich,** a strange specialty of **drive-ins, diners,** and cafes on the south coast of Massachusetts and Rhode Island east of Narragansett Bay (as well as at Nathan's of Coney Island), exists because Frederick Wong started the Oriental Chow Mein Company in 1926. Genuine chow mein sandwiches are built with noodles the family makes at the old building in Fall River. These noodles are crunchy, not soft as in chow mein elsewhere. And traditional chow mein sandwiches are meatless: simply noodles topped with sauced sprouts all on a plate along with a hamburger bun.

For those more familiar with typical Chinese-American chow mein, the concept is a little weird. It is certainly not a sandwich you can pick up and eat, and while a bun floating in chow mein at first seems anomalous, an eater soon discovers that it is a mighty handy tool for mopping up the last of the gravy from the plate.

CINCINNATI CHILI

Cincinnati chili first was served by Greek immigrants who came to town in 1922, after having sold chili dogs for a while in New York. It is now the specialty of dozens of Queen City eateries, including the Gold Star and Skyline chains. The foundation for every serving is a bed of well-cooked spaghetti noodles arranged on a thick oval plate, and, on top of that, ground meat sauce—a little hot and a little sweet with a distinctive formation of Greek spices. Recipes for the sauce are guarded like Fort Knox gold; unique ingredients include nutmeg, allspice, mace, and ground chocolate. Usually, the sauce is topped with kidney beans, raw onions, and shredded Wisconsin cheddar cheese—a total of five layers, leading to the moniker *five-way chili.* It is possible to order *four-way* (hold the onions) or to ask for a *haywagon* (hold the beans, too, and pile on the shredded cheddar). Oyster crackers are a customary garnish. Cincinnati chili parlors supplement their menus with double-decker sandwiches and **Coney Island** hot dogs piled up like five-way.

Cincinnati Five-Way Chili

Bearing no resemblance to any Southwestern "bowl of red," Cincinnati chili has a cult and culture all its own. Part of the culture is secrecy. No Cincinnati chili chef gives out the recipe, but many years ago we did manage to secure one by sending a dollar to a lady over the border in Kentucky who advertised in the back of a Midwestern housewife's magazine that she knew how to make the real thing. With minor adjustments, it worked for us, and it closely approximates some of the city's best brews. Feel free to fiddle and fuss to your own taste, and if you are missing cardamom or coriander, substitute something else. Five-way practically demands that you reinvent the recipe and make it your own.

1 pound ground beef
1 tablespoon cooking oil
2 medium onions, chopped
2 cloves garlic, minced
1 cup thick barbecue sauce
½ cup water
½ ounce unsweetened chocolate, grated
1 tablespoon chili powder
1 teaspoon pepper
¼ teaspoon ground cumin
¼ teaspoon turmeric
¼ teaspoon allspice
¼ teaspoon cinnamon
¼ teaspoon ground cloves
¼ teaspoon ground coriander
¼ teaspoon ground cardamom
½ teaspoon salt
Tomato juice, as needed
9 ounces spaghetti, cooked and lightly buttered
1 16-ounce can red kidney beans, heated and drained
1 pound Cheddar cheese, finely shredded
Oyster crackers, for garnish

1. Brown the meat in the oil with half the chopped onion and all the garlic, stirring to keep it loose. (Set the remaining onion aside to top the chili when it's done.) Drain any fat from the pan. Add barbecue sauce and water and bring the pan to a boil. Add the chocolate, spices, and salt. Cover the pan and lower the heat. Simmer 30 minutes, stirring occasionally. The chili will thicken as it cooks. Add tomato juice as necessary to create a brew that ladles up easily. Allow the chili to rest at least 30 minutes in a covered pan at room temperature. (Chili can be refrigerated and reheated to serve.)

2. To make each plate, put a layer of spaghetti down, top it with hot chili, then a few beans, then the reserved chopped onions to taste. Pat on the cheese so the chili's heat can begin to melt it. Serve immediately with oyster crackers.

4 SERVINGS

CIOPPINO

James Beard's second book, *Cook It Outdoors*, published in 1941, was billed as "a man's book written by a man." It was filled with recipes for hearty, two-fisted fare, **cioppino** being one of his prime examples (although, curiously, spelled "chippino"). A devil-may-care West Coast bouillabaisse with as many recipes as it has cooks, it is a fish stew originated by the Italian fishermen who settled San Francisco's North Beach in the late nineteenth century. They took the day's catch, usually including crab, shrimp, clams, scallops, and mussels, and cooked them all (including shells) with flatfish in a seasoned tomato-wine sauce. As the Italian community became a tourist attraction in the twentieth century, the colorful dish took on symbolic character and has since become as much a San Francisco signature as sourdough bread (with which it customarily is served).

CITY CHICKEN

Remnant of the pre-Depression era when "a chicken in every pot" was a symbol of prosperity, **city chicken** contains no chicken. It is pork or sometimes pork combined with beef or veal ground up and fashioned to resemble chicken: either as chunks on a skewer or as a mock drumstick. Its survival as a menu item, however tenuous, is ironic considering that chicken, once so dear, is now generally cheaper than pork and beef and frequently is substituted for them in sausage, chili, and burgers that yearn to be more nutritionally correct. A more subtle irony is that the modifier *city* once used to imply the seat of sophistication rather than a place of social decay. Nowadays, most mindful eaters prefer their food to be country-fresh, not city-slick. The few old-time places where we have encountered city chicken are blue-collar taverns and **diners** in western Pennsylvania and upstate New York as well as in West Virginia and Ohio.

CLAMBAKE

Like the Carolina **pig pickin'**, the Yankee **clambake** is a ritual that goes back to the seventeenth century and continues as a way not only to eat well but to honor regional culinary heritage. Clambakes are featured at large family gatherings, town picnics, political rallies, and seaside fairs. As practiced today, the featured ingredients include not only steamer clams but also lobsters, corn on the cob or corn kernels scraped into the pot with plenty of butter, potatoes, and sometimes sausages and flatfish as well. (Along the southern shore of Lake Erie, around Cleveland, a different kind of clambake takes place in the autumn: It features clams, chicken, sweet corn, and sweet potatoes.)

The Downeast method of cooking is to heat stones in a fire pit constructed on the rocky shore and burn wood down to ashes. The food is then set atop the ashes and hot stones among layers of seaweed and covered with either more seaweed or damp canvas tarps for a couple of hours. It is a tricky procedure to keep the heat relatively stable for that long as well as to layer the food so that it is all ready to eat at the same time; many modern cooks continue to use an open fire but steam the food inside metal pots.

Peaks Island, Maine: a classic clambake on the rocks.

CLAM CAKE

A **clam cake** may be sweet or briny or some of both, but it rarely is very clammy. Unlike a great **crab cake,** which accentuates the crab and minimizes its medium, clam cakes are all about the dough. In fact, you could think of a clam cake as a **doughboy** with bits of chopped clam included. Common on seafood menus throughout southern New England as a necessary companion for clam chowder, clam cakes are made from a batter leavened by baking powder and perhaps including a shot of clam juice. The batter is formed into a sphere a little bigger than a golf ball and deep-fried. A clam cake may also be shaped into a flatter form, in which case it will most likely be called a *clam fritter.*

Clam cakes: a shore dinner staple.

COAL CANDY

Coal candy is a unique confection invented in Pottsville, Pennsylvania, by Catherine Mootz of the Mootz Candy Store sometime in the 1950s, when the region's coal industry was thriving. It is intensely licorice-flavored, packaged in large, irregular chunks that are black and shiny like nuggets of freshly mined anthracite. It comes in boxes, in miniature miners' buckets, and in toy train cars; it is sometimes sold with a little toy hammer that can be used to smash big pieces into bite-size fragments. Whereas the traditional Christmas code says that boys and girls who have been bad get a lump of coal in their stockings, that practice is reversed in the mining towns of Pennsylvania, where only good children get stockings full of coal candy.

COCHON DE LAIT

In southern Louisiana, **cochon de lait** means more than suckling pig. It suggests a high-spirited *fais-do-do* (Cajun party) at which the long-cooked, butter-tender pig is a featured culinary attraction, possibly alongside a **crawfish boil** and cauldrons full of **jambalaya.** Some sit-down restaurants in this part of the world do serve cochon de lait, either as an entree or the filling of a **po'boy,** but the traditional place to get it is outdoors, at a buffet line, where the open pit–cooked pig is doled out as it is cut, affording eaters the opportunity to choose among the very soft white meat, the chewy parts from outside (known as *bark*), and crunchy strips of skin. Of course, Zydeco music should be wafting through the air.

COFFEE MILK

What is your official state drink? Not every state has one, and most of those that do play it safe and make it milk. But there are other choices, some obvious (orange juice in Florida, cranberry juice in Massachusetts), some obscure (Kool-Aid in Nebraska, water in Indiana). But such arcana pale compared to

Rhode Island's passion for **coffee milk.** Like chocolate milk, but coffee flavored, it is omnipresent on menus in **diners** and cafes, available in every market and convenience store, and a favorite among home cooks who make it using readily available coffee syrup. Historians speculate that its popularity derives from the state's rich Italian heritage and the Old Country tradition of gentling strong coffee with a lot of milk and sweetener. Rhode Island coffee milk, as popularized at drugstore soda fountains in the 1930s, tends not to be strong at all; it is milk that is slightly sweet with a hint of caffeination.

Add a scoop of ice cream to coffee milk and you have what Rhode Islanders know as a *coffee cab,* short for *coffee cabinet.* Whirl it in a blender and you've got what the rest of the nation might call a coffee **milk shake** and what Bay State neighbors know as a *frappe.*

COFFEE SHOP

◇◇

A **coffee shop** is not a coffee house. The terms are conflated in the Starbucks era, but there is scant synonymity. A coffee *house,* like Starbucks, is all about the coffee, including a catalog of fancy espresso drinks at dollar-per-ounce prices (see **coffee talk**). A coffee *shop* rarely offers more than regular and decaf, and the waitress will keep pouring as long as you keep drinking. Coffee *house* food is pastries and prefab sandwiches heated in the microwave. Coffee *shops* serve great platters of breakfast, hot lunch with gravy and double-decker sandwiches, pie and pudding for dessert, and maybe even dinner, too. In a coffee *house,* one can sit with a laptop in an easy chair and connect to the Internet. In a coffee *shop,* you sit at the counter, or maybe in a booth, and connect with human beings: your dining companion, the waitress or short-order cook, or perfect strangers sitting nearby.

The coffee shop is the **diner**'s more respectable cousin, offering a similarly broad menu but on nicer plates with sprigs of parsley. Most coffee shops are urban—oases for shoppers or business folks in need of decent food at a fair price with no folderol or wasted time. They reached their apotheosis in the mid-twentieth century in southern California, where the most glorious of them still thrive: places like Pann's in Los Angeles, with its dramatic "googie" décor, like a tailfinned Cadillac mated with a spaceship, and Hob Nob Hill in

Hathaway's Coffee Shop, Cincinnati, Ohio.

San Diego, where the staff are as efficient as nurses in an operating theater. However stylish, polite, and efficient they may be, coffee shops never are pretentious. Come as you are, no reservations required, eat well and pay little, and walk out with spring in your step.

COFFEE TALK

"Cup o' joe" will not suffice as an order in a twenty-first-century coffee house. First, you must specify size. *Small, medium,* and *large* may work in some places, but Starbucks has replaced such confusing terms with *tall, grande,* and *venti,* as well as the stealth (unlisted) size known as *short,* plus 2010's new sizes, *plenta* (128 ounces) and *micra* (2 ounces).

A single measure of espresso is known as a *shot* or a *solo*; a double is a *doppio* and four is a *quad.* There is no special term for three shots of espresso; it simply is a *triple.* A *red-eye* (also known as a *shot in the dark*) is brewed coffee with a single shot of espresso; a *black-eye* contains two shots, a *green-eye* three.

Other words to know:

Americano: Espresso cut with hot water.
Au lait: With milk.
Breve: Add half-and-half.
Cappuccino: Espresso, steamed milk, and foam.
Con panna: Espresso topped with whipped cream.
Dry cap: A cappuccino with less milk and more foam.
Frappuccino: A Starbucks concoction of coffee, sweetener, flavoring,
    and ice.
Half caf: Fifty percent decaffeinated coffee.
Macchiato: Espresso and foam.
Misto: Coffee, steamed milk, and a bit of foam (Starbucks version of *café
    au lait*).
Mocha: Espresso, steamed milk, and chocolate with whipped cream on top.
Skinny: Skimmed milk instead of whole.
Soy: Soy milk instead of cow's milk.
Wet cap: A cappuccino with more milk and less foam.

Latte art in Portland, Oregon.

JOE COLEMAN

In 1980 **Joe Coleman** of Wheeling, West Virginia, went to Boston and set sail on a fishing trawler. "I did every job you could do on that boat," he says. "I stood watch, I swabbed the deck, I hauled 'em in and stacked them in the hold. I followed the fish from the water to the pier to the auction. Then I rode in the front seat of the truck that carried the fish back to Wheeling. I trimmed it, I breaded it, I fried it, I made a fish sandwich from it, and I ate it."

The fisherman pictured behind Joe Coleman is his father, who started the business.

You can be sure the sandwich Joe Coleman ate that day was delicious. His seafood shop in the city's century-old Centre Market House has earned national renown for the simple perfection of its fish sandwich: two pieces of soft white bread holding a cluster of steaming-hot fillets. The golden crust on the fish is cracker meal, thin as parchment. When you break through it, your sense of smell is tickled by a clean ocean perfume, and as the pearl-white meat seeps its luscious flavor, you are tasting a brand-new food, like no other fish sandwich ever created.

Joe is the third generation of Colemans to work in the Wheeling market. His grandfather started selling chickens there prior to World War I. When the chicken business nosedived in 1914, his grandfather bought a retail/wholesale fish business in the market. He sold oysters from Maryland, lobsters from Maine, and fish from the Great Lakes and the Atlantic Ocean. After World War II, he came up with the idea of selling sandwiches of Lake Erie pickerel. But by the 1960s, lake fish was growing scarce, so Joe's father, Raymond Coleman, switched to frying North Atlantic pollock. He also invented the term *Canadian white fish* for a blander alternative to the ocean-sweet pollock that is used in Coleman's traditional sandwich. "Canadian white fish is really just cod," Joe Coleman explained to us. "But too many people associate cod with the taste of cod liver oil. When my father renamed it, sales took off!"

Joe Coleman likes to remind people that he runs a fish market, not a restaurant . . . despite its being the most popular eating place in West Virginia's northern panhandle. Every meal he serves is presented in a bag. Those who want tartar sauce or cocktail sauce must place an order for it, at ten cents or fifteen cents per ounce, respectively, and they must apply it to the fish sandwich themselves. "Charging separately for tartar sauce was my dad's idea," Joe told us. "He believed that it wasn't right for those who don't want it to carry the cost for those who do. Out-of-towners sometimes ask me, 'Why isn't your fish sandwich on a nice bun?' I will tell you why. I don't believe in buns any more than I believe in tartar sauce. What I believe in is quality fish."

CONCH CHOWDER

The sea snail known as a *conch* (pronounced "konk") has been so important in the culture and diet of the Bahamian-ancestored residents of Key West that they refer to themselves as Conchs and to their atoll as the Conch Republic. **Conch chowder,** made with chopped nuggets of the sweet marine meat, along with vegetables, a good measure of pepper and spice, and, perhaps, a shot of sherry, is now served throughout the Florida Keys. Harvested also for their beautiful shells, conchs are protected in U.S. waters but more plentiful in other areas of the Caribbean. Conch meat has long been considered an aphrodisiac.

CONCRETE

To understand the appeal of a **concrete,** you first must know that in much of the Midwest, *custard* is not pudding; custard is similar to soft-serve ice cream, but enriched with eggs. Because Ted Drewes Frozen Custard, the estimable St. Louis **drive-in,** never trademarked the term *concrete*, it now is widely used by any **milk shake** maker who wants you to know how thick his is. As Ted Drewes famously serves it, a concrete is a milk shake made with **frozen custard** blended so thick that the server hands it through the window to a customer with the paper cup that contains it upside down and topless. Nothing spills out. Needless to say, straws are pointless when drinking—or would it be *eating*?—a concrete.

Ted Drewes, a former tennis pro, began selling custard with a traveling carnival in 1929; it wasn't until 1959 that his son, Ted Jr., came up with the ultimate product. Pestered by a neighborhood boy named Steve Gamber, who never was satisfied with how thick his milk shake was, the younger Drewes made a shake with no milk whatsoever, just custard and flavoring. He handed it to Gamber upside down. Drewes called it a "concrete" because at the time many St. Louis ice cream shops were selling extra-thick drinks that they called "cement shakes." As any mason can tell you, concrete contains cement, but it is heavier, denser, and stronger.

CONEY ISLAND

Coney Islands are a sprawling subset of **hot dogs.** They are a little bit different in each part of the country, their common element a blanket of meaty chili. The chili that tops all Coneys tends not to be too hot, but it always has a constellation of seasonings that are distinctly Greek, for virtually every Coney Island restaurant was founded by Greek immigrants.

Curiously, one of the few places in America where the term isn't heard is Coney Island in Brooklyn, New York. **Hot dogs** got their start in Coney Island, but by 1913, the folk belief that hot dogs might actually contain dog flesh had become so widely held that the Coney Island Chamber of Commerce forbid the use of the term "hot dog" on signs or menus. Instead, the immensely popular boardwalk snacks were referred to as "Coney Islands." Many of the country's Coney Island shops were opened by hot dog men who got their starts in New York, but why the "Coney Island" moniker continues to thrive everywhere except its point of origin remains a mystery.

No city is more passionate about Coney Islands than Detroit, where dueling next-door neighbors Lafayette Coney Island and American Coney Island each have partisans for their red weenies topped with chili, onions, and mustard. The most effulgent Coneys are constructed in Cincinnati chili joints, the best of which is Camp Washington Chili, where the chili dogs are crowned with an impossibly big bouquet of shredded cheese. El Reno, Oklahoma, better known for its aromatic **onion-fried burgers,** serves extraordinary Coney Islands topped with chili and also bright, pickly-sweet, mustard-colored slaw.

Tulsa, Oklahoma: Coney I-Lander's signature weenie.

CONGEALED SALAD

In the South, when you see **congealed salad** on the menu, expect more than square cubes of translucent Jell-O. *Congealed salad* is the regional term for a Jell-O salad, meaning the colored gelatin is dotted with carrots or coconut shreds, Fun Mallows, fruit cocktail, or nuts, and instead of being clear, it may be opaque, thanks to the addition of cream cheese, sour cream, cottage cheese, or Miracle Whip. In restaurants that specialize in **meat and three,** congealed salad is usually listed on the menu among the vegetables, along with macaroni and cheese.

Sparkling like precious stones, trays of congealed salad beckon in the cafeteria line.

Congealed salad frequently is listed among the vegetables at meat-and-three restaurants of the South.

THE CONTINENTAL

There's all kinds of food foolishness on twenty-first-century television, but the silliest show ever was broadcast in 1952 on CBS at 11:15 Tuesday and Thursday evenings. No food was eaten or cooked during *The Continental*, but it was a unique education in how to be an epicure. Renzo Cesana played a suave, Italian-accented bachelor who looked straight into the camera and yearningly addressed each member of his audience (presumably female) as if she were his date for the evening. Viewers never saw her; everything was from her point of view. He welcomed her to his apartment, removed her stole, and escorted her to a table set for two, where he proffered a single rose. By candlelight, he sipped champagne and whispered sweet nothings to the camera for fifteen minutes until fade-out, weaving the conversation around such dreamy subjects as his bucolic fiefdom (its exact location never specified), the pleasures of fine wine, and his connoisseurship of all things beautiful. He didn't serve food or eat during the program. Of course not: It would have been impolite for the host to chew during what was essentially a fifteen-minute monologue. (We must assume that while he prattles on, his date has a mouthful of pasta, for she never replies.)

The Continental was just too weird for audiences and went off the air after only three months, but its fame as a pinnacle of preposterousness has lived on in television's gastronomic folklore. Poor Renzo Cesana was forever after typecast as a candlelight lothario for whom fine dining was prologue to seduction; in fact, he came to call his performance as the unctuous host "my Frankenstein's monster," and even into the 21st century, Christopher Walken was doing Renzo Cesana bits on *Saturday Night Live*.

CORN BREAD

Varieties of **corn bread** abound all across America, from the big yellow squares that accompany a Yankee **boiled dinner** to blue corn cakes in New Mexico and **corn dog** jackets everywhere. Corn bread in the South may be laced with oinky **cracklin's;** at the Cornbread Cafe in Eugene, Oregon, triangles of corn bread that come with every meal are purely vegan.

Corn bread sandwiches barbecue in Nashville, Tennessee.

In much of the mid-South, the term *corn bread* refers to a corn cake.

Fragile corn bread is especially good for crumbling into soups or onto hot vegetables.

Skillet corn bread at Zarzour's in Chattanooga, Tennessee.

Generally speaking, corn bread tends to be sweet in the North and more savory in the South, where it often appears in the form of *corn dodgers,* oval or tubular little corn cakes that may be cooked in cast iron molds that make them look like little ears of corn. Expect corn dodgers or muffins in the bread basket at most **meat and threes.**

In Tennessee, particularly around Nashville, *corn bread* is the term for a griddle-cooked pancake that comes alongside a meal and is extremely useful for pushing food around on a plate and sopping up gravy. The same flat cakes may be used in lieu of bread to make a barbecue sandwich.

Also see: **hushpuppies, jonnycake, spoonbread.**

A barbecue tray at the Skylight Inn of Ayden, North Carolina, includes a tile of chewy corn bread.

CORN DOG

Corn batter wrapped around a **hot dog** on a stick, dunked in the deep fryer long enough for the batter to become a crisp-surfaced blanket of sweet bread: That is a **corn dog.** The dog can be found in convenience stores everywhere, generally in the same holding box as 1000-year-old wieners and anorexic fried chicken. But not all corn dogs are repulsive. The Cozy Dog of Springfield, Illinois, dating back to 1946, is a noteworthy good one. Any state fair that didn't have them would be practically Communist. Corn dogs are good at state fairs because the turnover is quick (so they are made just moments before you eat them); they are eminently portable; and in true state-fair spirit, they are a diplomatic union of animal husbandry (swines) and agronomy (corn), at once nutritionally balanced—meat and vegetable in a single foodstuff—yet seductively dissolute.

Who invented them is up for grabs. It may have been Cozy Dog, but it has been pretty well documented that the Texas State Fair was selling "Corny Dogs" prior to World War II. And "Pronto Pups" were available at the Minnesota State Fair as early as 1941. The history mystery is whether the original Corny Dogs and Pronto Pups were presented on sticks. Being on a stick defines the dish.

Cozy Dog, Springfield, Illinois.

Zingerman's of Ann Arbor, Michigan, offers swanky corn dogs with a trio of interesting mustards.

CORNELL CHICKEN

In 1946, Robert Baker, a University of Pennsylvania master's degree student with an undergraduate degree in pomology, created something unusual to serve at a dinner for the state's governor. Baker, whose goal in life was to encourage people to eat more chicken, devised a tomato-free marinade with which to baste chicken parts as they cooked over charcoal. The dish was much loved by all in attendance, and when Baker moved to Cornell University in 1957, he took the recipe with him. As **Cornell chicken,** served at Baker's Chicken Coop booth at the annual New York State Fair in Syracuse, it was a hit for over five decades. Long a favorite of backyard barbecuists throughout New York's Southern Tier, Cornell chicken's primary role is as picnic food at fund-raisers, political rallies, and church suppers. Slow-cooked over charcoal, the chicken comes off the grill with a gold glaze and plush meat.

Cornell chicken was just one of Dr. Baker's creations. He also invented chicken nuggets and turkey **hot dogs.** Known as the "Edison of the Poultry Industry," he got America's cooks to think of chicken in terms of its parts rather than as whole birds, and he was inducted into the American Poultry Hall of Fame in 2004, two years prior to his death. Before the memorial service in his hometown of Lansing, New York, the Methodist church hosted a Cornell chicken barbecue.

Cornell chicken is picnic food.

Cornell Chicken

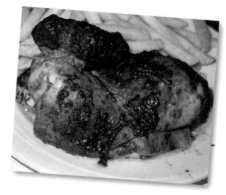

1 large egg
1 cup vegetable oil
2 cups cider vinegar
3 tablespoons salt
1 tablespoon poultry seasoning
1 teaspoon pepper
1 chicken, disjointed

1. Beat the egg well in a medium-size bowl. Whisk in all the remaining ingredients, except chicken. Set aside a cup of the sauce to use for basting the chicken as it cooks.

2. Place washed and patted-dry chicken parts in a shallow dish and coat them with the remaining sauce. Cover the dish and refrigerate the chicken for 24 hours.

3. Grill the chicken over a charcoal fire, basting frequently.

COUNTRY HAM

As different from canned ham as espresso is from Sanka, **country ham** is the aristocrat of pig meat. It delivers a haymaker salty punch, but it also is exquisite and complex. Like veined cheese, sourdough bread, and vintage wine, it tickles taste buds by teetering toward the refined side of rot. It usually is sliced wafer-thin.

Country ham stars at breakfast. The Loveless Cafe serves it with red-eye gravy, grits, eggs, biscuits, and house-made preserves.

Country ham is revered throughout the South, where artisans rub the whole ham with salt (sometimes sugar or pepper), then cure it while it sheds moisture and its flavor magnifies. Traditional producers age hams a minimum of six months, and some will keep a few special ones hung up for years. To connoisseurs, the older the ham, the finer its character. Some hams are hickory-smoked, giving them a softer taste, but even they are imbued with such concentrated piggy potency that a mild-mannered

Breakfast at the Southern Kitchen, New Market, Virginia. Whole hams are available for sale at the cash register.

King of breakfast sandwiches: a ham biscuit.

plate partner is essential. Sandwiched inside a fluffy buttermilk biscuit, country ham sings. In concert with a serving of sweet stewed apples or tomatoes, it's symphonic.

CRAB CAKE

Few prepared foods vary so dramatically in quality and price as **crab cakes.** A five-dollar-or-less one likely will be made of little filaments of crab amid a mass of seasoned breading, and it probably will be deep-fried. Along the Eastern Shore of the Chesapeake Bay, it is not uncommon to pay more than $20 for a crab cake that combines maximum crab and only enough filler to impart a wink of noncrab texture, convey the spice, and frame the meat from which the cake is made. The filling will be so negligible that when you eat one, you may find yourself believing that the sphere on your plate is all crab and nothing but crab, somehow raised to stratospheric succulence by the process of being mounded together and cooked.

Jumbo lumps make Chesapeake Bay crab cakes the best.

Although there is an inarguable pleasure about a fried crab cake's crunchy exterior breaking and giving way as your teeth sink into its moist insides, the best ones are not fried. They are broiled—only long enough for the meat to warm and for the surface of the mound to develop a gossamer gold crust. The crust is thin enough to clearly show the big white nuggets of crab that compose the cake, some of them so large that they defy dispatch by a single bite. There are Maryland cooks who insist that good cakes should contain at least some claw meat and backfin body meat, which tend more toward shreds than chunks, but connoisseurs prefer cakes made of nothing but jumbo lumps, the formal name for the choicest meat, picked from the hind leg area of the blue crab. Jumbo lump crab is costlier (as are the crab cakes made from it); these large pieces possess the silky weight that makes Maryland's beautiful swimmers the stuff of culinary legend.

CRAB FEAST

A Chesapeake Bay **crab feast** is one of America's messiest meals. Hard-shelled blue crabs, steamed in a kaleidoscope of spice, are presented as a great pile dumped onto a tablecloth that is disposable brown paper or several layers of newsprint. It is the eater's job to retrieve the meat by using pick and mallet (and stacks of napkins or, more conveniently, rolls of paper towels).

Getting the meat from hard-shelled crabs can be even more difficult than working on a lobster, so here, briefly, are the steps you need to know:

1. Twist off the legs and claws. Crack the claws and pick out the meat, which should come out in one or a few big hunks. There may be a small amount of meat in the legs, but you will have to crack them and dig to get it out.

2. Pull up the apron on the underside of the crab and pull the shell off. Remove the gills and, unless you are a liver-lover, scrape away the greenish-yellow stuff.

3. Snap the body half, revealing large lodes of meat, easily extractable using only fingers. Beyond the big chunks, smaller cavities contain meat that can be gotten with a pick or knife.

Pitchers of beer are needed to slake thirst induced by all the digging as well as by the spice.

CRACKLIN'S

Even halal and kosher cooking have their own version of **cracklin's** (made from fried chicken skin), but it's pork cracklin's that rule throughout the American South. Small nuggets of pork rind, roasted or deep-fried, are laced into **corn bread** to add immense richness or sprinkled on a salad for luxury's sake. In Cajun Louisiana, pop-in-the-mouth cracklin's are as popular a snack as **boudin;** in fact, nearly every butcher who slaughters hogs to make boudin naturally has plenty of material to make cracklin's, which are vigorously infused with hot pepper and sold—still warm—by the bagful. Hot, crisp, seasoned pork fat: Could there be anything more recklessly sybaritic? At first bite, a cracklin' crunches, and there may be a few striations of chewy meat (like deep-fried bacon), but after that first crunch and a chaw or two, it dissolves into a salacious slurry of pork and pepper without peer in the world of snack foods.

Cracklin's from T-Boy's Slaughterhouse, Mamou, Louisiana.

CRAWFISH BOIL

The premier party meal of Cajun Louisiana, a **crawfish boil** is an outdoor event that takes place in the spring, when crawfish are at their peak (and at their cheapest). The boil master cooks the crawdads with plenty of spice in a big cast iron pot, adding corn on the cob and potatoes precisely timed so that all will be ready at once. Serving traditionally is done buffet-style: The cooked crawfish are piled up in an elevated pirogue, the shallow-draft canoe that is used to traverse the bayous, and eaters help themselves.

The traditional serving vessel for serving crawfish at a crawfish boil is a canoe.

When anthropomorphized, crawfish are as happy as the people who eat them.

CREAMY GRITS

The term **creamy grits,** when found on the menu of a Lowcountry restaurant, is not adjectival fancy. Creamy grits are to ordinary grits what chocolate mousse is to chocolate milk. Instead of being made with water like the pale, ground-corn cereal so often served as a breakfast non-entity in **diners** throughout the South, creamy grits are cooked long and slow with plenty of butter and milk or cream, resulting in pale ochre grain that is smooth, dense, and luscious. While they are some-

A Lowcountry classic at the Old Post Office restaurant on Edisto Island: shrimp and creamy grits.

times served at breakfast, creamy grits' supreme destiny is to occupy a dinner plate as bedding for a school of barbecued shrimp, ham, or sausage.

CRUMB CAKE

In the metropolitan New York area, **crumb cake** is not just a generic term for coffee cake with crumbs on top. It refers to a pastry that is significantly more crumb than cake. The benchmark versions have so little cake that you might think of one as merely a conveyance mechanism to hoist streusel from plate to mouth, but that would be wrong. The cake provides creamy balance for the crumbs; the two elements together are morning coffee's best friend. Crumb cake is offered in countless **diners,** prewrapped by the piece in cellophane and sold to-go. (Do not

Heavy crumb cake from B&W Bakery of Hackensack, New Jersey.

attempt to eat crumb cake while driving.) Crumb cake is of Polish or German ancestry and is on the same family tree as Pennsylvania Dutch **shoofly pie.**

CUBAN SANDWICH

A perfect storm of multiple ingredients, the **Cuban sandwich,** also known as a *Cuban mix* or simply a *Cuban,* is a sheaf of roast pork chunks, sliced ham, at least one kind of cheese, puckery pickle slices, mustard, mayo, and hot sauce all packed into a torpedo of crusty Cuban bread. Most Cubans in Tampa, where it is said the sandwich was invented, include Genoa salami. Most in Miami do not. Tampa Cubans tend also to be outfitted with lettuce and tomato. The sandwich would fall to pieces as constructed, but it attains poise and harmony in a hot *plancha,* the Spanish toaster that is basically a toothless waffle iron. The heavy top of the *plancha* presses down on the assembled sandwich, causing all the different flavor notes to bond as one resounding chord inside the crisped loaf.

Hail the Cuban sandwich!

CUISINART

The **Cuisinart** brand name has become nearly as generic as Band-Aid and Kleenex, used to describe any food processor. It is so much a part of the essential food-prep battery that it is hard to believe it was hailed as a modern miracle less than forty years ago. When it first hit the market, the Cuisinart's sheer power seemed so radical and its whirling blades so awesome that a branch of sick humor sprung from it (*Q: What's green and goes 100 miles per hour? A: A frog in a Cuisinart*), and to this day, all manufacturers of food processors engineer their product so that the snap of the work bowl clicking into locked position ensures that fingertips are out of danger—a reassuring sound, like a bank vault *ker-chunk.*

Despite its sudden popularity in America in the late 1970s, the Cuisinart was not new. It had been discovered in 1971 by retired physicist Carl Sontheimer, who was fascinated by the possibilities of a restaurant food preparation machine he came across while traveling in France. Sontheimer modified the tool for home cooks by lengthening the feed tube and creating the fail-safe lock. He then began demonstrating its infinite uses to such important tastemakers as James Beard, Julia Child, and the editors of *Gourmet* magazine.

Sontheimer had a formidable task: to prove that his was a serious cook's tool, not yet another electric corn-popper, egg-cooker, or infrared broiler that had momentarily fascinated amateur cooks of the 1950s and 1960s, but was then soon relegated to attics or to yard sales. His greatest achievement was differentiating the food processor from the Veg-O-Matic, the most infamous culinary thingamajig of all time, bought by nine million people in the 1960s, thanks to televised ads that touted its ability to hack up any fruit or vegetable in the blink of an eye. Ron Popeil, whose father and uncle before him had sold millions of Chop-O-Matics, Mince-O-Matics, and Dial-O-Matics, had positioned his miracle nonelectric appliance as a cheap little gadget, the TV pitchman screaming its myriad virtues to viewers like a blazing Tommy gun, concluding his breathless spiel with a less-than-reassuring promise: "IT REALLY WORKS!"

The Cuisinart, with its vaguely Gallic name ending in the word *art*, was clearly not a cheesy as-seen-on-TV gadget. America's aspiring cooks came to see it as equivalently necessary to the preparation of world-class meals as extra-virgin olive oil. That it saved time and effort (the selling point of so many kitchen gizmos) was ultimately less significant than the fact that it allowed an ambitious cook to do things that had previously been the province of experts with complicated tools: to blend pâtés, to whip a mousse, to slice vegetables as finely as if they had slid from a master chef's mandoline. It was a big first step in the fashion of putting professional equipment in lay kitchens.

DATE SHAKE

Dates were unknown to most Americans when groves of date palms were planted in California between Palm Springs and the Salton Sea in the 1890s.

For decades, they remained obscure, exotic curiosities. Then in the 1940s, Russ Nichol, proprietor of a local fruit stand, figured out a way to lure travelers along old Highway 111 to give dates a try: the **date shake.** Made by adding finely chopped date crystals or date puree to the blender along with ice cream and milk, a date shake is wanton luxury that radiates the taste of sunshine. It has since become a signature dish not only of the Coachella Valley but of shake shacks and smoothie bars along the coast in Orange County. Even today, a date shake puts one in mind of a vintage California where sunshine and fresh fruit defined a healthy way of life.

DEBRIS

Apocrypha says it was named for the mess that remains after a hurricane, but Creole **debris** (say "DAY-bree") is too good to have so ignominious an inspiration. The name needs no such clever explanation: Debris is the shreds left on a cutting board after a hunk of meat is carved. Beef is its most common source, and as it is typical for New Orleans chefs to cook a roast long and slow to such extreme tenderness that it wants to fall apart as soon as a sharp knife approaches, there usually is plenty of debris to gather. It is thrown into a **po' boy** sandwich with or even without the beef; it can be used to flavor grits; it is

A bowl of debris at Mother's cafeteria in New Orleans.

cosseted alone in a biscuit; and at the venerable Mother's cafeteria on Poydras Street, it can be ordered in a bowl for spreading onto whatever else you happen to be eating at breakfast, lunch, or supper.

Like Kansas City's **brownies** (burnt ends), debris is so in demand that many restaurants circumvent the carving process and make it by pulling apart an extremely tender, gravy-sopped roast. There is nothing really awful about that practice, but debris connoisseurs like the real thing because it offers more crunch from the roast's edges and more streaks of melty fat.

DEEP-DISH PIZZA

An American original, **deep-dish pizza** was introduced in Chicago in 1943 at Pizzeria Uno. The restaurant was opened by former football star Ike Sewell and restaurateur Ric Riccardo, who had originally conceived a Mexican eatery. But after the place was decorated, they sampled a meal and Riccardo became ill— so ill that it is said he ran away to Italy. When Riccardo returned, he and Sewell removed the Hispanic decor and made their place a pizzeria. They decided that normal **pizza,** as served in some Italian restaurants around town, wasn't hefty enough for Chicago appetites. So they came up with the recipe for deep-dish.

Cooked in a high-walled round pan, deep-dish pizza verges on being a casserole, its thick, biscuity cornmeal crust loaded with mozzarella cheese and chunked tomatoes. Big sheets of fennel-spiked sausage are a common option. Deep-dish offshoots include the **stuffed pizza,** which adds a top crust and makes the whole thing look more like a traditional pie; *pizza souffles,* for which the cheese on top is whipped up and can contain pesto or spinach; and **pizza pot pie,** an upside-down version decanted into its crust tableside.

Chicago + Naples = deep-dish pizza.
STEPHEN RUSHMORE

DELI LINGO

Waiters in classic Jewish delis tend to be crabby no matter what, but they treat you even worse if you act like a greenhorn. Here are ten basic terms you should know before ordering:

Blintzes: Crepes rolled around sweet pot cheese and fried in butter.
Chicken-in-a-pot: A stew/soup in golden broth with tender vegetables.
Kasha varnishkes: Bow-tie noodles with buckwheat groats.
Knish: A potato dumpling with the atomic weight of lead.
Knoblewurst: Garlicky salami.
Kugel: Noodle pudding that can be either sweet or savory.
Latkes: Potato pancakes, served on the side of sandwiches or as a meal.
Novie: Short for "Nova Scotia lox," meaning sliced smoked salmon that isn't too salty.
"Oy vey": An expression of exasperation; the waiter's mantra.
Schmaltz: Rendered chicken fat, often spread on dark bread like butter.

DEVONSHIRE

Pittsburgh's own version of the Kentucky **hot brown** is known as turkey **devonshire:** a hot, open-face sandwich of sliced turkey and bacon on toast, smothered with cheddar cheese sauce. It is said to have been created in 1934 at the Stratford restaurant by Frank Blandi, who went on to become one of the city's best-known restaurateurs. Steel City chefs do not hesitate to elaborate on the formula, substituting crab, chicken, and/or vegetables for the turkey or garnishing the sandwich with tomatoes . . . or even with French fries, like a Springfield, Illinois, **horseshoe.** Needless to say, utensils are required.

DINER

What exactly makes a **diner** a diner? The original sense of the word described a restaurant that was movable. The first lunch wagons in the Northeast (precursors by 100-plus years of the current food truck phenomenon) were pulled by horses to wherever business might be good. As they became popular and grew larger, they were trucked from the factories that made them either whole or in pieces. While not as mobile as a lunch wagon, one of these prefab eateries could be hoisted off its plot and moved to a new location where business might be better.

It all began with a sandwich wagon operated by Walter Scott and pulled by his horse, Patient Dick, outside the offices of the *Providence Journal* starting in 1872. Scott served sliced rooster sandwiches, ham sandwiches, boiled eggs, and pie, as well as a novelty he christened the "chewed sandwich," made of cutting board scraps. There is no sure way of knowing, but Scott's food, if crude, may not have been all that bad. He baked his own bread and pies and once boasted that no one ever complained about his fowl sandwiches.

Worcester Dining Car Company Diner #812, manufactured in 1948.

As for ambience, however, diners always have been a walk on the wild side. Many of the early lunch wagons were made from beat-up and abandoned trolley cars and were known for the shady clientele they attracted. In the teens, a manufacturer named Patrick J. "Pop" Tierney went a long way toward improving their social standing by making them from scratch rather than from decrepit trolleys and, more important, introducing indoor toilets; Jerry O'Mahoney of Bayonne, New Jersey, manufactured diners that featured stained glass windows emblazoned with the motto PURE FOOD, CLEANLINESS, QUICK SERVICE, AND POPULAR PRICES. While by no means upper crust, diners were aiming to attract ladies and gentlemen. The term *diner* came into use in the 1920s because by this point, the moveable eatery had evolved from makeshift freight wagon to something that resembled a modern railroad dining car.

During the 1930s, when Chrysler Corporation introduced its teardrop-shaped "Airflow" cars and designers were infatuated with anything that looked windswept, diner companies streamlined their product and incorporated such modernistic material as glass bricks, stainless steel, and multicolored Formica. By 1950, there were an estimated 6000 of them in America. The diner as most of us know it developed an alluring personality midcentury as partner to the burgeoning network of American highways. In America of the 1940s and 1950s, the open-all-night diner became a prime symbol of a nation always on the move—an oasis on the long road, a place where roving sharpies shoot the breeze with fallen angels, and where gearjammers lay over for a mug of "forty-weight" coffee to fuel them on their way. Jack Kerouac began his novel *Visions of Cody* with a lyrically ambivalent description of an old diner with a smell that is "curiously the hungriest in America—it is FOODY instead of just spicy, or—it's like dishwater soap just washed a pan of hamburg—nameless—memoried—sincere—makes the guts of men curl in October."

The look of diners has evolved tremendously over the years, to the point that many restaurants that call themselves diners—located in strip malls or ordinary storefronts—bear no resemblance to a lunch wagon, a trolley, or a speeding railroad car. Nor do they necessarily look like any of the huge multi-room stone-encrusted Colonial and Mediterranean diners that appeared from the mid- to late twentieth century. So what is it, beyond architectural cues, that makes a place feel like a diner? First of all, there's the smell: a swirl of savory gravy and strong coffee and bacon sizzling on the grill along with oniony hash browns. A diner almost certainly has a counter and stools, and probably booths, too. Chances are good it is open early for breakfast and may serve the proverbial BREAKFAST ANY TIME. A place that calls itself a diner will not take reservations or have any sort of formal dress code. It will not be a romantic hideaway; it will be well-lit and family-friendly. Customers are always asked if they want coffee. While many people go to late-night diners to schmooze and palaver, you also can count on a diner to be efficient if you're in a rush: order taken right away, check delivered with the meal.

Despite their conventional cast of eccentric characters and an early reputation as purveyors of unsavory mystery meat, diners over the years have earned a reputation as places that dish out honest food at affordable prices. Some of this has to do with the fact that, at least in the classic smaller ones, so much of what is served is cooked and assembled before your eyes, at the grill behind the counter, where the chef can't pull a fast one and substitute shoelaces for spaghetti and a shoe sole for your veal cutlet. But there is also something about the aesthetics of classic diner fare that makes people want to trust it. Pot roast, pork chops, apple pie a la mode: nothing coy or pretentious about these blue-collar basics.

DINER LINGO

Diners have a language all their own: weird names for ordinary foods. The slang was created not so much for efficiency—often the slang term is longer than what it really means—but for fun. While it has become rare to hear a waitress call out "wrecked cackleberries on a whiskey raft!" to let the cook know she wants scrambled eggs on rye toast, you still hear occasional vestiges of a time when counter culture prevailed. Here are a few basics:

40-Weight, Joe, Java, Mud: Coffee
Adam and Eve: Poached eggs
Axle grease: Butter
Birdseed: Cold cereal
Blowout patch: Pancake
Bronx perfume: Garlic

Bullets: Beans

Cats' eyes: Tapioca pudding

Clean the kitchen: Hash

Cow paste: Butter

Dog soup: Water

Down a quart: Coffee refill

Eve with a lid: Apple pie

Georgia: Coca-Cola

Graveyard stew: Milk toast

High and dry: Hold the butter and mayonnaise

Hockey puck: Well-done hamburger

Hound and hay: Hot dog with sauerkraut

Houseboat: Banana split

Lumber: Toothpick

Mud: Chocolate syrup

On the hoof: Rare

Pipe: Drinking straw

Put out the lights and cry: Liver and onions

Radio: Tuna (from "tune it down")

Sinker, life preserver: Donut

Through the garden: Add lettuce and tomato (to a sandwich)

Tube steak, bow wow: Hot dog

Walk it: To-go

Yellow streak: Add mustard

DIP

Western Kentucky barbecue connoisseurs order their meat *off the pit,* which means unsauced, with **dip** on the side to moisten it. Less like ketchup and more like smoky *au jus,* dip also is used to baste meat as it cooks. It contains Worcestershire sauce, vinegar, mustard, sugar, a small amount of tomatoes, a good measure of hot pepper or hot sauce, and the occasional shot of Kentucky bourbon.

DIRTY RICE

Dirty food is bad. **Dirty rice** is good. In the latter, "dirt" means bits and pieces of turkey or chicken giblets, liver, and maybe skin that are cooked with the rice, giving it a smudged look and a rich, chickeny flavor. While enough dirt can make it a meal, dirty rice usually comes as a side dish with roast duck, smoked sausage, pork chops, or fried chicken. A Cajun dish almost always made with the **holy trinity** of pepper, celery, and onion, dirty rice is found on **soul food** menus throughout the Deep South.

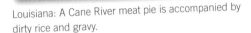

Louisiana: A Cane River meat pie is accompanied by dirty rice and gravy.

DITCH

In the bars of Montana (which has some of the most colorful bars in the country), the signature drink is a **ditch,** known formally as a *whiskey ditch.* A Big Sky cognate of Texas *bourbon and branch,* it is a mix of whiskey and water—usually half-and-half—on ice; and in the classic cowboy bars, it is about as fancy a drink as you can get. Its etymological apocrypha is that during Prohibition, in order to make what little whiskey they had last longer, tipplers mixed it with water and hid their stash in a nearby ditch.

DIXIE DOG

Dixie dogs are not known as Dixie dogs in Dixie. They are called *slaw dogs* or simply **hot dogs.** But because they come from the South and nearly every place that sells them is in the South, the Dixie dog moniker has stuck and has now begun to appear on menus outside the South where vendors make a point of honoring regional differences. Creamy-cool coleslaw is what makes this hot dog variation unique; it almost always comes in concert with meaty chili sauce, and chopped raw onions and yellow mustard complete the package. Tube steak historians believe that this variation first was configured in Huntington, West Virginia (where it remains immensely popular), at Stewart's root beer stand, which opened in 1932 with popcorn the only food on its menu. The next year, proprietor Gertrude Mandt developed a chili sauce and started serving hot dogs. Exactly when slaw became an option is lost in the mists of time.

DOGGIE BAG

The history of leftovers would be difficult to trace, but the **doggie bag**'s origin is clear. In 1946, so as not to embarrass budget-conscious customers at his Steak Joint restaurant on Greenwich Avenue in New York, proprietor Dan Stampler came up with the idea of suggesting they take their steak bone (and whatever meat remained on it) home "for the dog." Mr. Stampler designed a bag with a picture of his Scottish terrier on it and he called it a doggie bag. In 1947, the Bagcraft Corporation of Chicago, Illinois, began manufacturing them, and two years later Janice Meister, whose husband cofounded Bagcraft, wrote what may be the most widely disseminated poem of the twentieth century:

> *Oh where, oh where have your leftovers gone?*
> *Oh where, oh where can they be?*
> *If you've had all you can possibly eat,*
> *Please bring the rest home to me!!*

The poem, titled "Doggie Bag," appeared on more than 150 million bags, the verse surrounded by cartoon faces of five happy canines, four with tongues wagging. (The fifth, a boxer, appears glad but more businesslike.) An annotation above the image of the slavering pack of canines says, "This special greaseproof bag is provided with the compliments of your host." Unlike professional poets Maya Angelou or Dr. Seuss, Mrs. Meister received no royalties for her work. She granted it free in perpetuity to her husband's company, which she took over when he died in the early 1980s. She wrote only one other published poem—the little-known "*Ode to Potato Chips*"—for a Chicago snack manufacturer.

Even today, when many restaurants serve portions so large they inevitably wind up in take-home containers for next-day human consumption, the term *doggie bag* frequently is used to describe whatever the food is packed in. There is seldom pretense that the uneaten porterhouse will wind up in doggy's dish; indeed, fine restaurants send home leftovers in swan-shaped foil wrappers and carry-handle shopping bags as nice as those from a high-tone department store. But still, the white lie endures, rooted in archaic etiquette that says polite people do not gnaw bones, either in restaurants or at home, and that taking a bag full of food to reheat and eat is less couth, not to mention less humane, than serving a deserving pooch.

DOORYARD FRUIT

The best-known **dooryard fruit** is the Key lime, but there are many others, especially valued along the Overseas Highway through the coral keys from Miami to Key West. Named because they are fruits that grow in people's yards just outside their doors, they are generally unavailable in supermarkets anywhere else and scarce even in the grocery stores of Key West. Because they grow wild, the flavor of a single variety varies dramatically, depending on where it grows and even which particular tree it comes from. The sour orange, for example, might be a little sweet, but it usually is too sour to eat out of hand. Like many dooryard fruits, it isn't glossy-magazine pretty; it is gnarled and asymmetrical. Cooks value the orange to make marinades; mixologists use it for tropical drinks. One of the most distinctive dooryard fruits is the calamondin, which looks like a miniature tangerine. It has leathery skin and is easy to segment; its flavor is as intense as the Key lime. The mango now is common in supermarkets, but ask any chef with a Caribbean repertoire, and you will learn that the dooryard variety is a different fruit altogether. Chef Doug Shook of Key West's Louie's Backyard restaurant described the difference as that between a flavorless tomato and one picked fresh off a garden vine. "There is nothing like hearing a mango bang off a tree onto your tin roof at night," he said, "then going out the next morning to pick it up and have it for breakfast."

DOUGHBOY

Rhode Island and Massachusetts shores are good places to eat seafood—plain or fancy, fried, broiled, or steamed. In this region, chances are good that the meal will include **fried dough.** A full **shore dinner** automatically includes savory **clam fritters** or **clam cakes.** A popular alternative, especially around the Narragansett Bay, is **doughboys.** Resembling New Orleans **beignets,** but sheathed in crystalline sugar rather

Doughboys are sold by sixes and dozens.

than powder, doughboys are made from a yeast-risen dough that is sweet enough to balance the briniest seafood, and they usually are served by the half-dozen. Doughboys always are eaten out of hand. As a snack while strolling along the shore or at a fair, they are a doppelganger for Italian zeppoli.

DOWNSTATE CHOWDER

It may come as quite a surprise to residents of the ocean shores of New England and of the Pacific Northwest that Edwards County, Illinois, is the Chowder Capital of the World. So ordained the county commissioners in 1958 as a salute to **downstate chowder,** also known as *southern Illinois chowder*. A closer cousin to **burgoo** and **Brunswick stew** than it is to the seafood and farmhouse **chowders** of the coasts, it is a hunter-farmer's dish made with beef and/or chicken (and, historically, squirrel) along with beans, cabbage, and tomatoes. Chowder season starts when tomatoes ripen and ends with the first frost.

Rarely a one-family meal, downstate chowder is cooked at church suppers, fund-raisers, and community events that are themselves known as "chowders." Large cauldrons are used over open fires and two cooks are necessary: one to continuously stir the stew with a long-handled paddle, the other, known as the bone picker, to grab pieces of meat, remove the bones, and return the meat to the pot.

DRIVE-IN

Before Ralph Nader, cars were fun. For generations of joy-riders, a purring V-8 was a vehicle for play and pleasure. Dining at a true and classic **drive-in** is an apotheosis of car culture. Cruise into the parking lot and find a space. Blink your headlights. Here comes running—or roller skating—a carhop to take your order. Moments later, you are presented a tray of cheeseburgers, fries, and root beers to be hung on a half-lowered car window. Turn up the radio and plow into an *alfresco, al auto* cheap-eats feast.

Long before 1948, when the brothers McDonald started serving fifteen-cent hamburgers and ten-cent **milk shakes** at their quick-service eatery in San Bernardino, California, drive-ins were a fact of culinary life in the United States. Today McDonald's and its ilk offer drive-through service, which means you receive your bagged chow then go on your way; but the *drive-in* has always been a more social event—entertainment as well as a meal. Chevy and Ford and Plymouth owners pull bumper-to-bumper like different breeds of animal gathering at a favorite watering hole. Off-the-menu thrills include the opportunity to show off that new pair of fuzzy dice hanging from the rearview mirror and to flirt with diners in the vehicle parked nearby. Perfumed by a swirl of high-octane fumes, luminous fresh-rubbed carnauba wax, and onions frying on the griddle, a drive-in is more than a fast-food restaurant. It is curbside Americana with a Chuck Berry beat.

The original attraction of drive-ins was speed. When the first "Pig Stands" opened in Texas, in the 1920s, tray boys became known as carhops because they literally hopped onto customers' running boards to take orders even before the arriving diners slowed to a stop. Like eager-to-please pump jockeys from the golden age of gas stations, carhops in search of big tips were polite, pleasant, and even entertaining. At the late Sivils' Drive-In outside Houston, tray girls wore satin majorette costumes and high white boots and patrolled the parking lot in military cadence, marching to the rhythm of music blasted by loudspeakers.

Although they may seem as much a part of pop culture's distant past as bobby sox and jitterbugging, drive-ins still exist all around the country. Many are virtual time capsules, doing business exactly as they did fifty years ago. Some maintain the *spirit* of car-friendly quick eats and camaraderie but no longer offer car-window service. Others are precious museum pieces, such as the legendary Porky's of St. Paul. Originally opened in 1953 by Ray Truelson, this burger-and-root-beer shop became known for its crisp, onion ring garnish. At one time there were four of them in the Twin Cities, but the business went belly-up in the 1970s. In 1990 it was revived in St. Paul in all its do-wop glory, without the carhops but still serving Twinburgers.

Being generally wieldy and quintessentially American, the **hamburger** is a pillar of drive-in cuisine. At the Sycamore Drive-In in Bethel, Connecticut, carhops deliver overstuffed, double Dagwoodburgers pocketed in wax paper. The proper companion is house-made root beer that can be either wickedly sweet or refreshingly brut, depending on whether yours is drawn from the top or bottom of the keg.

Root beer, known during Prohibition as "the temperance beverage," has been the axiomatic drive-in drink since the 1920s, when the first A&W stands opened in California. At Hires Big H, which has several curb-service outlets in Salt Lake City, Utah, root beer comes in five sizes, from "baby" to "large." And of course there are root beer floats to accompany a juicy quarter-pound Big H burger topped with bacon, ham, or pastrami, your choice of cheese, and crunchy onion rings. At Indiana's Mug 'n' Bun, where pork tenderloin sandwiches are the thing to eat, the root beer is as luxurious as dessert wine: dark, creamy, complex, and spicy.

Some of the most exemplary drive-ins are summer-only. At the first signs of spring, locals start cruising into the lot of Harry's in Colchester, Connecticut, waiting for come-hither smoke from the old drive-in's extra-thick, hand-formed hamburgers to start wafting from the grill. At open-year-round drive-ins in the temperate South, **barbecue** is as much the favored entree as hamburgers or **hot dogs,** and the preferred libation is **sweet tea.** An attendant at the Beacon of Spartanburg, South Carolina, once bragged to us that the kitchen used two tons of sugar every week to sweeten its tea, which is served in titanic glasses guaranteed to put the sugar content in any soda pop to shame. The Beacon's choice meal is known as Outside Pork A-Plenty, which is hacked-up hunks of hickory-cooked pork on a bun with cool slaw buried under sweet onion rings and a mountain of fried potatoes.

The biggest drive-in on earth, adored by all traveling trenchermen, is the Varsity of Atlanta where, until late in the twentieth century, curb boys used to *sing* the highlights of the menu. Serving 10,000 customers a day (twice that many when Georgia Tech plays at home), the Varsity is a virtual nation that even boasts its own language. Order "a Yankee dog, a ring, a string, and an FO"; you'll receive a hot dog with a yellow-mustard streak, onion rings, French fries, and an icy frosted orange drink. Our favorite story about the Varsity is told by Texas senator Phil Gramm. When he was at college in Atlanta, the *Journal-Constitution* had a party for all its paper boys. The organizer pulled in and ordered six thousand hamburgers, to go. Without missing a beat, veteran order-taker Erby Walker shot back, "Whatcha drinkin'?"

DRY LINK

◇◇

Dry link is the Texas pitmaster's term for a hot beef sausage that is pit-cooked long enough to lose the extreme succulence typical of sausages in the Lone Star **barbecue** belt. Sublime as the juicy links are, attention must be paid to these well-done tube steaks, known to pit men as dry links because so much fat has been rendered out of them. Extra time on the grate diminishes the wanton hedonism of the sausage and creates a leathery, crackle-textured skin, concentrating flavor into an edible epigram of beef, pepper, and smoke.

DRY RUB

◇◇

Dry rub is the way many barbecuists enhance the flavor of their smoke-cooked meat. It can be as simple as the salt and pepper Texas pitmasters use on brisket or a nuclear-fission secret formula containing anything from gunpowder to curry powder. Sugar often is included in the formula because it caramelizes as it heats and creates a glaze on the meat. There are two basic reasons to rub **barbecue** before it goes into the pit. The first and obvious one is flavor. Some chefs will rub their brisket or **rib** racks hours before cooking them, creating, in effect, a dry marinade that penetrates the meat. Many hours later, when the meat has cooked, the rub has become a crust clinging to the outside, known as the *bark,* supercharged with flavor. The second purpose of a thick rub is to encase the meat, shoring up juices that flow as soon as the bark is broken.

RON DUARTE

Ron Duarte, who lives above his family's hundred-year-old tavern in Pescadero, California, comes down for breakfast a little after 7 a.m. carrying an egg, the gift of a local farmer whose chickens, he rhapsodizes, lay "beautiful eggs, big brown ones." After greeting the handful of morning regulars who gather at Duarte's daily for coffee and conversation in the dining room before work, he walks into the kitchen. As his egg fries, he chats with the staff: "Have you guys done chicken and dumplings lately?"

About a quarter century ago, Ron Duarte instructed us in olallieberry pie baking.

"Last Wednesday," a cook answers.

"The pears?" Duarte asks, referring to a bushel of fruits just brought in from the backyard orchard.

"Ready for pie," comes the answer.

Mr. Duarte says he doesn't do much anymore; his kids, Tim and Kathy, run the place. But every detail matters to him, and he doesn't miss a trick. Walking through the back of the kitchen, he shows how the apple pie gets a flat crust, the pear latticework, so they can easily be distinguished. He shows off a box of Watsonville olallieberries, used to make Duarte's most popular pie.

Although his place remains the rugged old tavern it was throughout the twentieth century, Ron Duarte's respect for its food's seasonal correctness rivals that of any hifalutin' bistro chef in wine country. Mr. Duarte, who took over the business from his parents in the 1960s, cannot hide his happiness when Dungeness crab season starts in November, because that means the restaurant's *cioppino* is at its best. "We don't buy frozen," he says. "We like to get them live and cook them."

A huge garden in back of the restaurant, where much of the kitchen's provender is grown, helps explain Ron Duarte's seasonal savvy. Walking through rows of Swiss chard, heirloom tomatoes, leeks, and artichokes, he can tell you exactly when each is at its peak. It's the artichokes for which the restaurant is most famous. They can't grow enough in the family garden, but neither do they rely on a big foodservice supplier. "Those artichoke balloons you see in the store?" he asks rhetorically. "They drive me nuts." Artichokes from his backyard garden are grand, meaty things, used in the kitchen for the most basic preparation—steaming—where no other flavor vies with the thistle's deep green goodness. For sausage-stuffed artichokes, artichoke omelets, fried artichokes, and the restaurant's legendary cream of artichoke soup, supplies come from farms an hour south, around Castroville, the Artichoke Capital of the World and source of nearly all grown in America. (In 1951, a little-known starlet named Marilyn Monroe was the city's first Artichoke Queen.)

EGG CREAM

New York's iconic corner-candy-store drink, the **egg cream,** has only three ingredients, none of which is eggs or cream. It is chocolate syrup, whole milk, and seltzer. David Fox, whose great-grandfather started Fox's U-Bet Chocolate Syrup (the only proper chocolate flavoring for an egg cream) suggested that cream may indeed have been part of the original recipe, but too expensive for the average soda fountain customer. A Lower East Side mixologist once told us that his vintage soda fountain used to include eggs in its chocolate syrup, and that is how the drink got its ovarian moniker. It is certainly within soda fountain tradition to plop an egg into a **milk shake** for extra calories, but it would make no sense to add such ballast to this elegant drink. It is much more likely that the name comes from a well-mixed egg cream's foamy head with its intimations of egg-and-cream luxury.

Although nothing could be plainer than the list of ingredients, construction of an egg cream is an exacting craft and, in fact, cannot be done at home. Syrup goes into the glass first. Next, cold milk. Then, the drama (and the reason professional equipment is needed): Cold seltzer must be spritzed into the glass in a fast and furious jet off the back of a long-handled spoon. After about one second, the fountain handle gets pushed back so an easy stream can flow into the glass as its foamy head rises high. An experienced soda jerk hardly needs to stir at all because that original, split-second injection of seltzer got the milk and syrup mixing.

An egg cream must be drunk almost as quickly as it has been made. The foamy head fades fast and the champagne-chocolate tingle dissipates as you gulp it down. At the bottom of the glass you should see a streak or two of chocolate, still unblended. That is the way it should be, the "imperfection" like the small flaw Renaissance artists used to include in their paintings, just to let you know they were made by a human, not by God.

Egg creams normally are made in shapely soda fountain glasses. But Harold's New York Deli in Edison, New Jersey, uses mugs because they hold more.

Unlike wine, an egg cream adds no pleasure to other foods. It is a snack that wants nothing else, the only possible accompaniment being a single long pretzel stick.

99

CAROL FAY ELLISON

One of ten children who grew up with their mother making biscuits for the family, **Carol Fay Ellison** started work as a dishwasher at Nashville's Loveless Cafe in 1968. One day, when someone didn't come in for work, she filled in as a line cook, making eggs, ham, and sausage. "Oh, lordy, it was hot then," she remembered when we chatted with her in 2004. "If it was 100 degrees outside, it was 200 in the kitchen. You had to walk into the freezer to get cool."

Although she did nearly everything in the kitchen of the Loveless Cafe, Carol Fay Ellison was best known for her biscuits.

Gifted with her mother's expertise, Carol Fay soon became the biscuit person. Biscuits had always been an essential part of the cafe's meals; when they became her responsibility, she made a change or two in the recipe and created what became the signature dish of the legendary restaurant. "They had been using powdered milk, buttermilk, and water," she recalled. "But with powdered milk, you make a dough that chunks and gunks. So I took it out of the recipe." Precious few people apprenticed with Carol Fay to become proficient biscuit makers. "It can be tough teaching people," she said. "A lot of them don't want to put their fingers in the dough. And handling the dough just right is key."

As she described it, making the cafe's famous blackberry and peach preserves to accompany the biscuits was a far less exacting science. "All I do is add sugar to the fruit," she revealed. "We used to cook them on the stove in big old rondos. Now I've got a tilt skillet, and we make preserves every day."

After the Loveless shut down for remodeling early in 2004, Carol Fay's skills and experience were key ingredients in a new kitchen that would stay true to the cafe's culinary roots. "When we reopened, I did 149 hours in the first two weeks," she said with a serene smile.

Jesse Goldstein, vice-president of operations for Tomkats, the company that saved and revived the Loveless Cafe, told us that Carol Fay's presence in the new kitchen was essential, and not only because she was keeper of the precious biscuit recipe. As one who had been a vital part of the Loveless Cafe for well over a quarter century, she embodied an indomitable spirit that gave strength to those around her. "I love her," Jesse said without equivocation. "There is no one in the world better to hug, or to be hugged by." Carol Fay Ellison passed away in 2010.

ÉTOUFFÉE

Although the term **étouffée** is from French (*étouffer* = to smother), the étouffée of Cajun Louisiana always begins with the Spanish-kitchen **holy trinity** of celery, green peppers, and onions and a dark roux made from vegetable oil cooked low and slow with flour. Garlic, peppers, and a constellation of other spices are added, creating a heavy stock that combines with crawfish or possibly crab or shrimp (and even, on occasion, chicken) and is served over rice. (Heretical though it may be, one vendor at a recent New Orleans Roadfood Festival served alligator étouffée over **creamy grits.**) Although it doesn't have such thickening agents as the filé powder or okra used in **gumbo,** étouffée is thicker and heartier—more like stew than soup, served as a main course rather than an appetizer.

A pot full of crawfish étouffée at Robin's in Henderson, Louisiana.

FAIRY FOOD

Fairy food is northern Wisconsin's name for little blocks of spun caramelized sugar that are leavened so thoroughly that they virtually are weightless. The cubic-inch cubes come robed in a choice of dark or milk chocolate. As teeth cut through the outer layer, the cloud of candy inside evaporates into pure, disembodied molasses sweetness. Known locally also as *angel candy* and similar to Buffalo's **sponge candy** and the seafoam sweets found in resort areas on both the Pacific and Atlantic coasts, fairy food is a specialty of old-time candy stores such as Beerntsen's in Manitowoc, which has been the town confectioner (and ice cream parlor) since 1932.

FAJITAS

A true Tex-Mex dish from the days of the vaqueros, who made the most of the skirt steaks they got from butchered steers, **fajitas** were a little-known regional specialty until the last few decades of the twentieth century. Starting in 1969, when a man calling himself the Fajita King began selling skirt-steak tacos at county fairs and rodeos between Austin and San Antonio, they have become one of the most popular dishes on Mexican restaurant menus throughout the country. Fajitas outgrew the taco category in 1982, when George Weidmann, chef at the Austin Hyatt Regency introduced "sizzling fajitas" that came from the kitchen on a platter hot enough to make them sputter all the way to the table—a razzle-dazzle touch that has become a vital part of the presentation.

Fajitas now are available made with chicken, shrimp, and only vegetables, and it has become *de rigueur* to serve them sizzling on hot metal and accompanied by guacamole, salsa, cheese, and sour cream. Weidmann used sirloin in his breakthrough fajitas, but to the classicist, if it isn't skirt steak, it isn't truly a fajita. The logic is etymological: The word *fajita* is a form of *faja,* the Spanish word for "belt," which describes exactly where skirt steak comes from on a carcass.

FILBERT (HAZELNUT)

Every September, 99 percent of all the **filberts** grown in the United States fall from trees in a patch of the Willamette Valley west of the Cascades and north of Eugene, Oregon. Hazelnut Growers' specialty products sales manager Dave Daniels told us that the word *filbert,* which is also common in England but nowhere else, has uncertain roots. It comes either from St. Philibert, whose nameday is August 22, the date the English crop is ready to harvest, or possibly from the fact that the husk around the nut's shell resembles a *full beard*.

Because they are relatively large and not outrageously expensive, filberts often occupy lots of space in cans of mixed nuts. In the fall, when they are harvested, they are a popular ingredient in **milk shakes** throughout Oregon. One September morning, in a bacon-and-eggs hash house west of Portland, we threw out the topic, and nearly everyone at the U-shaped Formica counter got a piece of the conversation. "If a man says 'filbert,' he's a Northwester," one gent said, peering over the top of his *Oregonian*. "That's what we always used to call them, and we still do. *Hazelnut* is for people back East or in Europe. They don't know filberts."

FISH BOIL

The **fish boil** is an extraordinary outdoor-cooking ritual unique to the slim peninsula of Door County, Wisconsin, that juts into Lake Michigan east of Menominee and north of Sturgeon Bay. Whitefish steaks and red potatoes are gathered in separate nets to cook in a big iron cauldron over crackling hardwood. Once the water hits a rolling boil, the potatoes go into the pot, along with pounds of salt. At the twenty-minute mark, the fish is added to the cauldron along with still more salt. As the meal cooks, onlookers gather around the fire drinking beer or cider. Accordion music, played by the boil master between his chores, is customary. When he decrees the food nearly done, he tells everyone to stand back and tosses a pint of kerosene straight into the fire. Flames burst up, engulfing the cook pot and instantly jacking up the heat. In the flash of the blaze, the heavily salted water boils over and splashes down onto the inferno, nearly dowsing it. The big bang that signals the end of a fish boil isn't only for dramatic effect: It ensures the taste of the whitefish. A ratio of one pound of salt for every two gallons of water in the pot creates a buoyancy that makes ingredients want to float. As the fish cooks in a net, its oils rise and hover at the surface. The volcanic upsurge at the moment of the boil-over forces oils and impurities to cascade out over the

Boilover: Pyrotechnical shock and awe in Door County, Wisconsin.

edge of the pot, leaving nothing in the boiling water but clean-flavored fish steaks and potatoes.

Ingrained as the fish boil tradition is in Door County life, no one knows for sure when or how it began. Most people believe it was started by Scandinavian-ancestored fishermen. "Their boats were equipped with pot-bellied stoves," reflected Andy Coulson, proprietor of Fish Creek's White Gull Inn, which is famous for its dramatic fish boils. "All they needed to stock on board was salt and potatoes. Or maybe the fish boil began with bonfires on the beach when they came ashore to clean their catch." Coulson pointed out that for the old-time fishermen, as well as for crowds of contemporary visitors who come north to enjoy the cool breezes that waft in off Lake Michigan every summer, one big appeal of the fish boil is the camaraderie it inspires among large groups of people. The bonfire and boil-over bring strangers together in an ebullient mix of awe and hunger. "As a meal for six, it is inefficient," Coulson observed. "But for a dozen or more, it's a thing of beauty. This is Door County's answer to the all-American **barbecue.**"

FISH FRY

Fried fish are everywhere, but **fish fries** are a heartland affair. In a sprawling triangular swath of America bordered by the Hudson River, the Ohio River, and the northernmost beginnings of the Mississippi, the Friday night fish fry is as much a part of life as **barbecue** in the Carolinas. In shot-and-beer pool parlors, storefront cafes, American Legion halls, and woodland supper clubs, friends and neighbors gather over pitchers of beer and fish that ranges from common Atlantic cod to smelt to prized freshwater bluegill. Some fish fries are little more than simple sandwiches: crisp, hot hunks from the deep fryer between two pieces of white bread, with tartar sauce an option; most make fish the hub of a meal with a constellation of sides. Indigenous accompaniments are as dissimilar as Tater Tots and elegant potato pancakes, hand-parched wild rice and Rice-A-Roni by the box. All-you-can-eat is a popular way to serve; portioned-out fish fry dinners are always abundant.

Not all who enjoy the weekly custom are Catholic, although the old religious proscription of meat on Fridays is certainly how it started. Fish fry culture thrives in cities with large Catholic populations and communities that maintain strong European ethnic identity. Foremost among them is Milwaukee, where the ritual is so much a part of life that it is rare to find a restaurant that does *not* dedicate Friday night to it. The august downtown institution Karl Ratzsch's adds fried perch to a Teutonic menu known for crackling pork hocks and roast goose; Taqueria Azteca offers perch tacos and Mexican beer; even local KFCs do it

Fish fries are community events as well as restaurant meals.

during Lent. We have found fish fries in such culturally diverse eateries as the Italian Community Center, Benji's Deli, Silver Spur Texas Smokehouse, and the Bya Wi Se Nek Buffet in the Potawatomi Bingo Casino.

FISH TACOS

A dozen years ago, when we wrote a story in a national magazine about Ralph Rubio, the man who introduced **fish tacos** to the United States, we had to explain to readers what a fish taco was. "Popular as it is in San Diego," we wrote, "the fish taco is still virtually unknown elsewhere in the United States."

Few San Diegans had heard of it back in 1978, when Ralph Rubio, then a sophomore at San Diego State, traveled down to Baja with his pals on spring break. He was looking only for sun and surf, but was smitten by the fish taco stands he found all along the water in the village of San Felipe. There was one Baja vendor Ralph Rubio especially liked, a man named Carlos, who ran a hole-in-the-wall taco stand with a ten-foot counter and a few stools. "Mexican food in San Diego was so bland in those days," Rubio remembers. One day, Carlos agreed to share his recipe, which Ralph Rubio jotted down on a scrap of paper pulled from his wallet. Ultimately, he took the recipe he had acquired and opened his own place with a sign that said RUBIO'S—HOME OF THE FISH TACO.

There now are hundreds of Rubio's Baja Grills, specializing in fish tacos, throughout the West, and the dish Ralph Rubio imported has become as common as fajitas in Mexican restaurants throughout the country. Variations are plentiful, including those made with upscale grilled fish, but the classic configuration is chunks of deep-fried white fish in a spicy batter, bedded on a yogurt-mayonnaise sauce in a soft tortilla along with rough-cut shreds of cool white cabbage and a wedge of lime.

Rubio's Fish Tacos

2 cups flour, plus more for dredging
2 cups water
2 tablespoons beer
1 tablespoon garlic powder
1 tablespoon dry mustard
1 tablespoon oregano
2 teaspoons salt
1 teaspoon pepper
Oil for frying
2 pounds pollock or cod, cut into 1½ ounce strips (no bones)
1 dozen corn tortillas, the thicker the better
⅔ cup mayonnaise
⅓ cup plain yogurt
½ head white cabbage, shredded
Salsa fresca: tomatoes, yellow onion, cilantro, jalapeños, chopped to taste
Wedges of lime
Guacamole, shredded Jack and/or cheddar cheese, for garnish (optional)

Fish tacos at The Cottage in La Jolla.

1. Mix 2 cups flour, water, beer, garlic powder, mustard, oregano, salt, and pepper thoroughly to form a batter. Put some additional flour in a shallow dish.

2. Heat two inches of oil in a skillet to 370°F (or use a deep fryer). Dredge fish in flour and shake off excess. Dip fish in batter. Slip into hot oil. Fry until golden brown (about 4 minutes).

3. Warm tortillas on a very hot skillet. Place hot fish on the tortilla. Combine mayonnaise and yogurt to make white sauce. Top fish with sauce, cabbage, and salsa fresca. Squeeze on lime and add optional garnishes.

12 FISH TACOS: 4 SERVINGS

FIVE-CUP SALAD

Five-cup salad, aka *can-can salad, millionaire salad,* and *ambrosia,* is a kitsch classic that comes in countless variations, the one ironclad rule being that none of its ingredients can be fresh. That's the vital subtext of this pseudosalad: Nature, as expressed in such unruly tangled stuff as lettuce and forbiddingly crunchy things like carrots and radishes (not to mention smelly veined cheese), is inferior to the smooth and palliative comforts of culinary technology. Once a popular offering at ladies lunch (back when ladies lunched), it endures as an ingenuous tradition in heartland cafeterias and at festive family dinners that demand something pretty and sweet and not the least bit challenging either to cook or diner. The recipe's pillars are sour cream, canned pineapple (crushed or chunked), and shredded coconut. To this trio may be added mandarin orange slices, maraschino cherries, fruit cocktail, miniature marshmallows, chopped walnuts, shredded American cheese, Cool Whip, and (at Easter only) multi-colored Fun Mallows.

Five-Cup Salad

Throughout much of the heartland, the word *salad* does not necessarily mean green leafy things and virtuous vegetables. A salad can be any sort of refreshing side dish that is not an entree or vegetable. Some such salads are so sweet that they could pass as dessert—Five-Cup Salad being a prime example.

> 1 cup shredded coconut
> 1 cup mandarin oranges, drained
> 1 cup crushed pineapple, drained
> 1 cup sour cream
> 1 cup miniature marshmallows

Combine all ingredients.

4–6 SERVINGS

FLANNEL CAKES

No relation to **red flannel hash, flannel cakes** are the name applied by Hollywood's oldest restaurant, Musso and Frank Grill, to dime-thin pancakes that are wide enough to eclipse a full-size dinner plate. Served only at lunch, they can be a simple, straightforward meal, but they also make a grand companion to such stalwart Musso menu favorites as lamb shanks, sauerbraten, and corned beef and cabbage. The term *flannel cake* dates back to the mid-nineteenth century, when it was applied to oatcakes. It was a not-uncommon term for any kind of pancake in much of the mid-South into the mid-twentieth century, but we have seen no contemporary reference to flannel cakes other than at Musso's.

FLAUTAS

The Spanish word for "flute" is **flauta.** In a Mexican restaurant, flautas are small corn or wheat tortillas tightly wrapped around a shaft of shredded beef or chicken (or less commonly, pork), then deep-fried to a crisp. They are tightly enough wound that they do resemble little flutes, and nothing other than the meat—moist and well-spiced—is included. Guacamole, salsa, sour cream, lettuce, tomatoes, and/or hot sauce are served as companions. Always presented warm from the fry kettle, flautas are eaten as Emily Post suggested eating a firm spear of asparagus—by hand.

Flautas with all the fixin's in Tucson, Arizona.

MONICA FLINN

In Tucson in 1922, just ten years after Arizona became a state, a young widow named **Monica Flinn** opened a small cafe. Daughter of a stonemason who had come from France to carve a church portal in the mid-nineteenth century, she named her place El Charro, after the master horsemen of Mexico. In the beginning, it was a one-woman operation. It is said that when a customer placed an order, Monica stepped into the kitchen, scurried out the back door, and convinced the grocer to give her provisions—for which she would pay once the customer paid her. Early menus warned, "No service for less than 10 cents."

El Charro changed location three times, eventually coming to the old family home that Monica's father had built in the neighborhood once known as Snob Hollow, just outside the early Spanish *presidio.* By the time she moved to this final location, Monica and her restaurant had become essential facets of Tucson culture. You could count on an El Charro float in the grand parade for the annual *Fiesta de los Vaqueros;* and when movie production companies came to shoot westerns at Old Tucson (a frontier-town set), the Hollywood cowboys and cowgirls made El Charro their place for good times. John Wayne used to play cards and have martinis with Monica, and young Ronald Reagan was a fan of her cooking.

Politician Thomas Dewey was a visitor, too, but he had no more success at El Charro than he did running for president in 1948. During the campaign, he sat down, unthinkingly picked up a broad flour tortilla, and tucked it in his shirt collar, thinking it was a napkin. After losing the election, he came to Tucson to rest and one day decided to return to El Charro for real Mexican food. He ordered chili con carne. But being unfamiliar with the cuisine, he grabbed a whole pepper from the table and took a chaw. Observers say he opened his mouth to gasp, but no sound emerged. Secret Service men rushed forward as a wave of red moved up from his neck to singe the roots of his hair. His eyes, filled with a surprise beyond belief, bulged. Like all gringo pepper-eating novices, he gulped quantities of water. This helped not at all. The Secret Service didn't know whether to reach for their guns or fans.

Now run by Monica's descendants, El Charro remains a defining Mexican restaurant of the American Southwest. Claims are made (and disputed) that it was she who invented the **topopo salad,** the **chimichanga,** and the cheese crisp. Day of the Dead festivities at El Charro include the creation of a shrine to Monica. Laid out around her photograph are a rosary, bright flowers, traditional Day of the Dead food items (sugar skulls, cookies in the shape of skeletons), and Monica's favorite cooking tools.

FLUFFERNUTTER

In 2006, the Massachusetts state legislature spent a full week debating the question: Should the **fluffernutter** become the official state sandwich? On one side, nutritional worrywarts griped that the combination of Marshmallow Fluff and peanut butter on white bread contributed to the scourge of childhood obesity; against them stood history-minded partisans for whom the fluffernutter sandwich was a proud culinary legacy. One state legislator declared, "I'm going to fight to the death for Fluff."

Outside New England, few people know what the sandwich is; many aren't even familiar with Marshmallow Fluff! The spreadable airy white confection first appeared early in the twentieth century, as Marshmallow Crème (invented in 1917 in Somerville, Massachusetts, by Archibald Query) and as Snowflake Marshmallow Crème (invented in 1913 by Amory and Emma Curtis of Melrose, Massachusetts). During World War I, when patriotic citizens sought to get their protein from sources other than beef and to find alternatives to wheat flour, Ms. Curtis published a recipe for the Liberty Sandwich—Snowflake Marshmallow Crème and peanut butter on war bread (made with oats or barley). It was not until 1960 that the combo was named *fluffernutter*, thanks to a creative ad agency seeking to sell more Marshmallow Fluff. (Rice Krispie Treats, originally made by combining the cereal with Fluff, were invented in 1966.)

Fluffernutter never did become Massachusetts's official sandwich, but October 8 has been proclaimed National Fluffernutter Day.

FRENCH DIP

At one time, the **French dip** was a signature dish of Los Angeles, where it was created. But it is now ubiquitous, especially west of the Mississippi, where its aliases include *wet beef* and *beef Manhattan*. The beef is warm, sliced thin, and bunned in a torpedo roll. Hot mustard or horseradish is also part of the presentation. But what distinguishes a French dip from such regional comparables as the upper Midwest's **hot beef** and New Orleans's roast beef and **debris** is that natural beef gravy, known by the curious non-noun *au jus,* is served alongside the sandwich in a cup for pouring or dipping.

Despite that fact, neither Philippe the Original nor Cole's P.E. Buffet, the two restaurants that claim to have invented French dip, serves it with gravy on the side. Both moisten the roll with gravy before the sandwich is assembled and (optionally) moisten it again after it is put together (known as double dipping). Philippe's version of its birth says that a cafeteria counterman—or possibly proprietor Philippe Mathieu—was preparing a roast beef sandwich for an impatient customer one day in 1918. The sandwich slipped out of its maker's hand into the gravy trough. Rather than wait for another one to be assembled from scratch, the customer said, "I'll take it just like that." Cole's P.E. Buffet claims that its kitchen made the first French dip to satisfy a customer whose teeth were so bad that he asked for his sandwich to be softened by a soak in gravy before it was served.

FRIED BOLOGNA

Most people's image of bologna is a circle of pale pink lunchmeat about ¹⁄₁₆ inch thin; when such people see **fried bologna** on a menu in the mid-South or Southwest, it is easy to understand why they'd disrespect it. But not all bologna resembles a Crayola-colored coaster. If it is sliced thick, made of pork and beef, well seasoned (usually with garlic), and fatty enough that it develops a dark, wickedly savory crust when it sizzles on a skillet, fried bologna is a sandwich that commands loyalty. A variation popular in Memphis, as well as in Oklahoma and Texas, is *barbecued bologna.* Known to derisive outsiders as *Okie Sirloin,* it is a full cylinder of bologna that smokes low and slow in the pit until the outside is a beautiful dark bronze and the inside still weeps garlicky juices. Sliced thick and served on a bun (in Memphis, with slaw included), barbecued bologna is almost always sopped with tangy red sauce.

FRIED CLAMS

The clam may be just one frequent-fryer among North Atlantic seafoods, but unlike shrimp, scallops, oysters, and cod, it has engendered cult adoration. Fried clamophiles (who care only for juicy whole-belly clams; no rubbery clam strips) debate who-makes-the-best with the fervor of **barbecue** boosters in North Carolina and **custard** connoisseurs in Wisconsin.

Clam connoisseurs insist on whole-belly fried clams, as opposed to clam strips.

The best clams for deep-frying—steamers large enough to pack a salty savor—are hand-raked at low tide from beds in the Essex River on the North Shore of Massachusetts. Breaded in cornmeal and fried in oil that traditionally is at least half lard, a **fried clam** is a crusty, pale gold nugget big enough to be one greedy mouthful, a heavy piece of food that resembles a bulbous cartoon ring (the neck) set with a giant stone (the belly). The belly yields the distinctive marine smack of a freshly opened mollusk. On the very finest fried clam platters, the bellies vary in size, making each and every piece a unique eating experience. Some are, in fact, scarcely bigger than a Virginia peanut, making a package with more crust than clam, in which the chewy neck provides the prime sensation and the silky morsel of oceanic meat plays second fiddle. On others, the belly is large enough that it reminds you of a steamer or a clam on the half-shell, with a nectareous clamitude that has the quality of being cooked and yet maintains its fresh, briny wallop.

Best of the best: Fried clams at the Clam Box, Ipswich, Massachusetts.

According to oft-repeated culinary lore, the fried clam was invented on July 3, 1916, at the still-thriving Woodman's of Essex in Massachusetts. The Great Moment is supposed to have occurred when Chubby Woodman, proprietor of what then was a small raw bar, tossed a few clams into the oil he was using to cook up the newly invented snack food Saratoga chips (**potato chips**). On the other hand, historians have found mention of fried clams well before Woodman's revelation, including an article in the *New York Times* on May 12, 1912, warning that "fried clams are generally unwholesome for persons of weak digestion."

FRIED DOUGH

While its name earns no points for cleverness, **fried dough**—a piece of yeast dough that has been fried—claims passionate devotees throughout New England, where it is ubiquitous at local and regional fairs and in amusement parks. Resembling a thick, knobby pancake and occupying most of the white paper plate on which it is sold, fried dough is food truck fare. It is always made just moments before getting eaten (like so much fried pastry, its appeal fades as it cools) and can be had two basic ways: sweet, spread with melted butter and cinnamon sugar or maple sugar, or savory, brushed with red tomato sauce. Chocolate sauce, garlic, and melted cheese are other possible toppings Nearly every vendor we have seen officially bills what is sold as fried dough, but nicknames abound, including *beaver tails, whale tails, frying saucers,* and *elephant ears.* Fried dough should not be confused with *funnel cakes,* which are of Pennsylvania Dutch origin and are formed from unleavened dough, making them more crisp than chewy.

Fried Dough with Peanut Butter Topping
The classic formulation for fried dough is either sweet (a dusting of sugar or cinnamon sugar) or savory (pizza sauce). In New Hampshire and Vermont, we've eaten it topped with maple butter. Years ago, at the late, great Corky's pizzeria in East Hartford, Connecticut, we found it offered as dessert, topped with peanut butter.

It's a grand idea. The peanut butter was sweetened, its silky heft a tantalizing counterpoint to the fragile dough. The only obstacle to enjoying peanut butter–topped fried dough at Corky's was that Corky's also happened to be a first-class pizza parlor, where they used a brick oven to turn out pizzas with magnificently chewy yet elegant crusts, as well as gargantuan calzones loaded with sausage, cheeses, sauces, vegetables, the works! There was no way any ordinary appetite could want dessert after a Corky's meal. So we began to look upon these rounds of fried dough as snacks all by themselves.

4 tablespoons butter, softened
⅔ cup dark brown sugar
½ cup peanut butter
¼ cup milk
1 cup all-purpose flour
1 teaspoon baking powder
½ teaspoon salt
1 tablespoon vegetable shortening or lard
⅓ cup warm water
Oil for frying

1. First, prepare the topping: Cream together the butter, brown sugar, and peanut butter. Beat in the milk.

2. Mix the flour, baking powder, and salt. Cut in the shortening until the mixture is mealy. Slowly add water to form a ragged dough. Turn the dough onto a floured board and knead 2 minutes, or until smooth. Cover with a towel and let rest 15 minutes.

3. Heat the fat in a deep skillet to 375°F. Divide the dough into four equal balls and roll the first one out into a 6-inch circle. To keep it from puffing up, use a sharp knife to cut four or five 1-inch-long slits through the dough. Repeat with the other three balls.

4. Ease a circle of dough into the hot fat. Cook 30 seconds, or until brown, then turn it and cook the other side until golden brown. Drain on paper towels. Cook the other circles. Spread them with peanut butter topping while the dough is still hot.

4 FRIED DOUGHS

FRIED GREEN TOMATOES

When the Spanish explorer Cortés returned to Europe with tomatoes, the New World nightshade created a scandal. A red ripe tomato reminded people so much of human flesh that eating one seemed improperly erotic. One solution was to eat the tomato when still green and therefore less fleshlike and not sweet. No one knows if that is how **fried green tomatoes** came to be, but Louis Van Dyke, the late proprietor of the Blue Willow Inn of Social Circle, Georgia, where fried green tomatoes are a signature, suspected they first were made by Italians who dredged tomato slices in semolina and deep-fried them, creating a versatile dish that is good companion to any meal or a fine snack with beer, lemonade, or ice tea.

Fried green tomatoes were an icon of the Southern kitchen for decades before Fannie Flagg's best-selling 1987 novel *Fried Green Tomatoes at the Whistle Stop Cafe* and its subsequent film version made them known to Americans beyond the South. They continue as a symbol of homespun Southern cooking, though frequently now they are used as a down-home note in an upscale dish: a base for **crab cakes,** folded into a deluxe BLT, or a puckery layer in eggs Benedict.

FRIED PIE

Fried pie, a popular dessert throughout the South and signature sweet of Atlanta's Varsity Drive-In, is a single-serving crescent of piecrust pastry dough pinched around traditional fillings—apple, peach, apricot, sweet potato—and deep-fried until brittle. Unlike a slice from a whole pie, a fried pie is portable. Among favorite convenience-store snacks around the Gulf Coast is a Hubig's "New Orleans Style Pie," a fried pie made by a company founded over a century ago in Texas. Hubig's pies, made

Fried peach pie at the Family Pie Shop, De Valls Bluff, Arkansas.

with fruit or sweet potato filling, are packed in a sturdy crust with a sugar glaze, and although they readily crumble, they often are spotted in the hand that a driver does not have on his steering wheel.

FRITOS PIE

Casseroles layered with corn tortillas go back to Mesoamerica, but the **Fritos pie** (or, if you wish, *Frito pie*) cannot, by definition, predate 1932. That is when Fritos were patented by Elmer Doolin, who got the recipe from a street-corner vendor and started selling them at his lunch counter in San Antonio. (Doolin subsequently invented Cheetos.) Long before Fritos, Mexicans had enjoyed eating *fritos* (small *f*), which simply means "little fried things," but it was Doolin who figured out how to mass-produce the curly little corn chips, and it has been reported that it was his mother, Daisy Dean Doolin, who first put them into a baked casserole with chili and cheese.

Some thirty years later, at the Woolworth's lunch counter in Santa Fe, cook Teresa Hernandez got the idea to create an individual Fritos pie by simply slicing off the top of a single-serving bag of chips and ladling in chili, then cheese, onions, lettuce, and tomato. She planted a plastic fork and, because Woolworth's was right on the Plaza in the heart of town, her creation became a popular portable meal that visitors and locals could enjoy while on the stroll or sitting on a park bench.

Like Fritos themselves, Fritos pie is no longer strictly regional, but it is especially popular across a wide swath of the Southwest from Arkansas through Texas and Oklahoma and into New Mexico. Variations encountered include *Flagstaff pie* in Amarillo and the Hot Springs *spread*, which also includes **tamales.**

Santa Fe's Five and Dime serves its Fritos pie in the bag.

FROGMORE STEW

A gallimaufry of shrimp, sausage, new potatoes, onions, and chunks of corn on the cob that all get boiled in the same pot with a hail of crab-boil seasonings, **Frogmore stew** was named for the coastal community of Frogmore, South Carolina, on the island of St. Helena near the Georgia line. In the early 1960s, Richard Gay of the island's Gay Seafood Company created it to feed mass quantities of fellow National Guardsmen, and it remains a favorite dish for big picnics, festivals, and political rallies. Although the U.S. Post Office abolished Frogmore in the 1980s, locals still like to call the dish by the obsolete town name in honor of its history. It also is known as *Beaufort stew* and the more descriptive *Lowcountry boil*.

Frogmore stew, aka Lowcountry boil, at Bowen's Island outside Charleston.

FROZEN CUSTARD

In Wisconsin, St. Louis, and much of the Midwest, *custard*'s first meaning is not pudding; it is a frozen dessert that looks like soft-serve ice cream but is significantly creamier. With less overrun (pumped-in air) than most ice cream, **frozen custard** is dense and silky smooth; and because it contains eggs as well as cream, it is luxuriously rich. At all the best custard shops, it is made fresh and served directly from the machine that produces it, and while some places, such as Kopp's of Milwaukee, offer literally hundreds of different flavors over the course of a year, plain vanilla is probably the best way to understand its back-to-basics appeal. See also **concrete.**

Excellent custard makes ice cream seem austere.

Milwaukee custard stands top sundaes with crunchy toasted salted nuts.

FRY SAUCE

Throughout the Plains, all the way to the West Coast, **drive-ins** and burger joints, as well as **loosemeats** shops in Siouxland, offer **fry sauce** to accompany French fries and onion rings. Ranging from Ranch-dressing-white to salmon pink, it is a mixture of mayonnaise and ketchup that can be doctored up with chopped sweet pickles or onions or other spices. A Utah drive-in chain, Arctic Circle, says it first created fry sauce in 1948 from "a tasty, tangy mixture of tomato concentrate, lemon juice, eggs, and a whole bunch of other ingredients."

GARBAGE PLATE

In the same reprobate family of outrageous belt busters as a **slinger,** a **horseshoe,** and **poutine,** the Rochester **garbage plate** was first created by **diner** man Alex Tahou during the Great Depression as a means of delivering maximum nutrition for minimum cost. Originally known as *hots and potots*—*hots* being the upstate New York term for **hot dogs**—the hash house extravaganza was renamed by Alex's son Nick, who

The last word in kitchen-sink cuisine: A garbage plate at Nick Tahou Hots, Rochester, New York.

became a local legend as the proprietor of an eponymous open-all-night cafe, Nick Tahou Hots. There never was one single way to make a garbage plate, but as the name suggests, it necessarily includes many disparate ingredients, all presented on a sturdy cardboard plate. The base typically is fried potatoes and/or macaroni salad or possibly baked beans. Atop the starch(es) go a brace of grilled hot dogs, **hamburgers,** or cheeseburgers, or your choice of sausage, chicken, ham, fish, egg, or a grilled cheese sandwich. These typically are garnished with chili, mustard, ketchup, and chopped raw onions. Bread is also provided; it is helpful for pushing ingredients around on the plate.

GATEAU SIROP

A moist, perfumy spice cake sweetened with dark sugarcane syrup, **gateau sirop** is a dessert and coffee an' staple in cafes and fine dining rooms in Louisiana Cajun country, where cane sugar is harvested. Whipped cream is a welcome crown; at the venerable Prejean's of Lafayette, it comes gilded with Frangelico cream sauce; at Cafe des Amis in Breaux Bridge, it is dotted with roasted pecans and available a la mode.

GERBER SANDWICH

No city has more unique and peculiar dishes than St. Louis, ranging from the now-popular **toasted ravioli** to the somewhat less-loved brain sandwich (once a local bar staple). Some, like the curious **St. Paul,** are virtually unknown elsewhere. The **Gerber sandwich** is another strictly local passion. A sauceless cognate of French-bread **pizza,** it is a ham sandwich made on a length of Italian bread that is well buttered and garlicked and topped with the St. Louis–favorite **Provel cheese.** Ruma's Deli claims to have invented it, along with an even more obscure sandwich, known as the Prosperity (hot roast beef on garlic bread topped with gravy and Provel cheese). Ruma's offers normal-topping French-bread pizzas as well as more typical thin-crust St. Louis pizza, both of which also are topped with Provel cheese.

GHETTO FRIES

Ghetto was the nickname of an employee of Max's Italian Beef restaurant on Chicago's North Side. Six or seven years ago, Ghetto came up with a wild combo of French fries topped with the carnivorous natural gravy used on Italian beef, plus barbecue sauce, plus Merkt's cheese, plus **giardiniera,** plus chopped onions, plus hot peppers. The kitchen-sink dish was dubbed **Ghetto fries** after its creator, and everything was copasetic until 2005, when a local television station, apparently on a slow news day, aired a story noting that some customers were "raising their eyebrows" at the possible offensiveness of the name. The story raised no eyebrows whatsoever, except for one blogger who suggested that if "the word 'ghetto' is politically incorrect, we should now refer to them as 'low-income housing' fries."

Ghetto fries likely never will be known by their P.C. name, "low-income housing fries."

GIARDINIERA

Giardiniera, meaning "from the garden," traditionally is a mix of bite-size pieces of broccoli, carrot, cauliflower, olives, and peppers in a spicy marinade. On the Italian table, it is a relish to accompany meat on a plate or part of an antipasto platter. In Chicago, it is something else: the same ingredients chopped finely enough that they can be spread with a spoon. Ranging from sport-pepper hot to nearly sweet, giardiniera is the fundamental condiment for **Italian beef** sandwiches, its pickly zest pairing so well with meat, bread, and gravy. Although the giardiniera concept dates back centuries in the Old Country, it is believed that giardiniera first appeared in Chicago sandwich shops in the late 1920s.

Giardiniera for Beef Sandwiches

In Chicago at Al's #1 Italian Beef, which claims to have invented the Italian beef sandwich, the giardiniera formula is not written down, but proprietor Chris Pacelli opened up the thirty-gallon tub in which a batch of it was fermenting, stirred it with a long wooden spoon, and gave us a few expert tips. He especially warned against using too much garlic or too much red pepper, thereby creating a condiment that calls attention to itself. A good giardiniera should have just enough zest to underscore—but not overwhelm—the deep, mellow savor of the juicy beef. These measurements make enough to generously top six long sandwiches.

3 celery ribs, minced
1 small clove garlic, minced
½ red pepper, seeded and minced
1 plum tomato, finely chopped
2 tablespoons small capers with 1 tablespoon of caper juice
½ teaspoon dried crushed red pepper flakes
1 teaspoon dried oregano
⅓ cup olive oil
2 tablespoons lemon juice

1. Combine all ingredients, toss to mix, and cover. Let the mixture steep at room temperature for at least 24 hours, preferably 48, tossing a few times each day.

2. Spoon onto hot beef sandwiches.

GOETTA

Cincinnatians accompany breakfast with griddle-cooked slices of the pork and pin-oat loaf known as goetta.

For Cincinnatians, **goetta** (say "getta") is a soothing taste of home. A pork and pin-oat loaf that is cut into thin slices and fried, it is similar to **scrapple** but usually more rugged-textured, the oats a significant presence. It is primarily breakfast meat, served plain alongside eggs or pancakes, but also frequently adorned with syrup or apple butter. Goetta is found nowhere beyond greater Cincinnati, where, like New Jersey's **pork roll,** it has a legion of loyal fans—who in recent years have invented goettaburgers and even goetta-topped **pizza** (both of which can be sampled at the annual Goettafest in Covington, Kentucky, on the other side of the Ohio River). Originally created by German peasant cooks as a way to stretch the meat supply, it has become a celebrated icon of Old World culinary heritage.

GOLD BRICK SAUCE

Milk chocolate melted with butter and studded with toasted pecans makes **gold brick sauce,** which hardens as soon as it is poured onto cold ice cream, creating a gilt-like sheath. The concept is based on the Gold Brick candy bar introduced by Elmer Candy Corp. of New Orleans in 1936: a bar of milk chocolate and pecans named because it cost a dime when other candy bars were a nickel. Elmer's continues to make the candy, as well as its much-coveted Gold Brick Sauce, which the company notes was the world's first hard-shell topping for ice cream. It also hardens when poured on fruit. While Elmer's owns the name, generic forms of gold brick sauce are available up and down the Mississippi River, as well as in Chicago.

GONADS

◇◇

A man's yen to eat **gonads** does not necessarily reflect either homosexual tendencies or machismo, but it is a fact that at least nine out of ten people who enjoy eating testicles are of the masculine persuasion. Out of embarrassment, sexual panic, or a sense of humor, virtually no one calls a ball a ball. Whether the organs are harvested from a rooster, sheep, pig, or bull, they go by such names as *Rocky Mountain oysters, prairie oysters, swinging beef, tendergroin, calf fries,* and *cowboy caviar.* Pop culture has mined a nice little vein of comedy from a tenderfoot's misunderstanding of these terms, as seen in Baxter Black's poem "The Oyster," in which a cowboy squirms as an Eastern lady tells him how she likes to pry open oysters with her knife, and in the movie *Funny Farm,* in which Chevy Chase sets the town record for eating calf fries before he understands the painful reality of what they are.

Rarely found outside the West and Great Plains, gonads tend to take the role of hors d'oeuvres, usually served deep-fried in bite-size pieces with cocktail sauce. Their flavor is vaguely organy, similar to sweetbreads, although deep-frying usually eclipses whatever subtleties of taste testicles may have. Historically, they were a special occasion treat enjoyed by cowboys at the end of a day of castrating young male bovines.

GOOEY BUTTER CAKE

◇◇

Supposedly created in the 1930s when a now-forgotten St. Louis baker mixed the wrong ingredients for a cake but decided to bake it anyway, **gooey butter cake** is a low-rise pastry with a tender crust around the edge and a middle that is custard-soft and supersweet. Center cuts are dripping-moist; outside segments tend to be a balance of gooeyness and plain cake. A continuing passion in St. Louis (but nowhere else), gooey butter cake originally was simply the fixin's for yellow cake with extra butter, cream cheese, and powdered sugar, but city bakers have taken the idea and run with it. The Park Avenue Coffee Shop boasts seventy different flavors, about a dozen of which are made each day. Varieties include banana split, white chocolate raspberry, Amaretto, Butterfinger, and funky monkey. Gooey butter cake demands coffee; *St. Louis Post-Dispatch* food editor Judith Evans once described it as "the perfect Tupperware party food."

Gooey Butter Cake

Adapted from *St. Louis Days, St. Louis Nights,* published by the Junior League, this recipe is attributed to Fred and Audrey Heimburger, whose now-shuttered bakery was known for its excellent gooey butter cake.

Crust:
> 1 cup all-purpose flour
> 3 tablespoons sugar
> 1 stick butter, softened

Filling:
> 1 cup sugar
> 1 stick butter, softened
> 1 egg
> 1 cup all-purpose flour
> ½ cup evaporated milk
> ¼ cup light corn syrup
> 1 teaspoon vanilla extract
> Powdered sugar

1. Preheat the oven to 350°F. Oil an 8 x 8 x 1¾-inch baking pan. To make the crust, combine the flour and sugar. Cut in the butter until the mixture resembles fine crumbs and starts to cling together. Pat this mixture into the bottom and up the sides of the pan. If you are not making the filling right away, refrigerate the crust.

2. Prepare the filling by beating the sugar and butter until they form a light paste. Mix in the egg. Alternately add the flour and evaporated milk, mixing after each addition. Add the corn syrup and vanilla extract. Mix at medium speed until well-blended. Pour the batter into the crust-lined baking pan. Sprinkle with powdered sugar.

3. Bake 40 minutes. The cake will test "not done" in the center, and it will remain gooey as it cools in the pan. Forks are required!

9 SERVINGS

GORDITA

In Mexico and in the borderlands, if you want to call someone a fatso, but in the nicest possible way, you would call him a *gordito,* or if it's a girl, *gordita.* If you are in a Mexican restaurant in the Southwest and want to order a fat little cornmeal pocket filled with chili or carne asada or roasted vegetables, you ask for a **gordita.** These pleasingly plump little sandwiches usually come two or three to an order, and instead of offering the substantial crunch of a fried taco shell, they supply an earthy pillow to cushion whatever it is they are stuffed with.

Little Diner outside El Paso offers gorditas stuffed with chili con carne.

GRANDMA PIZZA

Invented in Nassau County, but now found occasionally in a broader New York orbit, **Grandma pizza** is cooked in a well-oiled pan like Sicilian **pizza,** but it is not as thick. It is large and squared off; cheese is applied sparingly, as are crushed tomatoes. Other toppings are rare. Also known as *nonna pizza,* it is believed to have originated at King Umberto in Elmont, New York, sometime in the 1970s. It remained an unknown menu special (based on a pizzaiolo's mother's recipe) until the late 1980s, when bakers Ciro Cesarano and Angelo Giangrande got together with a customer named Tippy Nocella and christened it.

Grandma pizza is a New York original, reminiscent of what Nonna cooked on Sunday.
BRUCE BILMES

GRANOLA

For a few decades starting in the hippie era, **granola** was a counterculture icon—as much an emblem of rebelliousness as torn jeans and tattoos. Now consumers pay extra for jeans torn in a fashionable manner, skin art is commonplace, and granola is as unsurprising an item in supermarket baskets as Cheerios. Yes, granola is a vestige of the '60s—but of the nineteenth century's '60s. It was created during the Civil War, when Dr. James Caleb Jackson, proponent of the Water Cure regimen (drink forty glasses per day) and follower of Sylvester Graham's strict antimeat diet, decided that the patients at his Our Home on the Hillside Sanitarium in Dansville, New York, needed something more to eat than water and graham crackers. He baked thin sheets of moistened whole wheat flour, crumbled them into bits, then baked them again, creating hard little nuggets he called Granula. Followers were told to fill a glass one-third full of the stuff, top it with milk, and leave it in an icebox overnight. In the morning, the sodden Granula was to be eaten alongside a cup of Dr. Jackson's Somo, a grain-based coffee substitute.

Jackson's crunchy particles became the first processed health food sold in America, and the first breakfast cereal as well. Some years later, John Harvey Kellogg, who was operating a sanitarium of his own in Battle Creek, Michigan, added cornmeal and oats to the formula and began marketing his own Granula. Dr. Jackson sued him, so Kellogg changed the name of his product to Granola. By the turn of the century, there were more than forty different companies marketing similar breakfast cereals that promised good health to people who ate them.

Breakfast cereal, originally proposed by food faddists whose programs also frequently included such radical ideas as temperance, celibacy, and women's suffrage, was entrenched in the mainstream

There is no granola more inviting than that served at the Cottage in La Jolla, California.

American diet by 1965 when long-forgotten (and trademark-expired) granola was resurrected. Its proponent was Layton Gentry, whom *Time* magazine called "Johnny Granola Seed" for having introduced Crunchy Granola, an all-in-one dry, portable meal perfectly suited to vagabonds, hippies living in communes, and any groovy character too stoned to cook. Writing for the Liberation News Service in 1969, Ita Jones recommended homemade granola to revolutionaries because it could be made in quantities big enough to feed a guerrilla army. She noted that it didn't spoil and was therefore perfectly suited for sit-ins, demonstrations, and anyone "occupying buildings for a length of time."

The *Wall Street Journal* ridiculed granola in a 1972 story titled "What Tastes Terrible and Doubles in Sales Every 60 Days?" in which granola was described as "something a horse might be fond of . . . about as chewy as leather—and not quite as tasty." Nonetheless, like so many anti-establishment affectations, it soon became big business; its connotations of naturalness and health made it an irresistible product for baby boom consumers yearning to remain forever young.

GRAPE-NUTS PUDDING

Grape-Nuts is an unlikely fun dessert. But in the world of New England cookery, which features such grumpy-named specialties as **boiled dinner,** slump, and grunt, the little brown pebbles of breakfast cereal (which are wheat and barley and contain neither grapes nor nuts) are inspiration for crazy stuff. There is no documentation as to when some bright cook surmised that a custard pudding could be improved by stirring in Grape-Nuts. Perhaps the cupboard lacked crackers for cracker pudding; some reports say it began as a back-of-the-box recipe from C. W. Post. Wherever it came from, **Grape-Nuts pudding** has been a dessert staple in New England (but nowhere else) for generations, and Grape-Nuts ice cream also is a favorite throughout the region.

Because the cereal is very hard and dense, it never completely disintegrates when it is stirred into pudding or ice cream. It becomes streaks of amber grain, offering textural contrast to its smooth medium as well as an earthy flavor to balance the frivolity of sweetened custard.

Grape-Nuts originally were marketed in 1897 to compete with Granula, which was the predecessor to Kellogg's **granola.**

Grape-Nuts Ice Cream

We've never figured out why Grape-Nuts became a staple in the Yankee kitchen and nowhere else in the United States, where it is considered mere cereal. Many New England restaurants with a sense of local history offer Grape-Nuts pudding for dessert, and several of the best ice cream parlors make Grape-Nuts ice cream, in which the cereal becomes a semi-savory note in sweet vanilla-flavored cream.

If you have an ice cream maker and a favorite recipe for 2 pints of vanilla, just add a cup of cereal to it. We use this rich formula.

6 egg yolks
⅔ cup sugar
3 cups cream
1½ teaspoons vanilla extract
1 cup Grape-Nuts cereal

1. Beat the egg yolks with an electric mixer at high speed until pale and thick. Slowly mix in the sugar, continuing to beat.

2. Warm 2 cups of the cream in the top of a double boiler.

3. Gradually add about a cup of the hot cream to the yolks, beating constantly. Then gradually add the warmed yolks back to the top of the double boiler with the warm cream. Over moderate heat, cook and stir constantly, using a rubber spatula to scrape the sides until the mixture is custard-thick. Remove the top of the double boiler from over the hot water and pour the mixture into a bowl to cool. Stir occasionally while cooling. When room temperature, add the remaining 1 cup of cream, the vanilla, and the cereal.

4. Freeze in an ice cream maker according to directions.

2 PINTS

GREEK PIZZA

◇◇

Greek pizza isn't really Greek, but it has a crust unique to pizzerias that are operated by Greek families. You always can spot such a place, because the kitchen will be stacked with round pans that contain resting dough ready to be topped. Cooked in its shallow pan, Greek **pizza** is thicker than **Neapolitan pizza** but thinner than Sicilian and leans more toward crunch than chew. Rather than being tossed and stretched, the dough is patted into the pan, and because it contains a significant amount of oil, it develops a lusciousness that suggests pastry as much as bread. Frequently, white cheddar is used instead of or along with mozzarella. Most Greek pizzas are found in the Northeast.

Yes, Greek pizza is an Italian-American dish.

129

GREEN BAY CHILI

In 1913, a Lithuanian immigrant named John Isaac opened a **diner** in Green Bay, Wisconsin. Chili John's signature dish was chili architecturally similar to **Cincinnati chili,** including spaghetti noodles as the bottom layer, but with the addition of pepper-spiked oil to provide whatever level of heat requested by the customer. By the mid-twentieth century, Chili John's style of chili was widespread throughout Wisconsin and beyond and known by its home city's name: **Green Bay chili.**

It has been claimed that Mr. Isaac was responsible for the invention of oyster crackers, the spoon-size hexagonal saltines that always are served as a companion to Green Bay chili because they are good for balancing the hot oil. The story is that he convinced manufacturers of large, old-fashioned store crackers to downsize so he could have a garnish for his chili. However, research indicates that oyster crackers have been around since the mid-nineteenth century, long before Green Bay chili was a gleam in John Isaac's eye.

GREEN CHILE CHEESEBURGER

The **green chile cheeseburger** delivers a stunning range of meat and heat, sharp capsicum bite and creamy melted cheese. Condiments may include a slice of raw onion, lettuce, tomato, mustard, pickle chips, and a sliced jalapeño. The burger has become such an emblem of New Mexico pop cookery that the governor of the state recently instituted the Green Chile Cheeseburger Challenge, for which judges anoint the best each year at the state fair, and New Mexico's tourism board has developed a hugely inclusive Green Chile Cheeseburger Trail, listing virtually every one in the state (www.newmexico .org/greenchilecheeseburger/).

At least two places in New Mexico claim to have invented the burger, sometime in the mid-twentieth century: Bert's Burger Bowl in Santa Fe and the Owl Bar in San Antonio. Both still are thriving, and the Owl Bar, along with the Buckhorn Tavern, attracts crowds of burger fans to a crossroads town off I-25 where there are few other attractions. A recent corollary is the *slopper* of Pueblo, Colorado—a hamburger or cheeseburger served open-face and topped with chili stew (not just chopped chiles).

The ultimate green chile cheeseburger is made at Bobcat Bite, a diner on the outskirts of Santa Fe.

Green Chile for Cheeseburgers

The chile on a green chile cheeseburger can be as simple as a whole roasted pod, peeled and seeded, draped across the top. Or the pod can be chopped. It should go without saying that using freshly roasted peppers rather than canned ones makes all the difference. In fact, good peppers and cheese are all that are needed to make a great GCCB. To give the sandwich extra pizzazz, prepare the topping as follows. This recipe makes a messy sauce, suitable for knife-and-fork burgers rather than for bunned ones.

2 tablespoons minced onion
2 cloves garlic, minced
3 tablespoons olive oil
1½ teaspoons flour
⅓ cup water
1 cup chopped roasted green chiles
Salt

In a heavy saucepan, sauté the onion and garlic in oil until soft. Sprinkle in the flour, blending well with a wooden spoon. Trickle in the water, stirring constantly, then stir in the chile. Bring to a simmer, stirring frequently. Reduce heat and stir 3–4 minutes. Add salt to taste.

CHILE FOR 4 GCCBS

GREEN CORN TAMALES

Just as Christmas is hot **tamale** season throughout much of the Southwest, late summer into early fall is time for **green corn tamales.** Traditionally made when local corn ripens and chile pods are harvested, they have in recent years become a year-round dish, thanks to corn trucked up from southern Mexico and chiles frozen at harvest time. Fresh corn on the cob is essential, because when the kernels are scraped off, enough juice comes with them to make a moist, full-flavored tamale filling. The filling is laced with roasted chiles (often with cheese), and the combo is tightly rolled inside a green (not dried) corn husk, which is steamed until the taste of earth and fire within are exuberantly married. Nobody makes just a few tamales and few people do it alone. Tamales are the inspiration for house parties where family and friends gather with bushels of corn, pounds of chiles and corn masa, and cases of beer, and everybody pitches in.

GRILLED PIZZA

Grilled pizza has antecedents in South American flatbread cookery, but it was introduced to the United States by accident. In 1980, the proprietors of Al Forno restaurant in Providence, Rhode Island, misunderstood a recipe that called for a brick oven and used their grill instead. The result was a huge success and put the restaurant on every foodie's radar; the popularity of grilling in general in the late twentieth century buoyed its fortune in other restaurants as well.

Grilled pizza was introduced to the country by Al Forno in Providence, Rhode Island. CHRIS AYERS AND AMY BRIESCH

Grilling is a favorite technique for home pizzaioli, who frequently make grilled pizza with store-bought crusts (thus avoiding the risk of too-floppy dough dripping through the grill grate). Grilled pizza is thin and very well oiled, topped with minimal ingredients.

GUMBO

Like Louisiana cuisine itself, **gumbo** is all about mixing, matching, blending, and creating something glorious from sundry elements. A staple of kitchens in New Orleans as well as in the Cajun countryside, its cooking canon has only a few rules: It should contain rice (cooked separately and added after the soup itself is made); it should start with a roux made of flour and fat (preferably lard); and it must be thickened as it cooks, using either okra or filé powder.

Bozo's gumbo, Metarie, Louisiana.

Rocky and Carlo's seafood gumbo, Chalmette, Louisiana.

Most gumbos are loaded with ingredients and radiantly spiced, and while virtually no element is taboo, the most commonly encountered varieties are seafood gumbo, made with crawfish, shrimp, crab, and/or oysters, and sausage gumbo, which almost always includes duck or chicken as well. During Lent, it is not uncommon to come across meatless *gumbo z'herbes*, featuring varieties of greens.

The soup's diverse roots are French (like bouillabaisse), Spanish (the inclusion of celery, onions, and peppers is basically *sofrito*), and Choctaw Indian (filé powder is ground sassafras leaves). Its name is derived from the African Bantu word *kingombo*, which means "okra." After Hank Williams Sr. recorded the song *Jambalaya* in 1952, which contains the line, "Jambalaya, crawfish pie, and filé gumbo," Cajuns translated the lyrics and made it an anthem of south Louisiana country folk. They sing, *"Jambalaya, des tartes d'ecreuvisse, file gombo . . ."*

HALF SMOKE

The **half smoke** belongs somewhere in the **hot dog** family, but its pedigree is dubious. Is it called a half smoke because it is only smoked halfway? Because it is a half-and-half mix of beef and pork? Because some cooks bisect it lengthwise before cooking it on a grill? One claim to fame with which no one can argue is that the half smoke is the one single dish that is unique to Washington, D.C. It mostly is street food, sold by corner carts, but it also is a signature of Ben's Chili Bowl restaurant, as well as of Weenie Beenie, a one-time D.C.-area chain that is now a single location in Arlington, Virginia. Basically a fat hot dog with a coarse texture and an elusive smoky taste, the half smoke is always served in a bun and is typically topped with spicy beef chili.

Ben Ali of Ben's Chili Bowl, where half smokes rule.

Half smokes on the griddle at Ben's Chili Bowl.

HALUSHKA

Uncompromised foreign food, **halushka** is good for American eaters to know about when dining in any of the great Polish or Slovakian restaurants of the Midwest, especially in northern Ohio. It is a dowdy-looking dish and therefore all too easy to breeze past when pushing a tray through a magnificent cafeteria line, such as that of Cleveland's Sokolowski's University Inn, where such big guns as bratwurst, kielbasa, pierogi, and Lake Erie perch steal the show. But main courses want companions, and there is none better than the buttery mix of little sautéed potato dumplings and sweet cabbage that is halushka, aka *halushki* or *haluski*. Egg noodles are a frequent shortcut substitute, but they cannot fully satisfy a halushka eater who has known the tender comfort of teeth gliding into a real potato dumpling.

HAMBURGER

Although it was named for a town in Germany and its ancestry goes back to tribes of Mongolian cowherds known as Tartars, the **hamburger** is as close as this country comes to a national dish. Exactly where and when it was invented is a hot topic among the hamburger's would-be hometowns. Origins arguments depend on a clear answer to the fundamental question: What is a hamburger? People have eaten ground beef for centuries. But *hamburger* history begins with the act of making the beef into a patty and putting it between slices of bread, or possibly in a bun or on a roll, thus making it a no-fork phenomenon, at least theoretically.

Credible claims of this occurrence come from New Haven, Connecticut (1900: thrifty

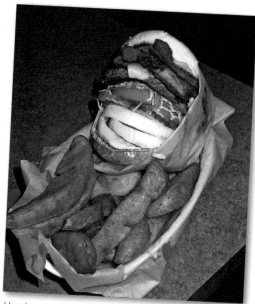

Hamburger: Hodad's, Ocean Beach, California.

sandwich-maker Louis Lassen finds a use for the trimmings of his steak sandwiches); St. Louis (1904: Fletcher "Old Dave" Davis of Athens, Texas, presents his ground beef sandwich at the World's Fair); Hamburg, New York (1885: the Menches brothers' sandwich stand at the Erie County fair runs out of pork, so beef is substituted); and Seymour, Wisconsin (1885: at the Outagamie County Fairgrounds "Hamburger Charlie" Nagreen flattens a meatball and serves it on bread). No one doubts, however, Seymour's claim to have made the world's largest hamburger—5520 pounds—in 1989, as part of the town's summer Burger Fest.

Hamburgers are less geographically specific than, say, **hot dogs,** but some parts of the country claim their own unique variation. West of Oklahoma City, along old Route 66, is **onion-fried burger** territory. Central Connecticut is home to about a half-dozen restaurants that all make **steamed cheeseburgers,** a regional specialty so geographically focused that even people in eastern and western Connecticut have never heard of it. Other significant subsets of the hamburger include the **green chile cheeseburger** (New Mexico), the **butter burger** (Wisconsin), and the **slider** (universal).

Hamburger: The Cottage, La Jolla, California.

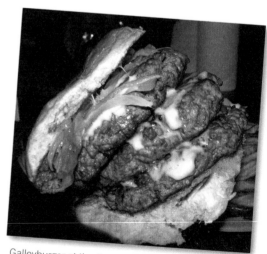

Galleyburger at the Anchor Bar, Superior, Wisconsin.

HANGTOWN FRY

Supposedly named for the summary justice meted out in Placerville, known as Hangtown in California's wild-west days, and first served to a miner who hit paydirt and demanded a meal composed of the most expensive items in the house, **hangtown fry** is a mix of fried oysters and scrambled eggs and, frequently, bacon. The oysters may be breaded or not, chopped or whole. The Platonic version is served at San Francisco's Tadich Grill, where it is made with six fried oysters and smoked bacon in a creamy egg frittata. Hangtown fry remains mostly a specialty of the Northwest coast, named the Official Dish of Placerville by local lawmakers.

HANKY PANKY

It is rare to find **hanky pankies** served in a restaurant, but go to a casual party in a home on the west side of Cincinnati and you very likely will be served them, always to be eaten in multiples. We are talking here about extremely humble food: a thimble's worth of seasoned sausage or sometimes ground beef with melted Velveeta atop a little tile of party rye. **Goetta** may be substituted for beef or sausage, and while it would be possible to use some other cheese, every hanky panky cook we know considers the smooth, melty texture of Velveeta just right for the dish.

How or why they got their goofy name remains a mystery, and in fact, not all who eat them call them that. We were chatting with a native Cincinnatian who knows quite a bit about local food, and yet he was puzzled when we brought up hanky pankies. But as we described them, we could see a light bulb illuminate above his head. "Ah, yes!" he said. "You mean what-you-eat-when-you-are-watching-football-on-Sunday! I didn't know they had a name." They also sometimes get the all-purpose sobriquet for any mess of food on toast, *S.O.S.*

FRED HARVEY

More than any other single person, **Fred Harvey** created a cuisine in America. The man who is said to have "civilized the West, one meal at a time" invented chain restaurants and chain hotels, pioneered cultural tourism, and "introduced America to Americans." The father of this nation's hospitality industry was dirt-poor when he immigrated to the United States from England in 1853, and although he died in 1901, the company he created grew and thrived well into the mid-twentieth century. While the business passed from him to his son, Ford, then to Ford's son, Freddy, the brand never changed. Harvey's biographer, Stephen Fried, deemed this a brilliant strategy because, long after Harvey's death, customers still felt "as if they were being taken care of by Fred Harvey himself."

To be taken care of by Fred Harvey implied quality and couth, an ethos so entrenched that in the 1920s the company battled Oklahoma's corporation commission all the way to the state supreme court over Fred Harvey's requirement that men wear jackets in Harvey House dining rooms. The company's civility wasn't only about etiquette. During the Depression, Harvey Houses became known as "the softest touches in the West" because their policy was never to turn away a hungry person, even one who couldn't pay.

When the young Harvey first sailed from London to New York, the very idea of a restaurant with a varied menu was new. In 1876, when he opened his first railway eating establishment in the Santa Fe's Topeka depot, train-station dining rooms were famously repulsive. Decades later, William Allen White referred to Harvey Houses as "beacons of culinary light and learning."

As the gold standard of hospitality in hotels as well as trains and train depot restaurants, Fred Harvey hosted everyone who was anyone. The company dispatched Hopis in its employ to greet Albert Einstein when he visited the Grand Canyon; Harvey's La Posada in Winslow, Arizona, had a special room reserved for Howard Hughes. M. F. K. Fisher wrote that dinner in a Fred Harvey dining car with her Uncle Evans when she was nineteen inspired her to care about food. Walt Disney, who created the character Mickey Mouse while riding on the Santa Fe, included a replica of a Fred Harvey restaurant in the original Disneyland.

HERMAN

Herman is a sweet sourdough starter that originally was birthed by a Virginia housewife whose 2½-year-old daughter gave it a pet name. Mom Gerrity was an avid baker, constantly making sourdough coffee cakes, but as her child, Amy, added flour, milk, and sugar every five days, there was always extra Herman they needed to give away, lest it take over the refrigerator.

Those to whom they gave it cooked with it, stirred it, and fed it, and brought containers full of their own surplus Herman to friends and neighbors, along with favorite sourdough recipes. Like an edible chain letter or a scene from Disney's *The Sorcerer's Apprentice,* Herman multiplied and even took on other identities, including Amish Friendship Starter. As one fan explained, "Herman is like faith. You can't buy it or sell it, but if you get some, you yearn to share it. And the more you share, the greater it grows."

After Harlene Hayer Watland received a Cool Whip container full of it from her Grandma Lorna in 1980, she began publishing *The Herman Sourdough Herald*, a monthly newsletter of recipes that ranged from Auntie Amy's Matrimonial Bars to Mango Peach Upside-Down Cake. "I still have my original Herman, who came to me wrapped in a baby blanket, and I feed him all the time," she told us many years ago. In 1990, Dawn Johnson collected recipes and Herman lore in a book titled *The Best of the Herman Sourdough Herald 1980–1990.*

HERO

To our knowledge, no one has catalogued all the sandwiches in America made on tubular lengths of bread, and there is no complete dictionary to explain their names. Some are so distinct they are a separate category altogether: **French dip, Italian beef, po' boy, banh mi, Cuban sandwich.** Others contain familiar ingredients and have names that need little explanation: a *zep* (western Pennsylvania) resembles a zeppelin; likewise, a *torpedo* (the Bronx) is shaped like a torpedo. But even some obvious names might be tricky.

Garnishes are vital in a Delaware Valley hoagie.

Take the *sub* or *submarine,* known throughout the Delaware Valley. The common and seemingly logical story is that they were named after the long, loaf-shaped ships of the silent service during World War II. But Tom LaRocca, longtime employee of the venerable White House Sub Shop in Atlantic City, offered another perspective: "Atlantic City said 'submarine' long before this place opened [in 1946]," he told us, explaining that the length of bread used to make the sandwich was always known as a sub. "Because it is not a full-size loaf. It is sub-sized, like a compact car."

Philadelphians call the same sort of sandwich a *hoagie.* One explanation is that Italian workers at the city's shipyard, known as Hog Island during the first World War, brought bunned lunches that became known as *Hog Island sandwiches,* and eventually *hoagies.* Most sandwich shop menus in the city offer both **cheese steaks** and hoagie cheese steaks, the latter including lettuce and tomato along with steak and cheese, but the classic hoagie (known in many places throughout the east simply as the *Italian special*), is strata of capicola, salami, and provolone with chopped iceberg lettuce, sliced tomatoes, and raw onions, a good drizzle of oil, and—optionally—roasted peppers, either sweet or fiery long hots. Some contend that hoagies always are cold or at least contain cool lettuce and tomato, whereas subs are hot; but the lines between the two are indistinct.

One of the least satisfying explanations afloat for a commonly used term is that people in Westchester County, New York, call their long sandwiches (hot or cold) *wedges* because, once assembled, the sandwich is cut on an angle and is therefore wedge-shaped. Likewise, the sandwich known as a *grinder* throughout southern New England is supposed to have gotten its name because one must grind one's teeth to eat it. Those theories will have to do until a substantiated account is uncovered.

At least the prevailing New York word for the sandwich has a solid source. In 1936, *Herald Tribune* food writer Clementine Paddleford observed Italian working men eating very large sandwiches from their lunch boxes and referred to them—the men as well as the sandwiches—as *heroes.*

HOLY TRINITY

Just as *mirepoix* (finely chopped onion, celery, and carrot) is a foundational ingredient of countless French dishes, so is the combination of onions, celery, and green peppers in the Cajun and Creole cuisines of Louisiana. Known as the **holy trinity,** the three elements are finely chopped and usually sautéed in butter to become the base for **jambalaya** or **étouffée** or, when blended with a bit of flour, the roux that starts a **gumbo.**

HOPPEL POPPEL

A nonsense phrase from an old German nursery rhyme about a nosy child who peeks into the stew pot, **hoppel poppel** (sometimes written as *hoffel poffel*) is a higgledy-piggledy breakfast for which each cook has a unique recipe. The foundation is eggs scrambled with chunks of griddle-fried potato and usually grilled onions, too. Ham, bacon, or sausage almost always is included, unless the kitchen is kosher, in which case the meat will be nuggets of beef salami. Deluxe versions include peppers and mushrooms and can be draped with melty cheese. Some home cooks supplement the formula with squares of sturdy bread that toast on the griddle and contribute serious crunch to the mix. Occasionally found in restaurants in Iowa and Wisconsin, hoppel poppel is a Sunday morning tradition on farmhouse tables as well as a frequent entry in locally published cookbooks.

Kosher hoppel poppel made with beef salami at Benji's Deli in Milwaukee.

HOPPIN' JOHN

Hoppin' john is a mostly edible good luck charm. *Mostly* edible, because not everyone should completely polish off their portion from the serving dish. One person will get a dime that has been buried in the mixture of black-eyed peas, rice, tomato sauce, and sausage or salt pork. That person is the ultra-lucky one, but Lowcountry lore says that all who eat hoppin' john at the beginning of the new year will be blessed with good luck—and if they accompany the rice and beans with greens, they'll likely make some money, too. While no claims are made for its ability to bring good fortune when eaten between January 2 and December 31, hoppin' john is a welcome coastal cognate of Creole **red beans and rice,** eaten with gusto alongside **soul food** meals throughout the year. How hoppin' john got its name remains a mystery. It may be a verbal corruption of the French-Caribbean name for black-eyed peas, *pois pigeons.*

HORCHATA

Throughout the American Southwest, at taco trucks and Sonoran **hot dog** stands and in Mexican restaurants plain and fancy, the nonalcoholic drink menu features **horchata.** A rice milk beverage that varies from sake-thin to **milk shake** rich, it always is at least slightly sweet, and its starchy character makes

it an especially effective emollient when eating very spicy food. It is always served on ice and often with a dusting of cinnamon on top. An Oaxacan restaurant called Guelaguetza in Los Angeles serves the most over-the-top variation, which includes chopped almonds, cantaloupe, and aromatic sweet cactus juice.

Horchata at El Norteño in Albuquerque, dusted with cinnamon.

HORSESHOE

Nobody eats **horseshoes** outside of Springfield, Illinois, where they are as much a passion as the locally loved chilli (yes, with two *l*'s). Conceived at the Leland Hotel in 1928 as an open-face ham sandwich that resembled a horseshoe on an anvil, with French fries scattered around like shoeing nails, the term has come to mean a giant plate of food that goes far beyond any reasonable definition of sandwich or any resemblance to equine footwear. Local taverns and **diners** pile 'shoes with **hamburgers,** pork tenderloins, fried chicken, whitefish, or even just vegetables, along with about a kilo of French fries and a flood of cheese sauce. It's the sauce that can make a horseshoe sing. Canned cheese sauce, which some Springfield shoe makers use, is easy and bright, but it cannot match the silky orange emulsion that starts with a roux in the city's top hash houses, where beer frequently is added to the recipe, giving the sauce a hopsy verve that balances its heft.

Shoes have become immensely popular for breakfast. Made with bacon or sausage and hash browns, and with cream gravy as a substitute or supplement for the cheese sauce, morning horseshoes are frequently available in downsized versions known as *pony shoes.* As is true of the Rochester **garbage plate,** variations are nearly infinite . . . as is the number of calories in a full-size one.

A Springfield, Illinois, breakfast horseshoe with cheese sauce and sausage gravy underneath the hash browns.

HOT BEEF

In the upper Midwest, **hot beef** means something other than roast beef that happens to be hot. It is the centerpiece meal of countless town cafes, as well as a respected entree at wedding banquets, silver anniversaries, and church suppers. The beef must be a pot-roast tender jumble of dark chunks and shreds, the mashed potatoes and gravy freshly made.

Eating a portion of hot beef demands some dexterity with knife and fork. The traditional way to do it (assuming you are right handed) is to grasp a fork vertically in the right hand, tines curved upward, just the way you'd grip a bicycle's handlebar, and hold a piece of soft white bread gently folded in the left. Slide the fork under a heap of beef like a shovel and use the bread to push the right amount of meat into balance on the fork. About every three bites, the leading edge of the bread has become so soaked with gravy that the fork is used to sever the moistened part and add it to the next forkload of beef. Hot beef often is served as a sandwich, but experienced eaters know to ask for extra bread to aid in pushing the meal around on the plate.

HOT BROWN

Chef Fred Schmidt of Louisville's Brown Hotel invented the **hot brown** in the 1920s to provide partygoers from the hotel ballroom an alternative to their

Louisville's hot brown, as made at Lynne's Paradise Café.

usual ham-and-eggs wee-hour meal. As he made it, the sandwich consisted of sliced turkey on white toast topped with Mornay sauce and Parmesan cheese, broiled until bubbly. When removed from the broiler, the top was criss-crossed with bacon strips and lengths of pimiento pepper. The hotel's name became affixed to the dish, which has since become a Kentucky trademark, available in many alternative configurations: with ham in addition to the turkey, with tomatoes instead of pimientos, with crab meat instead of turkey. There are even **hamburger** hot browns and vegetarian hot browns. The traditional version remains a featured attraction on the menu of what is now the Camberly Brown Hotel.

HOT CHEESE SANDWICH

Hot cheese sandwich? Is there really a need to define that simple term in this lexicon? Yes, if one is referring to the hot cheese sandwich that is a specialty of weenie shops throughout Fall River, Massachusetts. It is unlike an ordinary sandwich made of cheese slices or spread. Sharp cheddar, grated so it looks like it's been through a ricer, is kept warm in a vat on a steam table. Miraculously, or perhaps because of the addition of some kind of starch, it does not clump or melt. It is scooped out and put into a soft burger bun, preferably along with

A Fall River hot cheese sandwich benefits immensely from an application of Coney Island sauce and a sprinkle of raw onions.

145

a spill of meaty Coney sauce (typically used on **hot dogs** along the Southeast coast) and a spoonful of chopped raw onions: a wicked-good harmony of sharp, sweet, and spicy. In the shops that sell it, the same cheddar is offered as a topping for hot dogs, **hamburgers,** and chouriço sausage sandwiches.

HOT CHICKEN

Fried chicken is comfort food. **Hot chicken** is discomfort food—in the best sense of the word: crisp-fried chicken imbued skin to bone with peppers' fire that can range from quite hot to white hot. While some variations are found outside of Nashville (Keaton's of Statesville, North Carolina, is a sterling example), it is a signature of the Music City, where at least a dozen different restaurants make it their specialty. It

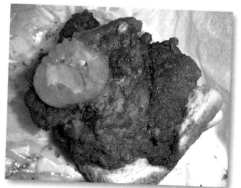

Allegedly mild versions of Nashville hot chicken tend to be ferociously hot.

originated at the still-thriving Prince's Hot Chicken Shack a couple of generations ago, when proprietor Thornton Prince's girlfriend, wanting to get even with him for his carousing one night, sopped his fried chicken in a painful amount of hot sauce. Instead of screaming for mercy, he yelled for joy, and hot fried chicken soon became Prince's trademark.

Hot chicken may be cooked in deep fryer or skillet, and its heat can be elevated in several different ways: The batter in which it's coated may be laced with pepper, the frying oil itself can be spiced, or it can be brushed with a pepper-hot paste either before or after being battered. It always is served with white bread, which sops up the spicy chicken juice and becomes a delicious hot companion, as well as with tart pickle chips, which may themselves be peppered.

Nashville hosts a Hot Chicken Festival every Independence Day.

HOT DISH

Like Yankee **shore dinner** and mid-South **meat and three, hot dish** (sometimes written *hotdish*) is a misleadingly plain term for a rousing culinary phenomenon. In the upper Midwest, hot dish is never a side dish and never trivial; it is the deluxe casserole at a church social, Independence Day party, or fiftieth wedding anniversary. While others may bring beans, salad, pie, and cookies, it is the accomplished cooks who assume hot dish responsibilities. A full meal in a casserole, it includes meat (beef most likely), vegetables (usually canned), and starch in the form of rice, noodles, Tater Tots, and/or a topping of biscuits, cornflakes, or crumbled Ritz crackers. Cream of mushroom soup is a common denominator.

A phenomenon we have noted whenever hot dish is served is that it never is anonymous. That is Gail's Tater Tot casserole or Brenda's tuna bake or Linda's pork roll supreme. Indeed, at almost any community potluck event, even less important foods are referred to by their creators' names: Martha's baked squash, Betty's ambrosia salad, Jim's bread and butter pickles.

HOT DOG

Despite the **hot dog**'s prominence as an all-American food, there is absolutely no agreement among Americans about what exactly constitutes a right and proper one. For specific iterations, see **Sonoran hot dog, ripper, New York System,** and **half smoke.** Here is the story of the hot dog in general—actually, stories, because there are a few competing ones.

Perhaps it started at the prolific St. Louis World's Fair of 1904 (also credited with ice cream cones and **hamburgers**). Antoine Feuchtwanger, a sausage vendor at the fair, had a problem. With each piping-hot link he sold, he lent the customer a glove to alleviate any worry about getting greasy fingers. However, souvenir-hungry fairgoers were walking off with his gloves. Feuchtwanger convinced his brother-in-law (who happened to be a baker) to make him elongated mini-loaves of bread. He sliced the bread down the middle and he began selling the sausages stuffed into the little breads as a package deal. Not only were his worries about stolen gloves over; customers loved the idea because the buns kept the sausages from dripping on their clothes. Ta-da! The hot dog was born.

A better-known alternative theory credits the hot dog's nativity to Charles Feltman, a vendor with a pie wagon along the then-rustic byways of Coney Island, New York, at the end of the nineteenth century. When a nearby restaurant began serving hot sandwiches for lunch, Feltman became anxious about losing business. He didn't have space to cook anything elaborate, so he fixed up a small charcoal stove and a pot of water. He boiled frankfurters and sold them two at a time, nestled inside rolls so that customers could eat a hot, cheap lunch standing up. Feltman's invention was so successful that he abandoned the pushcart and opened a restaurant selling sausages in buns at a dime apiece. According to an account by amateur hot dog historian Murray Handwerker, among

Two dogs in full dress.

Nathan's of Coney Island: Where America's hot dog culture began.

the up-and-coming entertainers who performed at the Coney Island resort were a sausage-loving duo named Eddie Cantor and Jimmie Durante. They could not afford Feltman's ten-cent product, so they convinced one of his employees, Nathan Handwerker (Murray's father), to open his own hot dog place and sell sausages in buns at half price, a nickel each. So began Nathan's of Coney Island.

The apocryphal story about how the hot dog got its name dates back to the opening day of the 1900 baseball season at the Polo Grounds in New York. Harry Stevens, head of catering, wanted to sell customers something that would warm them up and that would be easy to eat in the bleachers as well as easy to vend throughout the ballpark. He equipped his men with thermal boxes and supplied them with the long, skinny links popularly known as dachshund sausages, stuffing them into warm buns. He instructed the vendors to deal their sausage sandwiches with this cry: "They're red hot. Get your dachshund sausages while they're red hot!" The concept was an immediate success: Ballparks and hot dogs have been wed ever since. But they still didn't have their name. Legend says that the christening came about in 1903, when T. A. Dorgan, a San Francisco sports cartoonist, moved to New York and began working for the *Evening Journal.* Dorgan was so amused by the way Harry Stevens sold sausages at the ballpark that he drew a cartoon lampooning Stevens's vendors and their peculiar cry. In order to make the cartoon easy to read (or possibly because he could not spell *dachshund*), he labeled the sausages "red hot dogs" and drew pictures showing miniature pooches nestled in rolls, barking at one another. It's a great story, but Dorgan's seminal cartoon has never been found.

Regardless of its origins, the edible canine joke went over way too well. Sausages of any kind had long been a suspect food, even before 1906, when Upton Sinclair wrote *The Jungle,* describing the repulsive parts of animals that went into processed packaged meats. As early as the mid-1860s, the Whiffenpoofs of Yale used to serenade in jest: "Bologna sausage is very good, And many of them I see; Oh where, oh where is my little dog gone? I guess they make 'em of he!" Well into modern times, hot dogs have retained their shady reputation. "There's damn good reason we should never sell hot dogs," McDonald's president Ray Kroc declared before he died in 1984. "There's no telling what's inside a hot dog's skin." Hot dogs continue as a favorite touchstone for twenty-first-century muckrakers seeking to instill food fear in consumers.

HOT FISH

Throughout the South, but especially in the soul food restaurants of Nashville, **hot fish** is not just fish that is hot. It is fried fish—most often whiting fillets—that are served splotched with a daunting measure of red hot sauce. Hot fish almost always is served as a nominal sandwich, meaning the fillets are placed between two or four slices of white bread, but the fillets always are too large actually to hoist between bread, so the custom is to break off pieces by hand or, rarely, with a fork, using the bread to hold the fish and to dampen the heat of the sauce. Crisp-skinned and hugely succulent, well-fried whiting has forceful enough fish flavor that it cannot be eclipsed by Texas Pete, Frank's Louisiana hot sauce, or Tabasco, no matter how much is applied. Slices of raw onion, dill pickle chips, and smooth yellow mustard are the standard complements. A full hot-fish dinner will include the sandwich, **hushpuppies,** coleslaw, and meat-sauced spaghetti.

A Giant King hot fish sandwich at Eastside Fish in Nashville.

HOT LINK

Two very different sausages go by the name **hot link,** in Chicago and Texas. Hot links in Chicago are available mostly on the South Side at soul food barbecue parlors. They are ruggedly cut pork spiced with sage, pepper, and fennel, slow-cooked in the pit to a point where the ends develop a crunch but the inside is as succulent as a breakfast link. Those who like the ends ask for

Texas smoke house portrait: A sausage ring propped up by a pile of brisket slices and sided by white bread.

150

theirs well-done, which offers extra chew. Chicago hot links are served slathered with hot, tangy red barbecue sauce and accompanied by French fries and white bread.

A Texas hot link is all-beef, cooked by indirect heat so that the natural pork-gut casing bursts with juice as soon as it is severed with a knife or simply broken apart. It is so juicy that sauce would be redundant. Preferred side dishes are raw onion slices, pickles, a hunk of orange cheese, and, of course, slices of white bread that are especially handy for sopping up juices. (See also **dry link.**)

A common variation of the hot link throughout Texas barbecue country is the *sausage ring*, a horseshoe-shaped, string-tied gut packed with beef (and sometimes also a measure of ground pork) and, usually, plenty of pepper.

HOT TRUCK

Like the word **barbecue, hot truck** has several meanings. It is a destination: the food truck that parks at 635 Stewart Avenue at the edge of West Campus at Cornell University in Ithaca, New York. It is the cuisine served by that food truck. And it is the language used to describe that cuisine.

Ithaca's Hot Truck, inspiration for French Bread Pizza.

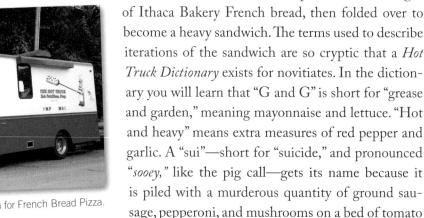

Hot truck, the food, is a hot submarine—baked open-face on a length of Ithaca Bakery French bread, then folded over to become a heavy sandwich. The terms used to describe iterations of the sandwich are so cryptic that a *Hot Truck Dictionary* exists for novitiates. In the dictionary you will learn that "G and G" is short for "grease and garden," meaning mayonnaise and lettuce. "Hot and heavy" means extra measures of red pepper and garlic. A "sui"—short for "suicide," and pronounced *"sooey,"* like the pig call—gets its name because it is piled with a murderous quantity of ground sausage, pepperoni, and mushrooms on a bed of tomato sauce under a mound of melted mozzarella.

The original hot truck, created in 1960 by Bob Petrillose, was a PMP (Poor Man's Pizza): sauce and cheese spread on a butterflied half-loaf of French bread and baked in his truck's **pizza** oven. Ithaca folklore says that one of the students who assisted Petrillose in hot truck's early days took the idea to Cleveland and sold it to Stouffer's, begetting French Bread Pizza. In fact, Stouffer's VP of manufacturing in 1962, when the company introduced frozen prepared foods, was Cornell Hotel School graduate C. Alan MacDonald; French-bread pizzas were launched twelve years later, in 1974.

Hot Truck Sep Pep Pizza

When we sought a recipe from the Smith family, who now run the Hot Truck and the Shortstop Deli, both of which sell French-bread pizzas, they suggested the Sep Pep, which is a WGC with mushrooms and pepperoni. What's a WGC? Simple: wet garlic with cheese. What's wet about the garlic? In Hot Truck lingo, wet means tomato sauce. According to our *Hot Truck Dictionary,* the WGC has less cheese than a double PMP (which is, of course, the original basic formulation of bread, sauce, and cheese).

Garlic Sauce
> 1¼ sticks butter (10 tablespoons)
> 1 tablespoon granulated garlic

In a medium bowl, microwave the butter until completely melted. Add the garlic and mix thoroughly.

Pizza Sauce
> 1 cup tomato juice
> 2 cups pizza sauce with basil
> 1 tablespoon granulated garlic
> ½ tablespoon salt

In a medium bowl, mix the tomato juice, pizza sauce, garlic, and salt. Stir thoroughly.

Pizza Subs
> 2 full loaves hearty French bread (about 24 inches total)
> 3 cups sliced mushrooms
> 3 cups shredded mozzarella cheese
> 2 cups sliced pepperoni
> 1 tablespoon oregano

1. Preheat oven to 375°F.

2. Cut the French bread loaves in half and slice them open horizontally ⅓ from the top. (This will allow the French bread to lay flat in the oven to prevent burning edges.)

3. Use a brush to spread the Garlic Sauce onto the French bread.

4. Use a ladle or spoon to spread the Pizza Sauce on the bread, being sure to cover it out to the edges (to prevent burning).

5. Divide mushrooms and mozzarella among the bread. Spread ½ cup (about 20 slices) of pepperoni across each half loaf. Sprinkle on oregano.

6. Transfer the sandwiches to a baking sheet and bake until all the cheese is melted and the French bread is golden brown, 8–10 minutes. When cooked, fold the top half of the French bread over the bottom half to make sandwiches.

4–8 SERVINGS

HUBBA WATER

Hubba water is the correct beverage to pair with Texas hot weiners in Port Chester, New York.

A specialty of Hubba (aka Pat's Hubba Hubba), a chili dog joint in Port Chester, New York, **Hubba water** is tap water with a light pink hue that comes from an infusion of Hawaiian Punch. There is so little pseudofruit juice that the sugary flavor is barely perceptible (especially to chili-ravaged taste buds), but frankfurter *bec fins* contend that its slight sweetness teases forth all the hot pepper zest of the chili dog. At Texas Chili, a competing **diner** one block away, the same beverage is known as *Texas water*.

HUEVOS RANCHEROS

Of Mexican descent and once distinctly Southwestern, **huevos rancheros** (meaning "ranch-style eggs") have gone the way of **fajitas** and are known all over the United States in countless variations. The dictionary definition is a couple of chili-smothered fried eggs atop corn tortillas, sided by refried beans and rice or potatoes. Salsa frequently takes the place of chili and flour tortillas may be substituted for corn. The eggs might be scrambled, with or without cheese. Variations include *huevos Mexicana,* for which eggs are scrambled with jalapeño peppers; **migas,** which includes strips of corn tortilla along with the scrambled eggs; and *chilaquiles,* which is like migas but more about the sauce or chili than about eggs, which may be excluded altogether.

Huevos Rancheros, Christmas: Topped with both red and green chili.

HUGUENOT TORTE

Neither of European heritage nor a torte, the **Huguenot torte** is a moist, rugged-textured cobbler made of chopped pecans and chopped apples, bound with eggs, sweetened with sugar, flavored with vanilla and spice, and served under a crown of whipped cream. It is considered a signature dish of Charleston, South Carolina, where it was concocted at the Huguenot Tavern in the 1940s, but while it may remain a standard in history-conscious home recipe files, it is rare in restaurants. It is always on the menu, however, at the Middleton Place Restaurant at Middleton Plantation in South Carolina.

153

HUMMINGBIRD CAKE

Triple-layered with cream cheese frosting, **hummingbird cake** contains mashed bananas, crushed pineapple, and chopped pecans. It rarely is found outside the South; a recipe with this name first was published by *Southern Living* magazine in 1978. Although one would assume that the cake was named simply because it is sweet enough for a hummingbird to love, culinary genealogists trace it back to the Doctor Bird, a swallow-tailed hummingbird that lives only in Jamaica and a banana cake from there that was its inspiration.

Fruity and well-frosted, hummingbird cake has Jamaican roots and is now a Dixie favorite.

HUSHPUPPIES

Hushpuppies are spheres, tubes, or squiggles of cornmeal batter that are deep-fried so the outside gets dark and crisp while the inside stays steamy. They may be laced with onions; some are a bit sweet. Supposedly named because they originated as little lagniappes tossed to dogs who were begging for food around the fry kettle (or possibly because Confederate soldiers gave them to their dogs so the dogs would hush and not give away their position), hushpuppies started as a companion to fried fish, catfish in particular. But in the 1950s, Warner Stamey began serving them at his legendary **barbecue** restaurant in Greensboro, North Carolina, and they have since become a necessary side dish on trays and plates of barbecue throughout much of the mid-South. Following Stamey's style, pups in the Piedmont region tend to be more tubular than spherical.

Tubular hushpuppies, as served at Bill Spoon's in Charlotte, are found throughout North Carolina.

Spherical hushpuppies at the White River Fish Market, Tulsa, Oklahoma.

INDIAN PUDDING

Despite the name, **Indian pudding** is not a Native American dish adapted by colonist cooks. It got its name simply because early settlers considered anything made with corn to be "Indian" in nature. In its most primitive form—beaten corn, boiled with milk—it kept the Pilgrims alive, and as the first adaptation of an English recipe (for wheat meal and milk, known as "hasty pudding"), it signifies nothing less than the beginning of American cookery. Its fundamental mixture of cornmeal and molasses tastes like history, as basic a foodstuff as bread itself. An extremely long cooking time—up to ten hours—is necessary to soften the corn and for the flavors to meld, and although some restaurants add raisins or other flavorings, the only traditional add-on is a scoop of vanilla ice cream. Indian pudding usually is served as dessert by the steaming bowlful, but, like apple pie, it can be found in town cafes serving double duty as breakfast.

Indian pudding is dark and serious, but it welcomes a scoop of ice cream on top.

Indian pudding is one of New England's founding comfort foods, but for newcomers to Yankee cooking, it is, to say the least, an acquired taste. How well we recall many years ago sitting at a shared table in Boston's Durgin-Park (a bastion of culinary tradition) and recommending it to a North Carolinian who had just enjoyed a meal of prime rib. He took our advice and spooned into it. "Grits for dessert!" he exclaimed, looking not a little befuddled.

IN-N-OUT SECRET MENU

In-N-Out **drive-ins,** hugely popular in the West and gradually growing eastward, do what McDonald's once did: offer a simple, efficient menu. In fact, it is four items long: **hamburger,** cheeseburger, double-double (two patties, two slices of cheese), and French fries. Plus **milk shakes** and soda pop.

As any In-N-Out devotee can tell you, there is much more than that. The **secret menu,** not posted on the wall but programmed into the restaurant cash

There is nothing secret about this In-N-Out Double with French fries.

register, offers myriad choices. Say any of these terms to the order taker and he or she will understand:

2-by-4: Two beef patties, four slices of cheese.

4-by-4: Four beef patties, four slices of cheese.

Animal-style: Mustard-coated burger topped with grilled onions, pickles, and cheese spread.

Mustard grilled: Animal-style (mustard coating), but without the pickles and cheese spread.

Protein: Substitute lettuce for a bun.

Wish burger: Just vegetables. No meat and no cheese.

Flying Dutchman: Two patties sandwiching two cheese slices, hold the bun.

Extra toast: Crisper bun.

Root beer float: Half root beer, half vanilla milk shake.

Lemon-Up: Half lemonade, half 7-Up.

Neapolitan shake: Vanilla, chocolate, and strawberry milk shakes swirled together.

French fries also can be ordered well done, lightly cooked, topped with melted cheese, or animal-style.

IOWA PORK CHOP

In Iowa, the term *pork chop* has a different meaning than it does in most other places, where it refers to a modest triangle of meat about as thick as a slice of Wonder Bread and, sadly, sometimes as chewy as a dog toy. In fact, food-conscious citizens of the Hawkeye State rarely ever say the words *pork chop* without preceding them with *Iowa*. An **Iowa pork chop** is a grand and special cut, more prized than porterhouse in beef country or Dungeness crab in the Pacific Northwest. First off, it is as thick as a regal filet mignon, but, of course, it is broader by a factor of four, reminding one of a whole rack of lamb. The Machine Shed, outside of Des Moines, calls their version a double-cut chop, noting that it looks more like a pork roast. The inside spurts and sputters as a knife glides down through the caramel-colored crust and into the vast lode of meat. It comes topped with extremely savory pan gravy, which is less for the chop itself, which needs nothing but eager taste buds to attain its destiny, than for the great reef of mashed potatoes that accompany the chop on its plate.

ITALIAN BEEF

Unique to Chicagoland, **Italian beef** is a shaft of bread loaded with thin-sliced beef in garlicky gravy. It rarely is eaten while seated. Most joints that serve beefs (the word "sandwich" is redundant) provide a chest-high counter for customers to stand at, unwrap the butcher-paper serving shroud, and scarf 'em down. Regular beef eaters know that to avoid gravy dripping onto shirtfront and forearms, one must lean forward, elbows on the counter and feet back the way police position a man about to be frisked. This allows the eater to tear off big chaws of bread and beef as all the excess gravy and meat shreds fall onto the wrapper, which has become a handy drop cloth.

An Italian beef shop is not the sort of place where waiters patiently explain the menu—most have no written menu—and order-takers are famously brusque, so it is wise to get to the head of the line knowing Italian beef jargon. A request for "double-dipped" means the entire sandwich will be momentarily submerged in gravy after it's assembled. Conversely, "dry" tells the server to pluck a heap of beef from the pan with tongs and let excess juice drip away before inserting it into the bread. Say "hot" and the beef will be topped with the fiery pickled-vegetable relish called **giar-**

An Italian beef garnished with both giardiniera and peppers.

diniera; "sweet" refers to a garnish of roasted peppers. "Combo"—the only possible improvement for Italian beef (cheese is sacrilege!)—means the sandwich gets freighted with a length of charcoal-cooked Italian sausage.

Traditionally, Italian beef stands are in neighborhoods that also have vendors of *Italian ice,* the summertime slush that makes so good a sandwich companion or postprandial refresher.

JAMBALAYA

There are countless different recipes for the southern Louisiana stew **jamba-laya** and multiple apocryphal explanations of its name, among them:

Jambon (French for "ham") + *a la* + *ya* (West African term for "rice").
  The problems with this explanation are that ham is a rare jambalaya ingredient and *ya* means "sorghum."
Jamón (Spanish for "ham") + *paella.*
Jambalaia means "chaos" in Provençal.
Balayer is the Creole verb for whipping something together.

A cook named Jean was once asked to make a quick dish from whatever was on hand, the command being: *"Jean, balayez,"* which eventually was bastardized to *jambalaya.*

Despite the chaos and confusion that surrounds the dish—and frequently defines what is in the cook pot—there basically are two different styles. *Creole jambalaya* was, in fact, a version of Spanish paella in which tomatoes were substituted for saffron. *Cajun jambalaya,* which contains no tomatoes, tends to be a hunter's stew made with whatever swamp country critters are available, plus sausage. Like **gumbo,** jambalaya is aggressively seasoned, partly by the smoked and spiced meats it contains, but also by the cook who stirs it in the big iron pot using a paddle or shovel. The technical difference between jambalaya and gumbo is that in the latter, rice always is cooked separately and combined with the soup for serving. When making jambalaya, the rice is cooked with everything else, sopping up different flavors. But a more important distinction between the two is that gumbo can be thought of as quite sophisticated; jambalaya is a people's dish, often served at big picnics, fairs, and community parties.

JEWISH APPLE CAKE

It is mostly gentiles who cook something called **Jewish apple cake**; Jews more likely will refer to it as *German apple cake* or simply *apple cake* or *apple bundt cake.* The name may come from the fact that it is a recipe of German-Jewish

Jewish apple cake at the Dutch Kitchen, Frackville, Pennsylvania.

origin; its lack of milk, cream, and butter makes it suitable for dessert at a kosher meal that is either meat or dairy. Juice from the profusion of apple bits it contains as well as a good measure of vegetable oil make it extremely moist; its flavors usually include cinnamon, orange juice, and vanilla extract; chopped walnuts are an option. It is both a hearty dessert and an ideal coffee companion; in the latter role, it is sometimes made as individual muffins.

For reasons unknown, *Jewish apple cake* is a term that is fairly well known throughout eastern Pennsylvania and into Maryland, but almost nonexistent elsewhere—except in places to which Pennsylvanians and Marylanders have moved.

JIBARITO

First served in Chicago at Borinquen Restaurant in 1996, the **jibarito** is a Windy City gloss on the Puerto Rican *emparedado de platano*—a sandwich that replaces bread with flattened, twice-fried plantains. Between the crunchy plantains is a sheaf of spicy, thin-sliced steak along with cheese, lettuce, tomato, peppers, onions, and mayonnaise. Named for the *jibaros*—the hearty country folk of inland Puerto Rico—a jibarito may also be made with chicken, ham, or roast pork; some places even offer vegetarian versions. Although its inspiration was Puerto Rican, the jibarito has become a staple in Mexican and South American restaurants throughout Chicago.

San Francisco, 1927. New owners, none named **Joe,** buy a nine-stool ice cream parlor named Joe's. They build business by adding spaghetti and hamburgers to the menu. Joe's success begets New Joe's, then Little Joe's and Original Joe's. Modern-day Original Joe's on Taylor Street is in the same family as New Joe's but not related to the original Joe's and has nothing to do with Baby Joe's. Now that we've got that straight, here's the first question: Was it Joe's, the original New Joe's, or Original Joe's that first served the New Joe Special? Second question: Was the New Joe Special a haywire Americanization of a northern Italian spinach dish, or did a Joe's cook invent it as a stopgap measure when the kitchen ran out of everything but hamburger, spinach, and eggs? One credible tale of Joe's genesis is set in San Francisco's New Joe's, late one night. A hungry musician orders a spinach omelet but pleads with the chef to do something to make it more substantial. The obliging chef adds hamburger meat left over from the dinner hour.

Whatever the precise evolution of this gnarled little branch of Bay Area cuisine, this is certain: Joe is an egg dish that involves pan-cooked ground beef with an Italian flair. Add tomato sauce and it becomes a **sloppy joe.** Add anchovies, olives, and capers, and it's a **Sicilian Joe.** A **Special Joe** always has spinach—indeed, some New Joe Specials are little more than beef and spinach—but at Original Joe's in San Jose (since 1956), the modern archetype of the dish also includes onions and eggs and, optionally, mushrooms. Original Joe's menu alerts customers, "We are not associated with any other 'Joe's' restaurants."

Eggs, beef, and spinach make the Special Joe an especially bracing breakfast.

JOHN JOHNSON

When we met **John Johnson** in 1977, he was beaming with pride, having just bought Camp Washington Chili parlor from its founders, his uncle Steve Andon and Anastasios "Fred" Zarmbus. John had worked at Camp Washington since his arrival in America in 1951, so he knew the secrets of five-way chili as well as any cook in the chili-crazed city of Cincinnati. He explained to us with conspiratorial glee that when he took over, he actually tinkered with the hallowed recipe and improved it! The result was an American success story—a restaurant beloved by Queen City eaters for decades, now recognized far and wide as a roadfood original.

Camp Washington sets the standard for **Cincinnati chili;** and John Johnson, God bless him, has maintained his prototypical Midwest urban chili parlor as the open-all-night, democratic joint it always has been. He's kept the menu simple, too: chili available three-, four-, or five-way, as a "haywagon," or as the abundant topping for Coney Island hot dogs. And, lest we forget: Camp Washington remains a shining beacon of excellence in preparation of that little-known Cincinnati chili parlor specialty, the double-decker sandwich.

When this photograph of Mr. and Mrs. John Johnson was taken in the late 1970s, they had just bought the chili parlor from John's uncle and were proud as punch.

JONNYCAKE

A thick jonnycake, as made on the western side of Narragansett Bay.

The cornmeal pancakes known as **jonnycakes** are such a matter of pride in Rhode Island that state law decrees they can be made only from meal milled from flint corn and they must contain no sugar or flour. Furthermore, it is illegal to spell *jonnycake* with the letter *h* (albeit a misdemeanor, not a felony). East of Narragansett Bay, jonnycakes are broad and flannel-thin with a lacy edge. West of the Bay in South County, they are made from extra-thick batter poured onto the griddle in discs no wider than a coaster and nearly two fingers high. The little cylinders cook long enough to develop a crunchy crust and earthy flavor that begs to be gilded with real maple syrup. It is believed their name comes from Colonial times, when they were known as *journey cakes* because, once cooked, they were handy to carry on a trip.

JUICY LUCY

America's most dangerous **hamburger** was invented in 1954 in Minneapolis, but both Matt's Bar and the 5-8 Club, a good three miles apart on Cedar Avenue, have staked claims as the originator of the **juicy Lucy.** (Matt's Bar spells it *jucy Lucy.*) It is an inside-out cheeseburger, meaning the cheese is completely secreted inside the meat. As the beef cooks, the lode of cheese inside melts. If an unsuspecting eater takes a hearty bite of one hot off the grill, the molten center erupts and can seriously hurt tongue, lips, and fingers. Experienced eaters know to wait a while or to gingerly hoist the burger and take a dainty bite that reveals just enough of the cheese cavern that some of it can be dripped onto accompanying French fries. American, Jack, and Swiss cheese are the common fillings, but more exotic cheeses may be used, and the cheese can be supplemented by peppers, bacon, olives, or mushrooms.

JUMBO SLICE

You can get a large **pizza** nearly everywhere (except for places that have become sticklers for **Neapolitan pizza** regulations that decree fourteen inches, max), but if you want a **jumbo slice,** you must go to Washington, D.C. In this city, *jumbo slice* is not a synonym for *large slice.* It is much bigger than that, cut from a pie that is a full three feet in diameter, so outsized that two paper dinner plates are required to hold it and its surfeit of oil-weeping cheese and tangy sauce. To our knowledge, nobody defends the jumbo slice as an epicurean triumph, and as far as we can tell, few people ever have eaten one sober. The jumbo slice preferably is consumed during or at the conclusion of a night on the town. Its two leading purveyors, Jumbo Slice and Pizza Mart, stay open until just before dawn.

KEY LIME PIE

Like **Buffalo wings** and **fajitas** from south Texas, **Key lime pie** is a home-town dish that has became an American food icon. Once unique to the coral islands at the southernmost end of Route 1 in Florida, the sweet-tart, pale yellow, no-bake dessert is served in restaurants that range from deluxe steak houses to paper-napkin seafood shacks, and in variations beyond pastel custard on a graham cracker crust. Among the interesting permutations we have encountered are frozen Key lime pie on a stick from street vendors in Miami, deep-fried Key lime pie at several state fairs, Key lime **milk shakes,** and Key lime pie martinis.

True Key lime pie (or Key lime *anything*) is made from fruit dramatically different from the familiar, thick-rind Tahiti lime sold in supermarkets. The Key lime is smaller—about golf-ball size—with skin so thin that a two-fingered squeeze yields all its juice. That juice is brilliantly tart; when combined with sweetened condensed milk, its flavor creates a taste-buds balancing act of sugary opulence and citrus sourness. The truth is that many so-called Key lime pies are made not from genuine Key limes, but from the hybrid Tahiti lime. That is not an awful thing, but once you've tasted Key limes or an expertly made pie created from them, you will always know the difference. And you will always want pie that contains the genuine article.

Because they are too fragile to ship and store by the truckload, agribusiness wants little to do with Key limes. In the United States, they have become what residents of Florida's Keys refer to as a **dooryard fruit,** so named because it grows fairly wild in people's backyards, just outside their doors. Dependable sources for such fruit are rare and prized by cooks. Chef Doug Shook of Louie's Backyard restaurant in Key West, where Key lime pie is made on a spicy gingersnap crust, reveals only the first name of his supplier—Doris—and says that she makes it her business to know which yards have the good Key lime trees. She gathers them and squeezes them; Louie's uses the juice not only for pies but in an intoxicating ceviche marinade and as the sparkle in a vodka tonic.

In a genuine Key lime pie recipe, sweetened condensed milk is vital. When it first became available in the years after the American Civil War, Bahamian settlers in the Keys, having limited access to fresh dairy products, made pies with the canned milk along with juice of their native Key limes or sour oranges (another dooryard fruit), plus egg yolks for extra richness. Early in the twentieth century, Key lime groves thrived throughout the Keys, but after a 1926 Category 4 hurricane wiped them out, they were not restored or replanted. Since then, the Key lime has remained an elusive citrus legend . . . although Key Lime pie has been formally recognized as the official state pie of Florida.

KOLACHE

A **kolache** looks like a small version of the Danish pastry you'd have at breakfast in any **diner.** A really good one, still oven-fresh, as found on the shelves of bakeries in Czech communities of Texas and Oklahoma, leaves ordinary Danishes in the dust. It is so exquisitely tender that a too-eager grip will compress it into a blob. Its dough is sweet but ever so delicately so, and its filling is anything but cloying. Apricot, prune, and poppy seed paste are the traditional variations, but today's bakers address the twenty-first-century sweet tooth by also offering brighter, fruitier flavors, such as apple, strawberry, and blueberry—as well as kolaches made with cream cheese in addition to the fruit.

A savory variant of the kolache was invented early in the 1950s, when Wendell Montgomery of the Village Bakery in the town of West, Texas, decided to do something to improve sales of sausage bread. He convinced his mother-in-law to come up with a snack-sized version of the bread using the slightly sweet kolache dough and including short lengths of the sausage that local butchers make. Her inspiration was the Czech *klobasniki*, which is customarily filled with ground sausage. Old timers still call them that, although most are currently sold as *pigs in blankets,* the term *kolache* being reserved for those with sweet filling. Klobasniki have become a staple of kolache bakeries throughout the state, often including cheese and jalapeño peppers along with the sausage.

Although its ancestry is Czech, the kolache has become a signature breakfast pastry throughout Texas.

165

KRINGLE

In Denmark, a **kringle** is any pretzel-shaped pastry, sweet or savory. In Racine, Wisconsin, it is a broad oval of the flaky dough known as *wienerbrod* that is filled with fruit preserves, cheese, or nuts; baked; then iced with buttercream frosting or a clear sugar glaze. Large enough to feed six or eight coffee drinkers, it is served warm by the slice and, being a specialty of Wisconsin, with soft butter that is easy to spread for even further enrichment.

Kringles were brought to America by Danish settlers over a century ago, and while Racine is their best-known home, with at least three different bakeries that make them (and ship by mail), they also are found in Danish communities in Iowa, Illinois, California, and Washington state. Classic fillings include almond, pecan, and raspberry; in addition to these, Racine bakeries offer almond-macaroon, chocolate, date, apricot, apple, and a turtle kringle that is iced with chocolate and filled with rum-flavored caramel.

Bakeries in Racine, Wisconsin, will ship kringle, but kringle aficionados know that they are best when they are that-morning fresh.

LIMA BEAN SUPPER

In the foreground: A bowl of pork scattered with limas. In back: A bowl of limas in gravy. Not shown: Bowl of rice and empty bowl for bone disposal.

A Lowcountry **lima bean supper** has a drab name but can be a thrill to eat. As made and served in **soul food** restaurants in and around Charleston, South Carolina, it is an awe-inspiring presentation that, although built around beans and listed on the menu as such, includes a meal's worth of pork, often in the form of neck bones and pig tails. The meat on neck bones is tender enough that little effort is required to slide off bite-size pieces with minimal fork pressure; pig tails are as unctuous as sizzled fatback. A full lima bean supper arrives in at least two separate bowls: one full of soupy beans, themselves porkily spiced, the other heaped with brick-red meat decorated with a handful of beans. A third bowl might contain rice, and a fourth empty one can be used for bone disposal.

LIVERMUSH

Eaters not fond of **livermush** sometimes refer to it as a southern cognate of **scrapple,** but fans elevate it into a category of its own. Ground pig offal (including liver) and cornmeal are made into a loaf, which is cooked and cooled, then sliced. At breakfast, it will be fried to a crisp. At lunch, it may be fried, but it also can simply be sliced as lunch meat. It is a product of economic necessity—stretching the least expensive parts of a hog—and therefore is sometimes known as *poor man's ham* or *poor man's pâté.* Its culinary ignominy has earned it a cadre of contrarian devotees as well as an annual festival in its honor in Marion, North Carolina. At last look, the Livermush Facebook page had more than 12,000 fans. *Liver puddin'* is similar but made without the cornmeal.

LOBSTER ROLL

Eating a whole lobster requires knowledge (where's the meat?), skill (how exactly do you get it?), and physical labor (cracking, picking, and sucking). Eating a **lobster roll** is easy. A bun filled with picked lobster meat, it demands only to be lifted from the plate and put into one's mouth. The cold lobster roll—meat bound with mayonnaise and bits of celery loaded into a bun that may or may not be toasted—has been a New England shoreline staple for over a century. Known also as a *lobster salad roll,* it remains the more popular variation along the Maine shore.

Picnic table epiphany: Hot lobster and butter in a toasted, split-top roll.

In 1929, Harry Perry, proprietor of a seafood shack in Milford, Connecticut, came up with a new twist: the hot lobster roll. He eliminated the mayonnaise and piled warm picked meat bathed in butter into a toasted bun. Perry's invention was such a success that his restaurant soon sported a sign boasting that it was HOME OF THE FAMOUS LOBSTER ROLL. His outrageously rich creation became what *Connecticut* magazine editor Charles Monagan has called "Connecticut's greatest contribution to the world of regional cuisine."

LOGANBERRY JUICE

The loganberry was created late in the nineteenth century, when horticulturalist James Harvey Logan, trying to breed a heartier blackberry, accidentally planted blackberry bushes near raspberries. The resulting hybrid was a fruit that is dark red, big and juicy, with a bright, tart flavor all its own. None of this history is very relevant to **loganberry juice,** which, despite its name, tends to be much more about the flavor of sugar or corn syrup than any berry nature

A charcoal-cooked hot dog in Buffalo, New York, is not complete without an accompanying cup of loganberry juice.

has to offer. Little-known in most of the United States but popular at **hot dog** joints and fast food outlets in western New York state and up into Canada, loganberry juice (known to fans simply as *loganberry*) is bottled with and without carbonation and as syrup for do-it-yourselfers. Aunt Rosie's, an uncarbonated brand made by Pepsi, has some real fruit flavor, and it is the drink of choice among charcoal-cooked hot dog aficionados at the legendary Ted's of Buffalo, New York.

LOOSEMEATS

In 1924, David Heglin made a sandwich of steamed, seasoned ground beef to serve at a Sioux City restaurant he ran called Ye Old Tavern. It was a time when many Americans, worried about the ill effects of frying meat, turned to steam cooking as an alternative (see **steamed cheeseburger**). In 1934, Abe Kaled bought Ye Old Tavern, further antiqued its name to Ye Olde Tavern, and also tinkered with the formula for ground beef on a bun. Kaled and his wife, Bertha, sold their spiced-up sandwich, known as a "tavern," for a dime.

The pride of Siouxland: A loosemeats sandwich.

It inspired imitations for miles around, and by the time Ye Olde Tavern closed in 1971, Sioux Citians were smitten with the sandwich, which had come to assume many aliases in the places that served it, including Big T, Charlie Boy, Tastee, and, most popular of all, **loosemeats.** Like **Santa Maria barbecue** in the ranchland east of Santa Barbara or **Brunswick stew** in southern Virginia, loosemeats has become the favorite thing to dish out at fund-raising suppers; it continues to be a staple on school lunch menus; and it is served at virtually every **drive-in** restaurant and bar throughout the counties of Sioux, Plymouth, Cherokee, and Woodbury.

Loosemeats are customarily dressed with pickle slices, mustard, and a square slice of American cheese—a remix of the cheeseburger with fragmented harmony. Like *grits* and *burnt ends*, it is a name for which the singular form never is used, although it can be either singular or plural. Usually one sandwich is *a* loosemeats; a batch in the kitchen or a bowlful without the bun *are* loosemeats.

MALASADA

A subset of **fried dough** found in Hawaii and along the coast of New England from Cape Cod to Rhode Island, wherever Portuguese immigrants settled, the **malasada** (sometimes spelled *malassada*) is an anytime snack or a breakfast pastry. It is made either as a sphere, like a holeless donut, or stretched out flat like a pancake, cooked in hot oil until golden brown, then dusted with powdered sugar and served, preferably while still warm. Malasadas are available year-round in bakeries and at fairs and carnivals that sell eat-on-the-stroll indulgences, but as home-cooked food, they most often are found in observant Catholic kitchens at Mardi Gras time. The point of making them before Lent is to use up all the lard and sugar on hand. In Hawaii, Fat Tuesday is known as Malasada Day.

Malasadas, the Portuguese version of fried dough, are made by bakeries in southern New England and in Hawaii.

MALT

When a **milk shake** made with ice cream, syrup, and milk isn't rich enough, the next step is to make it a **malt.** Short for *malted milk shake*, malts first were concocted at Walgreen's Drug Store in Chicago in 1922. At the time, malted milk—made by adding a powder of malted barley and wheat flour to milk and flavored syrup—already was popular as a health-food drink for children and others who needed to gain weight. Soda jerker Ivar "Pop" Coulson figured out a way to make it even more fattening by adding ice cream. The malt was born, and it became such an emblem of soda fountain joy that the term *malt shop* became a descriptor for any confectionery where ice cream drinks star.

MAQUE CHOUX

In southern Louisiana, where it was developed by Acadians, based on a Native American dish, **maque choux** (pronounced "mock shoe") is so taken for granted that few people even think of it as a regional specialty. Unlike **jambalaya** and **boudin,** it has little cultural cachet, but it is a common presence on cafe **meat and three** menus, as well as in kitchens where home cooking prevails. Corn, peppers, and tomatoes are combined with onion and garlic and braised with plenty of fatback or bacon grease, then simmered with just enough chicken stock to keep them moist. While maque choux is a good side dish for almost any meal, it can become a meal itself if shrimp, chicken, sausage, or crawfish are added.

MATZOH BREI

Matzoh brei, which is Yiddish for "fried matzoh," is a standard of the Jewish kitchen that is somewhere on the breakfast spectrum near Tex-Mex **migas** and French toast. The basic formula is to scramble small pieces of the unleavened bread known as *matzoh* into eggs, and then to cook the mixture in a pan of butter or in the rendered chicken fat known as *schmaltz.* The ratio of matzoh to egg makes a huge difference in the nature of the dish. Is it basically an egg recipe with a hint of texture from a few bits of matzoh? Or is it all about the crunch of matzoh, with just enough egg mixed in so the matzoh can be fried? A well-balanced version will contain matzoh pieces that are softened just enough that there is no disturbing brittleness, but that still provide the kind of textural poise that no other bread or cracker could deliver. Matzoh brei may be served with applesauce or sour cream or even, untraditionally, with maple syrup.

MEAT AND THREE

No meal has a plainer name and few meals can be so baroque. Used through much of the South, but especially in Nashville, the term **meat and three** quite simply refers to a menu template that lists two to five entrees and one or two dozen side dishes. From these lists, a diner picks one entree and three sides. Among the sides will be vegetables, but also **congealed salads,** macaroni and cheese, spaghetti, and rice. **Corn bread,** hoecakes, and biscuits or dinner rolls are always provided on the side. **Sweet tea** usually costs extra. Variations include *meat and two* or *meat and three without the meat,* meaning an all-vegetable plate of three or four selections. While it is possible for a meat and three meal to be simplicity itself—meat loaf with mashed potatoes, glazed carrots, and butter beans—the list of side dishes likely includes a number of souped-up vegetable casseroles or soufflés in which squash, broccoli, or spinach is transformed into a luxurious indulgence by use of butter or margarine and bread crumbs. Greens and cabbage tend to be enriched by massive infusions of pig, in the form of fatback, **country ham,** or neck bones.

Meat and three without the meat: A four-vegetable plate at the Loveless Cafe.

There are no extraneous adjectives on this meat and three menu, but it will make a plate-lunch lover's pulse quicken in anticipation.

MEAT PIE

A half-circle-shaped pastry pocket about the size of a taco with a rugged crimp around its edges, the **meat pie** is as popular a snack in rural Louisiana as **boudin** sausage. Also made with crawfish, especially on Fridays and during Lent, it sports a brittle, golden crust that is crunchy near the crimp, pliant near its mounded center, and filled with a steamy portion of spiced ground beef. While frequently eaten out of hand as a walk-around snack, the meat pie also is served on plates with dirty rice and gravy, becoming a knife-and-fork meal. Lasyone's Meat Pie Kitchen in Natchitoches also offers a meat pie breakfast, with eggs and hash browns.

"I cannot explain for certain how meat pies first came to this place," James Lasyone told us many years ago. He believed it happened in the nineteenth century, when Natchitoches—the oldest settlement in the Louisiana Purchase, founded in 1714—was a thriving trade center and outfitting point for settlers heading West. By the mid-twentieth century, however, street-corner pie vendors were fading into history. Lasyone, who had grown up a sharecropper's son out in the country and had enjoyed the pies when his family came to town, became the butcher at a Natchitoches grocery store. When he wanted a meat pie, he knew which ladies to call. "Some were white, some were black," he remembers. "But there weren't many of them left." In the mid-1960s, he began experimenting with recipes to make his own pies. He sold some over the butcher's counter at the store, then in 1967 he opened his restaurant in a minuscule retail space near the meat market. It has since become a Southern food landmark.

The legendary crawfish pie of Cajun country.

Meat pie from Champagne's Bakery in Breaux Bridge, Louisiana.

MEDIANOCHE

Found mostly in Florida where the culinary heritage is Cuban, the **medianoche** is a variation of the **Cuban sandwich** made on lighter-weight, egg-enriched bread (known as *pan medianoche*) rather than the typical French loaf. Like a Cuban, it contains ham and roast pork, cheese, pickles, mustard, and mayo and is toasted inside a plancha so that all the ingredients meld together. The sweet bread develops a fine crunch and the whole sandwich is significantly less filling than a traditional Cuban, making it an ideal wee-hours snack. That is how it gets its name: *medianoche* means "midnight" in Spanish.

MENUDO

Menudo is a party dish and an afterparty dish, too. All along the Mexican border and through much of the Southwest, it is mostly a weekend item, partly because it takes a long time to cook, partly because it is an inexpensive way to feed a large number of people, and partly because it is alleged to be a hangover cure. Made from hominy and tripe and, usually, a good measure of red chiles, it is served with garnishes of onion, lime, and cilantro and sided by tortillas or *bolillo* rolls that are good for mopping the last of it from the bowl. Most restaurants

Hangover, be gone! Menudo to the rescue.

that make it offer menudo not only by the bowl but by the quart and gallon for taking home. One place on 12th Avenue in South Tucson advertises that any customer who brings in his own jug to be filled gets a $2 per gallon discount.

METT

Cincinnati, which earned the moniker Porkopolis because it once packed more pork than any other city on earth, is crazy for **metts.** *Mett* is short for *mettwurst,* a cured, deeply smoked, rugged-grind sausage, about twice as portly as a regular **hot dog,** firmly packed inside natural casing. As much a Queen City signature dish as **goetta** or **Cincinnati chili,** metts are made and sold by the city's old-time butcher shops.

There is no better place to enjoy a mett than at a table on the sidewalk just outside Avril-Bleh, a butchershop that dates back to the nineteenth century (house motto: "A link with the past since 1894"). Avril's display of tube steaks is a postgraduate education in oinky edibles. The curriculum includes

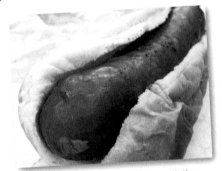

In the multisausage city of Cincinnati, the mett (short for mettwurst) is a street-eats favorite. Shown here: a cheese mett.

bierwurst, bratwurst, knockwurst, bockwurst (spring only), yard sausage (with garlic), tiny links, oatmeal rings, liverwurst, kielbasa, wieners (natural casing or skinless), Cajun andouille, smoked Italian and chorizo, and metts that are made regular, hot, super-hot, and Cheddar cheese–laced. Cooked at a sidewalk cart that sends the aroma of grilling pork through the neighborhood, metts are kingly sausages, their skin audibly crackly when severed by teeth, their insides, while not oozy, radiant with sweet pork flavor, smoke, and an energetic shot of spice. A true taste of Cincinnati!

MICHIGAN

Like its close cousins, the **Coney Island** and **New York System** wiener, the **Michigan** is a small frankfurter in a soft bun topped with vividly spiced beef sauce, bright yellow mustard, and chopped raw onions. It does not exist in Michigan, at least not with that name. It is unique to the Clinton County area of upstate New York, between the Adirondacks and Lake Champlain. Its history is uncertain, although it definitely was named in Plattsburgh.

Plattsburgh's love of Michigans began at the summer-only wiener joint known as Clare & Carl's.

The Michigan: Plattsburg, New York's unique take on the chili dog.

The most obvious place to look for understanding of the geographic dislocation is Detroit, and the popularity of chili-topped wieners there, starting with the opening of the first Coney Island stand in 1917. One story credits the Michigan's prominence in Plattsburgh to a short order cook who came from Detroit sometime in the 1930s and got Plattsburgh to love them. Another account says that after Clare Warn opened her summertime **hot dog** stand, Clare & Carl's, on Lake Shore Road in 1943, she tried to improve sales by topping her franks with a special sauce she invented. Her top salesperson was Eula Otis, a Michigander who is said to have gone around to locals saying, "I'm from Michigan. Would you like to try one of our chili dogs?" The state's name stuck.

Genealogy aside, it is important to note that in addition to unique seasonings in the sauce that give it a beguiling glow, a Michigan is distinguished by its bun—a soft, split-top affair similar to the rolls used in New England for hot dogs and **lobster rolls** (but never grilled). The bun is thick at the bottom and shored in at both ends, giving it necessary capacity as well as absorbency for customers who order Michigans "buried," meaning an arrangement that puts the onions underneath the hot dog, thus hoisting the chili sauce on top to a precarious level nearing overflow.

MICROWAVE OVEN

While not as significant as the cave dwellers' discovery of fire, the popularization of the **microwave oven** in the last third of the twentieth century revolutionized the middle-class kitchen, providing home cooks a world of shortcut recipes that formerly required time, care, and culinary expertise.

Microwaves seemed so miraculous in their early years that they inspired a rich vein of cautionary folklore about people who misused them. Little old ladies were alleged to have tried to dry rain-soaked Chihuahuas by putting them in microwaves, causing them to explode. Stoned hippies with the munchies put food in a microwave and stood bug-eyed at the oven door, waiting for it to cook, roasting their corneas instead. The theme of most such folklore was indolence. By trying to use the quick and effortless microwave instead of old-fashioned elbow grease, the perpetrator invited disaster. The moral was a Puritanical one: Laziness deserves punishment.

Although they were not popular enough to worry anybody until the late 1960s, the earliest ones actually predate TV dinners. And the first food known to be cooked by microwaves was an accident. It happened one day in 1942, when Percy Spencer, an inventor employed by Raytheon in Waltham, Massachusetts, was testing a radar component called a magnetron tube. Dr. Spencer liked chocolate. He liked it so much he often kept a bar in the pocket of his pants. After testing the magnetron, he reached for a piece of his chocolate bar and found he had a pocket full of goo. The chocolate bar had melted. He put a bag of corn kernels near the magnetron and they popped inside the bag. Next, he blew up an egg. He knew he was on to something big. As soon as the war was over, in 1946, Spencer created a prototype microwave oven. "Foods prepared with sealed-in flavor *quick as a flash*!" Raytheon boasted, sending out photographs of wieners in buns and hot apple pie a la mode emerging from the monstrously large, brushed metal machine they patented as the Radarange. They were "duds for a decade," according to the *Wall Street Journal*, which blamed their failure on "bilious grey meat and limp French fries." Still, Waldermar Kaempffert, science editor of the *New York Times,* wrote an article in the early fifties about a hypothetical family named the Dobsons, living in America in the year 2000: "Cooking as an art is only a memory in the minds of old people. . . . Jane Dobson has an electronic stove. In eight seconds a half-grilled frozen steak is thawed; in two minutes more it is ready to serve." (The Dobsons, by the way, eat mostly food made out of recycled sawdust, discarded paper tablecloths, and old rayon underwear.)

The earliest home-kitchen microwaves sold for more than a thousand dollars, but in the mid-1960s Keishi Ogura of New Japan Radio invented a compact electron tube that made cheaper, home-sized ovens a reality, and in 1967 Amana Refrigeration (which was part of Raytheon) introduced a $495 Radarange. Its instruction book raved, "Imagine, no after-meal clean up of pots and pans! In just a short time you will be using the Radarange for most of your food preparation. It will become the center of most of your food preparation. In fact, it will help you prepare 75–80% of the foods that you serve your family." Included in the book were recipes for the likes of "Chunky Pizza Sticks," "Rice & Spice Hamburger Casserole," "Chewy Chocolate Log," and "Pretzel Peanut Butter Pie."

No appliance has better fit the restless disposition of a nation in love with fast food. In 1989, when U.S. sales of microwave ovens were running over ten million per year, the *New York Times* reported that fast food restaurants were scrambling to fulfill the expectations of high-strung customers who had grown to expect instant eats from their home microwave ovens. "There are never any lines at home," said one food marketing consultant, explaining people's impatience with service in franchise restaurants that prepared victuals the old way, using fire and heat. "With the microwave, you just reach into your freezer and pop it into the oven and zap! It's done." That same year, an executive at Campbell Soup predicted that by 1992 automobiles would be equipped with microwave ovens, explaining "Food today is more of a maintenance function than pleasurable experience. . . . People are willing to accept something inferior as long as it is fast."

MIGAS

A popular breakfast dish on Tex-Mex menus throughout the Southwest, but especially around San Antonio and Austin, Texas, **migas** is (or, more correctly, migas *are*) scrambled eggs laced with strips of corn tortilla. Migas may

Migas at the Classen Grill, Oklahoma City, Oklahoma.

also contain diced tomatoes and onions, crumbled chorizo sausage, and melted cheese. When a hangover remedy is sought, hot jalapeño peppers will be added; and eaters frequently spritz migas with hot sauce or spoon on spicy salsa. Side dishes include refried beans, grits, and fried potatoes.

Named for a Spanish dish that uses leftover bread (the word translates as "crumbs"), migas made without sausage are especially popular during Lent.

MILK SHAKE

We were uninclined to include the term **milk shake** in this lexicon because everybody knows what one is. But fountain drinks in New England have a language all their own, and a milk shake in that part of the world is not ice cream, milk, and flavored syrup. Rhode Islanders call that combination of ingredients a *cabinet* and Yankees farther Downeast know it as a *frappe* or *velvet*. If you order a "milk shake" in Rhode Island, you will get milk mixed with flavored syrup, but no ice cream.

To further complicate the issue, if you head west to Buffalo, New York, and order a "frappe" you will get what looks like a sundae. The city's great ice cream parlors (and they truly are great) list both sundaes and frappes on their menus. Inquiries throughout Buffalo of mixologists and soda jerks about the difference between them yielded only a strong belief that a frappe is an especially exotic sundae.

And P.S.: If you tell someone in Massachusetts you want a "soda," you will get plain bubbly water. If you want what Midwesterners know as *pop*, ask for *tonic*.

MILLIONAIRE PIE

Millionaire pie is just that rich. A no-bake jiffy dessert made of cream cheese, coconut, Cool Whip, crushed pineapple, and chopped pecans on a graham cracker crust, it is frozen and served still chilled enough that it is easy to press down and sever a tidy piece with a fork. Like **five-cup salad** (also known as *millionaire salad*), its ingredient list is a welcoming one; creative cooks might include mandarin orange segments, sweetened condensed milk, shredded coconut, and even chocolate chips; Cool Whip and graham cracker

A cross-section of millionaire pie reveals pineapple chunks and mandarin oranges.

crust are essentials. When maraschino cherries or cherry pie filling is added (as at Furr's Cafeterias in the Southwest), it becomes **billionaire pie.**

MINORCAN CHOWDER

Minorcan chowder is a tomato-vegetable soup that looks like Manhattan clam chowder but definitely doesn't taste like it. The difference is datil peppers, grown only in and around St. Augustine, Florida, which give Minorcan chowder a fruity pepper punch. The shock and awe come on slowly, beginning with a glow at the back of the throat that soon blossoms to set tongue and lips tingling. Chopped clams, shreds of tomato, corn kernels, and hunks of potato ride a slow-rolling capsicum wave that swells with sweet-tart citrus zest.

There is no Minorcan chowder on the island of Minorca in the Spanish Mediterranean, nor anywhere other than Florida's northeast coast. The pastel orange datil pepper pods, which resemble habañeros, arrived in the late eighteenth century in the hands of Minorcans who came to work the once-ubiquitous indigo fields and finally settled in St. Augustine. They likely picked up the New World peppers in Cuba, as there are none in Spain, and while no Florida restaurant is entirely devoted to Minorcan cuisine, datil pepper–charged food is served in and around St. Augustine.

MINT JULEP

The **mint julep** has been the official drink of the Kentucky Derby since 1938. Well over 100,000 of them are drunk at Churchill Downs on Derby Day, but the sweet bourbon cocktail is a warm-weather favorite throughout the year and well beyond Kentucky. Dating back to the early nineteenth century, when alcoholic beverages were considered by some to be medicinal, the term *julep* can refer to any sweet libation that does something more than merely slake thirst. Consisting of bourbon, mint sprigs, muddled mint leaves, and simple syrup, with plenty of ice, mint juleps traditionally are served in silver beakers that expert drinkers know to hold only by the top and bottom edge so as not to transfer their hand's heat to the beverage. (The old Seelbach Bar in Louisville still uses silver cups.)

While the exact history of the drink is unknown, Vicksburg, Mississippi, claims to be the "first place anyone stuck a sprig of fresh mint into bourbon" and asserts that the mint julep was named for Mint Springs in the Vicksburg National Military Park. Other accounts credit Virginians for having invented it as a morning pick-me-up. Some historians trace the name back to an ancient Arabic drink called the *julab,* sweetened with rose petals, the petals ultimately replaced by mint.

MORNING BUN

The San Francisco Bay area is rich with bakeries that make excellent morning buns.

An unsticky sticky bun made with buttery croissant dough and veined with swirls of sugar and cinnamon, the **morning bun** first became popular in the San Francisco Bay area in the mid 20-aughts. Some reports say it originated in Wisconsin and traveled west; by 2010, it had become ubiquitous, even part of the regular lineup on Starbucks's pastry shelf. It is made in a muffin tin, giving it a dual personality, the stump compressed and rich like a farmland sweet roll with perhaps a thin web of caramel crispness like a chewy trivet all around the bottom, its top as light and flaky as a well-made croissant.

MOXIE

Since 1998, **Moxie** has been Maine's official state drink. Although it is owned by Kirin of Japan and its U.S. headquarters are in New Hampshire, no one can dispute Maine's claim on it. The inventor, Augustin Thompson, was born in Maine, and more important, Moxie is a soft drink with character well-suited to the stereotypical dour personality of the Pine Tree State. It is more bitter than sweet; even its bubbles are not so much frothy as they are sharp. Marketed in the late nineteenth century as a nerve tonic that prevented "softening of the brain," Moxie has come to be synonymous with such words as *chutzpah* and *cojones,* used to describe someone who is bold, unafraid, and in your face. We met just such a woman a few years back at a lovely lobster pound along the Downeast Coast,

Moxie is a good antidote for nutrition nags who wail about soda being too sweet.

where she was in charge of selling beverages. When we asked her for a bottle of Moxie to go with our **shore dinner,** she didn't hesitate to say bluntly, "No. You won't like it. You'll have Coke instead." That's moxie.

MR. BROWN AND MISS WHITE

The motto at Leonard's barbecue restaurant in Memphis is "Mr. Brown Goes To Town." It was explained to us many years ago by a waitress who said, "**Mr. Brown** was the term used for brown-meat **barbecue.** It is the outside of the shoulder that gets chewy from the sauce and the smoke in the pit. The inside part of the roast, which is moist but has very little barbecue flavor, is known as **Miss White.** People used to ask for plates and sandwiches of 'Mr. Brown and Miss White'." Racial harmony in the smoke pits of Memphis!

White and dark, crisp and soft, mild and intense: Pork barbecue is a study in harmonies.

MUFFALETTA

Central Grocery in New Orleans claims to have invented the **muffaletta** (aka *muffuletta, muffelatta*), which is named for the round Sicilian loaf that resem-

bles a double-tall focaccia. It happened in 1906, when Salvatore Lupo, proprietor of the French Quarter grocery store, sliced the loaf sideways and layered in salami, mortadella, capicola, and provolone, along with a thick ribbon of garlicky olive salad in the same genus as the **giardiniera** used on Chicago's **Italian beef.** A traditional muffaletta, as made at Central Grocery (which now exists for no reason other than to make and serve it), is almost a foot in diameter—enough sandwich for two—and is sold as a whole, half, or quarter. Some restaurants do offer it

A mini-muffaletta as served at the 2010 New Orleans Roadfood Festival.

heated; recipes extend to vegetarian versions; and there even are ones made on sliced bread rather than on a muffaletta loaf. Such variations test the limits of the word.

MUSHROOMS AND BUTTERFLIES

There are all kinds of popping corn in different degrees of hull hardness, size, shape, and color, and there are two different ends of the popped corn spectrum: flakes that are **butterflies** and flakes that are **mushrooms.** (*Flake* is the formal term for a single popped kernel.) Butterflies are flakes that sprout wings when they pop, extending far beyond the hull and offering more crisp crunch. Mushrooms are kernels that pop into smooth, round balls that are softer but lack butterflies' elegance. The distinction is good to know if you are making popcorn balls or caramel corn, as you want popping corn that yields mostly mushrooms—they are sturdy enough to be mixed—although in caramel corn especially, a measure of butterflies adds welcome texture.

NACHOS

Like **pizza** and yogurt, **nachos** are a formerly foreign food that has been totally absorbed by U.S. popular culture. All three dishes ascended concurrently in the expansive years after World War II, when so many middle-class Americans sought to broaden their cultural and culinary horizons. The moment of creation is supposed to have happened in 1943, at a restaurant in Piedras Negras, Mexico, when a group of U.S. Army wives came to eat and a maitre d' nicknamed Nacho realized that the kitchen's supplies had dwindled to little more than tortillas and cheese. Señor Nacho cooked the tortillas crisp, broke them into pieces, and melted cheese on top. He subsequently went on to open his own restaurant, named Nachos, and pretty soon the dish in its simplest form began to appear on Tex-Mex menus all along the border and up into the Southwest.

The introduction of **Cheez Whiz** in the early 1950s, and then Doritos in 1964, made nachos very easy to make as well as fun to eat, and in the mid-1970s they began appearing in sports stadiums and then at movie concession stands. Ordinary toppings include jalapeño chips, chopped olives, and salsa. Guacamole, seasoned ground beef, and refried beans are not uncommon. But there is no limit to nachos' anything-goes personality. "Nachos Jorge," a specialty of Pico's restaurant in Houston, are topped with peppered pork baked in banana leaves and shredded atop the chips along with marinated onions, black beans, guacamole, hot jalapeños, and melted Chihuahua cheese. We have encountered nachos topped with fried oysters, crab meat, Italian sausage, bratwurst, and sauerbraten (separately—not all on one heap of chips).

NAVAJO FRY BREAD

For many years while traveling the Southwest, we assumed that **fry bread** was some sort of **Fred Harvey** knock-off of **fried dough** or perhaps an outsized **sopaipilla** or simply something made by contemporary Navajo cooks to appeal to Americans' taste for just about anything fried in a bucket of fat. We were wrong. It is no exaggeration to say that fry bread is to Navajos what matzoh is to Jews—a simple dish with profound meaning that arises from the harsh

Hot from the kettle, sprinkled with powdered sugar and cinnamon, Navajo fry bread is a glorious snack.

tribulations of ancestors. When the U.S. Army rounded up Navajos after they surrendered to Kit Carson in 1864, the captives were marched 300 miles through winter snows to Bosque Redondo, near Fort Sumner along the Pecos River in New Mexico. Many starved on what is now known as the Long Walk, and many more died from harsh conditions on the reservation. The meager supplies issued by their captors included lard, flour, baking powder, and powdered milk, and from these they learned to make fry bread—broad discs of dough that puff up in hot oil and are delicious plain or as a partner for a bowl of chili or sugared for dessert. Fry bread also serves as the foundation layer of what is known as a *Navajo taco* or *Indian taco*, heaped with all the ingredients that normally would be stuffed into a corn or wheat tortilla.

Navajo Taco

The Navajo taco is a multicultural dish that is a little bit Mexican, Native American, and Anglo and even, arguably, Italian, at least conceptually, given its resemblance to pizza. Indeed, Navajo tacos are as open to creative variation as pizza, whether topped with lunchtime ingredients or breakfast. For the latter, fry the bread as directed, and spread the hot disc with a bit of butter and cinnamon sugar or top it with eggs the way you like them and cooked chorizo sausage.

Fry Bread

1–1½ cups flour, plus more for rolling
1 teaspoon baking powder
½ teaspoon salt
¼ cup instant milk
½–¾ cups water
Oil for frying

Taco Meat

½ cup chopped onion
2 cloves garlic, chopped
1 tablespoon olive oil
1 pound lean ground beef
2 cups pinto beans, drained

Toppings
>Grated Monterey Jack cheese
>Shredded lettuce
>Chopped tomatoes
>Chopped raw onions
>Chopped olives
>Sour cream

1. Mix together 1 cup of the flour, the baking powder, salt, and instant milk. Mix in ½ cup water, adding more or less and additional flour, if needed, to create a workable dough. Knead the dough about 5 minutes, cover, and let rest 20 minutes while you prepare the meat and assemble toppings of choice.

2. Cook the chopped onion and garlic in the olive oil until they soften. Add the beef and cook, stirring constantly with a fork so it doesn't clump up. When meat is browned, drain any excess oil and stir in the pinto beans.

3. Heat one inch of vegetable oil to 360°F in a broad, deep skillet.

4. Pinch off a sphere of dough about 2 inches in diameter and roll it out on a floured board until it is ⅓ inch thick and about 8 inches wide. Slide the disc into the hot oil, cook about 1 minute, flip, and cook 1 minute more. It will puff up, but if a part of it bubbles too high while cooking, puncture it with a sharp knife. The disc is done when it is light gold. Use tongs to remove it from the oil and drain it on paper towels. Continue until you have cooked all the dough. You should have 4-6 discs.

5. Spoon the beef and bean mix onto a disc and spread it across evenly. Add toppings of choice and serve.

4 SERVINGS

NEAPOLITAN PIZZA

Just about everybody in America has a good idea of what **Neapolitan pizza** is: your basic medium-thin-crust pie with a puffy edge, topped with tomatoes or tomato sauce, mozzarella cheese, and, perhaps, meats and veggies. But according to the experts, just about everybody in America is wrong.

In 2004, the Vera Pizza Napoletana (**V.P.N.**) association of Italy convinced the Italian Ministry of Agriculture to present true Neapolitan pizza to the European Union as a protected product like chianti, balsamic vinegar, and Asiago cheese. They were unhappy that **pizza** makers around the world were

An untraditional garden pizza being pulled from a traditional Neapolitan wood-fired oven at Pizzeria Lauretano, Bethel, Connecticut.

making pizza and calling it "Neapolitan" when, in their opinion, most such pies were bastards. When the stink arose, Neapolitan pizza makers all across America took notice and said, "Who cares?"

But in these days of artisan baking, some of the nation's most ambitious pizzaioli yearn to make their pizza exactly right and do proudly produce V.P.N.-approved pies. These are the qualifications a pizza must meet to make the grade.

♦ It must be cooked in a wood-fired dome oven at 800 degrees.

♦ Size can be no more than 14 inches in diameter.

♦ Flour must be extra-fine 00, preferably from Italy.

♦ It can be made only of fresh, nonprocessed ingredients, including basil, San Marzano tomatoes, and buffalo mozzarella. Forget Hawaiian pizza, cheeseburger pizza, and barbecue chicken pizza. Allowable configurations are marinara, margherita, Parmigiano-Reggiano, and prosciutto di Parma.

♦ The dough should be kneaded by hand or a low-speed mixer. No mechanical flattening of the dough is allowed; even a rolling pin is taboo.

♦ The bottom crust must be like a cracker and no thicker than a credit card. The outer crust can rise up and be dense and chewy. The latter should have a few charred black bubbles on its surface, proving the extreme heat of the oven.

NEWARK HOT DOG

The **Newark hot dog,** also known as an *Italian hot dog,* is one of several frankfurter formations unique to New Jersey. (See also **Texas weiner** and **ripper.**) It is a deep-fried all-beef tube steak—usually two; few customers order a single—inserted into half of a capacious circular bun known locally as *pizza bread.* The bread is sturdy and absorbent and can be squeezed open like a pita pocket to hold not only the **hot dog**(s) but also sautéed onions and peppers and a heap of potato chunks that have been either deep-fried or sautéed. Newark dog shops tend not to drain any of the toppings; they are forked directly from the griddle or frying cauldron onto the hot dogs and they in turn are dressed with the diner's choice of ketchup, mustard, marinara sauce, or fire-hot onion relish.

James Racioppi, proprietor of Jimmy Buff's hot dog restaurants, believes his grandparents, James and Mary Racioppi, originated Newark hot dogs during the Depression as a snack to serve friends who came to their North Ward apartment to play cards each week. "After a while, people started coming just to eat," Mr. Racioppi says. "So in 1932 they opened a store at 14th and 9th to sell the sandwiches. That was the beginning." Today at least a dozen different places in and around Newark sell the distinctive dog; most also offer Italian sausage sandwiches and some offer dog-and-sausage combos as well as meat-free sandwiches that contain only vegetables and potatoes.

James Racioppi of Jimmy Buff's shows off his specialty, the Newark hot dog.

A double Newark hot dog, aka Italian hot dog, is a full meal in a bun.

NEW YORK SYSTEM

Rhode Island **hot dogs** are known as **New York System** weenies, although there is nothing remotely like them in New York. (In New York City, that is. The **Michigan** of Plattsburgh, New York, is vaguely similar.) The logical explanation, which has yet to be proven in fact, is that nearly all of the Ocean State's wiener depots, which are remarkably similar, were opened by cooks who once had worked at America's frankfurter mothership, Nathan's of Coney Island. Even if that's true, however, the fundamental mystery remains: Where, when, and why did the hot dog, once a New York sausage with a German accent, get topped with distinctively Greek-seasoned sauce and proliferate all across the country (except New York) as a **Coney Island** weenie?

Rhode Island's small pink links—always known as *weenies,* never *hot dogs* or *frankfurters*—are smothered with fine-grind beef sauce that is moderately spicy and maybe a little sweet. Yellow mustard, chopped raw onions, and a shot of celery salt complete the picture. The "system" element of the name means they are made in a systematic way, by lining up multiple dogs in buns and dressing them assembly-line style. Old-time counter men can array a few dozen from wrist to shoulder, adding sauce and condiments with lightning speed. Hence the common local description of New York System dining: *wieners up the arm.* Providentians, who think nothing of having six for a midnight snack, fondly call them *gaggahs,* local dialect for "gaggers."

Mustard, sauce, and onions eclipse the New York System weenies they dress.

Application of the term New York System is ambiguous: It can be the style of preparation and service, the weenies themselves, or the name of the restaurant. For example, Olneyville N.Y. System restaurant of Providence serves New York System wieners using the New York System to prepare them.

New York System Sauce

Like all chili sauce recipes for hot dogs, the fine-grind beef that tops New York System weenies is made from formulae that are guarded as tightly as that for Coca-Cola. After careful study and a little prying, we came up with the following blueprint for producing a chili sauce in the style of New York System restaurants. It is eminently suited to franks of any pedigree, all-beef or porky.

½ cup finely chopped onion
1 clove garlic, minced
2 tablespoons vegetable oil
1 pound lean chuck, ground very fine
½ cup beef broth
2 teaspoons chili powder
½ teaspoon pepper
1 teaspoon allspice
½ teaspoon nutmeg
½ teaspoon celery salt
¼ teaspoon ground ginger
1 teaspoon ground cumin
1 tablespoon soy sauce

1. Sauté the onion and garlic in vegetable oil until soft. Add the ground chuck and cook until it is browned, stirring constantly with a fork or spatula to keep it broken up. Drain off excess oil. Add the beef broth and seasonings. Simmer 10 minutes or until all liquid is absorbed.

2. The sauce should be topped with mustard and raw onions. It is zesty, so use it sparingly. This recipe makes enough to dress 8–10 modest-size hot dogs.

NORFOLK-STYLE SEAFOOD

Norfolk = butter. That's all you need to know. If a menu in the Tidewater area of Virginia lists crab Norfolk (the most popular variation) or oysters or scallops or shrimp Norfolk, you can expect seafood swimming in the butter in which it has been sautéed. There may be a dash of lemon and a bit of spice, but nothing more than that. The only possible improvement on this bliss is when the crab is joined in its sauté pan by nuggets of Virginia ham.

OLALLIEBERRY PIE

Glossy black and knobby, the olallieberry looks like a jumbo blackberry. One bite of **olallieberry pie** underscores the difference. When olallieberries are cooked, heat releases regal sweetness more like serious wine than frivolous sugar; partnered with butter-rich crust, they are the ultimate bramble fruit. Ollallies grow only on a few hundred acres along the California coast and their season is brief—no more than six weeks of mid-summer—so when they are gone, pie makers frequently will substitute more readily available marionberries or blackberries. They make lovely pies, but once you know how special an olallieberry pie can be, there is no substitute.

OLD FORGE PIZZA

At least a dozen bars and restaurants in and around Scranton, Pennsylvania, serve **Old Forge pizza.** (Old Forge is a Lackawanna County borough.) A favorite coal-miners' snack from the mid-twentieth century, it is a rectangular pie with a thick crust vaguely reminiscent of Sicilian **pizza.** It comes single or double-crusted, red or white, and with usual and very unusual toppings, including eggs and breakfast meats for morning pizza. Even standard-ingredient Old Forge pizza is more American in character than Mediterranean: sunny tomato sauce, cheese that tastes like a mild blend of Italian and American varieties, and a uniquely puffed-up crust that develops because the pie is made in a pan well-greased with peanut oil.

Old Forge pizza, a Pennsylvania favorite.

Polish pizza is a subset of Old Forge, made with onion and kielbasa and cooked with so much oil in the pan that the crust develops a deep-fried crunch.

ONION-FRIED BURGER

Sometime in the 1920s, a restaurant opened in El Reno, Oklahoma, called the Hamburger Inn. Its specialty: the **onion-fried burger.** Not merely a **hamburger** with fried onions, it is a patty of meat that gets put on the grill with a heap of thinly sliced onions on top. The chef presses down, mashing the onions into the raw meat, and when the burger is flipped, he presses down again. By the time the hamburger is done, the onions and meat have become inseparable—a savory/sweet package with an especially enticing aroma. Dozens of burger restaurants have come and gone in El Reno since then, all opened by cooks who apprenticed at other onion-fried burger joints in town, and today there are four places in the city and a handful in its orbit.

"Onion-fried burger" is not listed on the menu of restaurants that serve it. In El Reno, when you order a hamburger, you will get an onion-fried burger unless you specifically instruct the cook to leave the onions out. All the usual hamburger condiments are available, plus a unique one: El Reno slaw. A pickly-sweet, mustard-colored hash of finely minced cabbage, the slaw is vaguely like relish, and it is more typically used as a topping for the **Coney Island** hot dogs that also are served at most local burger restaurants.

OYSTER LOAF

It is possible to think of an **oyster loaf** as a subset of the **po' boy,** and most of them are. But in many restaurants of New Orleans and out into Cajun country, the term has a nuanced meaning, defined by the bread with which the sandwich is made. French bread is not used for this type of oyster loaf. Instead, fried oysters are layered between extra-thick slices of pan bread that are buttered and toasted, not unlike Texas toast. In some cases, a whole pullman-style loaf is used, hollowed out to hold maximum numbers of oysters.

Its majesty, the New Orleans oyster loaf.

OYSTER ROAST

When an oyster is covered with wet burlap over smoldering charcoal, it wallows in its juices and the flavor intensifies. More warmed than cooked, it retains all the sensual mouthfeel of a raw one with the added lick of fire. Unlike urbane oysters that are bright and glistening in their clean marine liquor, presented on the half shell on a bed of crushed ice, **oyster roast** oysters can be quite hideous to see, bunches of them stuck together and smelling of the sea, all gnarled and splotched with *pluff*, the oysterman's term for the fine silt that sticks on them when they are harvested and clings to them when they are roasted, so that merely touching a cooked cluster will smudge your fingers.

The oyster roast is a cultural touchstone of the Lowcountry—a communal feast where amenities are minimal and camaraderie is huge. The rare restaurant that serves an oyster roast along the South Carolina coast is ebulliently colorful, parking lot paved with millions of crushed shells, tables topped with newspaper instead of cloth, oysters quite literally shoveled from the grate onto the table, where the only utensil provided is a knife to wedge into the place the oyster has begun to spring open. The knife is used to detach a slippery nugget of marine meat, then to bring it to the mouth. Once it is dispatched, the connoisseur tilts the shell back to drink down its warm, salty liquor. At Bowen's Island outside of Charleston, the big tables have holes in their centers, under which are garbage cans, so eaters can easily dispose of shells. The heavy kerplunk of emptied shells getting tossed into the cans sets a beat to which slurping and sucking sound a sweet melody.

OYSTER SKILLET

You can get oysters year-round in the Lowcountry, but during months spelled with the *R*, the height of oyster season, you can enjoy the best possible version in the form of an **oyster skillet.** A cast iron skillet is loaded with local oysters, suspended in a broth of oyster liquor, butter, garlic, and parsley. On the side will be a toasted baguette, crisp enough to break off long, crunchy tiles to push through the skillet, scooping up a few of the pearlescent little softies and at the same time moistening the bread with their marine juices. Proper companions hereabouts are **creamy grits** and **butter beans,** as served in perfect form by chef Philip Bardin at the Old Post Office restaurant on Edisto Island, South Carolina.

OYSTERS FOCH

A signature dish of New Orleans's Antoine's, and there listed on the appetizer menu as *huîtres á la Foch,* this impossibly opulent Creole creation is toast spread with fois gras pâté, topped with fried oysters, and crowned with Colbert sauce, a dark red-brown variation of hollandaise that includes tomatoes, veal stock, and sherry. *Bec fins* consider it perhaps the best dish at Antoine's, but hoi polloi like us might never have known of it had not the very swanky Antoine's opened its somewhat less formal and definitely less expensive Hermes Bar, where the menu is headed by an **oysters Foch** po'boy. This **po'boy** was a major hit at the 2010 New Orleans Roadfood Festival, where it staked its claim as the most deluxe street food ever served anywhere. Reflecting Antoine's venerable history (it's the nation's oldest restaurant), oysters Foch was named nearly a century ago to honor France's World War I Field Marshal Foch. The combination of ingredients was supposed to honor Foch's soldiers, the pâté representing the mud on their shoes, the sauce their spilled blood.

PAN ROAST

In Victorian times, luxury resort hotels in the Mid-Atlantic states offered guests a special way to enjoy oysters—in a **pan roast.** It is a warm and comforting stew made with just-shelled oysters, cream, a bit of chili sauce, and spice, served in a broad bowl on a square of thick toast. The tradition is carried on by the Oyster Bar in New York's Grand Central Station, where a seat at the counter affords a view of the roasts being made in vintage silver vessels that hearken back to a long-passed era of unabashed bourgeois extravagance. Pan roasts also are available made from shrimp, clams, lobster, or scallops.

PASTY

Citizens of Michigan's Upper Peninsula, who call themselves Yoopers, consider the pasty their own.

The **pasty** (say "pass-tee," not "pay-stee") began as a portable stew—meat and vegetables sealed inside a pastry crust—that Cornish miners in Northern Wisconsin and Michigan's Upper Peninsula used to carry with them for lunch. It stayed warm, it could be heated on the end of a shovel, and its filling was thick enough that it did not require major knife-and-fork work. Long after the mines closed, the pasty remained a popular dish in the northland where families from Cornwall had settled. And although it has been eclipsed by fast food, the U.P. still is rich with pasty shops. Traditionally, pasties are filled with beef or beef and pork with chunks of potato, rutabaga, and onion, but today between Sault Ste. Marie and Ishpeming you will encounter gourmet pasties filled with steak, **pizza** pasties with pepperoni and mozzarella, Reuben pasties, chicken pasties, even vegetarian pasties for meat-phobes and breakfast pasties filled with eggs and sausage.

PEANUT SOUP

Peanut soup at Middleton Place Plantation outside of Charleston.

If Virginia had an official state legume, it certainly would be the peanut. Virginia peanuts (actually grown beyond the Old Dominion, too) are bigger and fuller-flavored than any others. Eating peanuts is said to have been the reason the state's hogs earned a reputation for their delicious hams. In no other state will you find so many different variations on African **peanut soup.**

Known colloquially as "Tuskegee soup" after the university where George Washington Carver conducted his famous experiments that turned peanuts into everything from tile flooring to peanut butter, it is a dish that can

FRANK PEPE

When **Frank Pepe** came to America from a town called Maori on the Amalfi Coast southwest of Naples, he had no intention of becoming a baker, much less the Jupiter of twentieth-century **pizza.** "He learned to bake bread *here,*" says his grandson, Francis Rosselli, who grew up with him at the helm of Frank Pepe Pizzeria Napoletana. When Francis says *here*, he doesn't just mean America. He means here on Wooster Street, in New Haven, Connecticut, which, when Frank Pepe arrived in the teens, was a robust neighborhood with a business at every address. Francis points over his shoulder with his thumb, indicating the place where Libby's pastry shop now stands, and where his grandfather learned the baker's trade—at a business called Generoso Muro, which made bread and macaroni.

In 1925 Frank Pepe rented out a space at 163 Wooster Street and opened a bakery. He was illiterate and because he had a hard time keeping orders for bread delivery in his head (yes, in those days, bread was delivered just like milk), he decided to use the bakery to make the simple flat-breads that he knew from his homeland: thin rounds of dough spread with tomato, olive oil, garlic, and grated cheese, with anchovies the only option. They were cooked in the bread oven that then was heated by coke (a fuel derived from coal), emerging with an edge that offered a good chew and a bit of bituminous char. There was no home delivery, and there were no pizza boxes at the time; nor did the original place offer tables at which to eat. When a customer came in to buy a tomato pie to go, Pepe set it on a piece of corrugated cardboard called a flat and wrapped paper around it.

Pepe's original oven was at a restaurant known as the Spot in a building owned by the Boccamiello family. In 1937, once his tomato pies had gained a loyal following, he was evicted and the Boccamiellos continued in the pizza-making business. Ever resourceful, Frank Pepe bought the building next door, installing an oven and tables where customers could sit and enjoy what he advertised as "delicious Italian food" in the form of Neapolitan tomato pies. To come to a restaurant, sit down, and eat pizza was such a novelty that Frank had a hard time convincing authorities in Hartford to grant him a license to offer beer with his pies. Until that time, pizza was considered a corollary of bread-making; Frank Pepe had to drive home the point that people actually came to his place, sat down, and ate pizza—just like they would a regular meal.

Frank Pepe's welcoming personality helped make his Wooster Street establishment far more than just an eatery. Francis recalls that even into Grandpop's older days in the 1960s, he used to stroll around and chat with customers, sit at tables, and enjoy the company. Through the 1940s and into the 1950s, he opened at noon and did not close until 3 a.m. Francis explains: "The community was so vibrant then. People didn't automatically get in their cars and go somewhere else. This was their home, their social life, their friends and family. They came to Pepe's to be with each other and with Grandpop."

seem sophisticated or plain and that serves well as the companion for a sandwich at lunch or as the first course of an elaborate dinner. Versions of it are shockingly diverse, from an elegant broth just barely tinged with peanut flavor to cloddish brews that taste like watery peanut butter. Our gold standard has always been that served by the Southern Kitchen, a modest town lunchroom in New Market not far from I-81, where it is creamy but not too thick, just-right nutty-flavored, and laced with fetching onion sweetness. A cup is an ideal prelude to a dinner of Virginia **country ham** or fried chicken.

PEPPERONI ROLL

Little-known beyond West Virginia, between Cheat Neck in the north and the Little Kanawha River in the center of the state, the **pepperoni roll** is common in grocery stores, gas stations, and on restaurant menus in the area where

so many Italians settled and created an Italian-American-Mountaineer cuisine. Consisting of bread dough baked around twigs of pepperoni, it ranges from a tidy snack scarcely bigger than a cocktail frank in crescent roll dough to a meal-size platter similar to a calzone, complete with marinara sauce on top.

Conventional wisdom holds that the portable snack was invented in the 1920s by baker Giuseppe Agiro and popularized by his son, Frank "Cheech" Agiro, at the bakery they ran in Fairmont. The family's Country Club Bak-

The Country Club Bakery of Fairmont, West Virginia, makes a very simple pepperoni roll, easy to eat out of hand.

ery still supplies them to many markets in Mountaineer country and sells plain and perfect ones, warm from the oven, for under a dollar apiece. Aficionados eat them by the half-dozen.

A few years ago, we received a more nuanced account of the pepperoni roll's origin from a woman who signed her story "Granddaughter of two 1920s coal miners." She wrote, "My grandfather worked for the mines in the '20s and retired Vice President of the UMWA District 31. My mother, born in 1921 and still living, used to eat pepperoni baked in small loaves of bread that my grandmother made when she was young. The story I was told is that Giuseppe Agiro used to take a stick of pepperoni and a loaf of bread down into the mines as many other coal miners did at the time. Giuseppe's wife came up with the idea of baking the pepperoni right into the bread to make it easier to carry down into the mines. The idea caught on among the miners, and both of my grandmothers started baking pepperoni into bread. So did a lot of other miners' wives who had access to pepperoni. I don't know if Mrs. Agiro was making pepperoni rolls and giving them away or selling them to other miners. And I don't know which was the first bakery to package them as pepperoni rolls.

"The only reason I know this story at all is because when I was around 14 years of age (I'm now 52), we had relatives visiting from Italy. I didn't understand how they could be from Italy and not know what a pepperoni roll was. At the time, I thought pepperoni rolls originated in Italy."

PEZ

◇◇◇

No other candy is like Pez. It is eaten from a hidden orifice atop its own little altar, which is a pedestal with a head on top designed to remind the eater of a favorite character from folklore, movies, cartoons, or comic books. In almost every variation of the disgorging icon, the sweet brick of candy comes out of a mouth, like a food pellet from the beak of a mother bird, proffered to supplicants at a confectionery shrine.

The Pez experience, which elevates sugar-eating to a nearly spiritual event, seems so American, but actually its origins were in Vienna, Austria. Eduard Haas III, known in the candy trade as "the Wilber Wright of Peppermint," had made a fortune in baking powder before 1927, when he conceived the idea of combining peppermint oil with sugar and using heat, humidity, and compression to create tiny brick-shaped lozenges. He named his product Pez, from the German word *Pfefferminz,* and marketed it to adults as a breath mint.

For over two decades, Pez was sold wrapped in stacks that required the consumer to pick one, then rewrap the rest. In 1948, the Pez-Haas Company introduced the Pez dispenser, which could be loaded with a stack of candy the way staples are loaded in a staple gun, and which ejected the little bricks one-by-one from a flip-top. The first Pez dispensers had no funny heads on top. Known to collectors as "regulars," they were strictly utilitarian, resembling cigarette lighters.

In 1952, Pez came to America in a dispenser with Mickey Mouse's head on top. Plain peppermint candies weren't of much interest to American candy buyers, so fruit flavors (and fruit colors) were introduced, and dozens, then hundreds, of different heads were molded to fit on top of the dispenser. Snowmen, skulls, clowns, jack-o-lanterns, and witches have all been mounted, each with a lever at the back of its pate that causes the mouth (or neck) to open wide and regurgitate a candy. Mickey Mouse and Santa Claus are the all-time bestsellers, and the cast of heads is always growing, with about forty in production at any given time. Curiously, humans—living or dead—were taboo on Pez dispensers until the first decade of the twenty-first century, which produced NASCAR driver heads, Elvis heads, and Star Trek cast heads.

Pez never has advertised, but Americans like it enough to ingest over a billion tablets every year, and it has become an inexorable pop culture icon. Pez confuses the alien in *E.T.;* in an episode of the TV show *Seinfeld* titled "The Pez Dispenser," it causes Elaine to break into hysterical laughter at the most inopportune moment; and in Rob Reiner's sentimental 1986 movie *Stand by Me*, which gazed back on a 1960s childhood, Pez is the romanticized little lads' favorite snack. "If I could have only one food for the rest of my life?" one boy asks. "That's easy. Pez. Cherry-flavored Pez." An article about the company by Jeremy Schlosberg in *Connecticut* magazine attributed Pez's continuing success to its nostalgic connotations, calling it "a favorite of the generation that refuses to let go of its adolescence." Rare collectible Pez dispensers are valued at up to $10,000.

PICKLE-SICKLE

A proper **pickle-sickle** is not just excess juice from a jar of dill pickles that has been frozen. Correctly made, it contains real pickle squeezin's, which give it a chunkier flavor than mere brine. The term Pickle Sickle (without a hyphen) is in fact a trademarked name for blister packs full of pickle juice that are made in Seguin, Texas, and shipped to customers who freeze them and then eat them like stickless Popsicles. Pickle Sickle proprietor John Howard started serving them at his roller rink in 2007. As Howard once told a reporter, "There are a lot of closet pickle drinkers in South Texas."

No doubt, Texas is America's most pickle-happy state, but we have found good pickle-sickles throughout the Ozarks, where they are sold by the frozen cupful at convenience stores and independent ice cream stands—mostly to kids, according to the vendors with whom we've spoken. Year-round, there is no shortage of them in Atkins, Arkansas, where a pickle juice–drinking contest is always part of May's annual Picklefest.

PICO DE GALLO

In most Mexican-American restaurants, **pico de gallo** refers to rugged salsa, but in Tucson, it is something altogether different. This "beak of the rooster" is a bouquet of watermelon, coconut, pineapple, mango, and jicama that gets spritzed with lime juice and liberally sprinkled with a red-hot chili-powder mix. It is a heady fusion that can either marshal taste buds to attention for the meal to come or soothe them after a fiery meal just eaten.

Refreshing fruit, Sonoran-style: Pico de gallo as served at the Tucson restaurant that calls itself Pico de Gallo.

PIG PICKIN'

Tradition-minded Carolinians refer to a celebratory barbecue as a **pig pickin'**, the implication being that those who attend will have the entire hog from which to choose, meaning ham and shoulder meat, ribs, crunchy pieces of skin, snoots and ears and assorted gravies made from less desirable parts, maybe some sausages and trotters, plus corn bread dotted with **cracklin's.** Outdoors at a community picnic or indoors at a public eatery, pig pickin's are almost always presented buffet-style, and many of the region's most beloved **barbecue** restaurants continue the custom of serving them as a TGIF kind of meal, weekends only. Therefore, travelers be advised: If you are planning to visit a barbecue, especially in South Carolina, and most especially any day other than Friday or Saturday, be sure to call ahead to make sure the place is open.

PIG SANDWICH

The **pig sandwich** first was assembled in the 1920s by Leonard Heuberger of Leonard's barbecue in Memphis. Mr. Heuberger's idea was to pile shreds of sauced, smoked pork shoulder into a bun and top the pork with coleslaw—a yin-yang balance of hot and cool, meat and vegetable. The term *pig sandwich* actually has been trademarked by Van's Pig Stand in Oklahoma. (The Pig Stands—America's first **drive-ins**—go back to 1921, and among their myriad claims to fame in the gastronomic record book are that Van's invented Texas toast and onion rings and were the first restaurants to use neon signage. Van's pig sandwich includes a very finely chopped relish in lieu of slaw.)

In much of the South, waiters will not ask if you want slaw on your sandwich; it

A Memphis pig sandwich, as served at Payne's.

is automatic. Depending on where you are, the pork will be just lightly sauced with vinegar and peppers or sopped with tangy-sweet-peppery red sauce. Most pig sandwiches come in an untoasted bun or on white bread, but the GA Pig in Brunswick, Georgia, adds another note by griddle-toasting a sesame seed bun, thus including crunch to surround the soft meat within.

PIMIENTO CHEESE

Unless you've done some good eating in the South, the words **pimiento cheese** most likely will conjure up a little jar of Kraft processed cheese food (spelled *pimento* on the label) that is as valued for its usefulness when recycled as a little juice glass as it is for the mild cheese spread it contains. A lot of Southern pimiento cheese is every bit as bland as Kraft's: smooth orange paste enriched with mayonnaise and laced with bits of a red cherry pepper that delivers absolutely no heat and just a whisper of sweet flavor (but does give the cheese a festive appearance). On the other hand, cooks riff brilliantly on the concept, making versions with different kinds of sharp cheddar, adding horseradish or olive bits or other, more punchy peppers.

Pimiento cheese sandwich, Franklin, Tennessee.
BRUCE BILMES

Pimiento cheese is served with crackers or crudités as an hors d'oeuvre and on sandwiches (made with polite white bread, please). The late Ruby Seahorse Grill on Edisto Island, South Carolina, claimed to have invented the pimiento cheeseburger, which is now a popular alternative to regular cheeseburgers throughout much of the South. Golf fans all over the world know about pimiento cheese because it is the featured snack at the Masters Tournament in Augusta, Georgia.

PITZA

Originally a sign-maker's error, **pitza,** as served in a small area around Hazelton, Pennsylvania, is different from **pizza.** *Pitza* means sharp melted cheese edge-to-edge, along with sweet sauce atop a soft crust. It is not something you get by walking into a restaurant, placing an order, and waiting. Instead, it is served by the piece at room temperature in gas stations or convenience stores and usually eaten behind the wheel, while driving. This method of ingestion is possible because pitza is not oily or drippy. It is moist and soft, but totally wieldy. Roadfood.com contributor Mosca, who alerted us to its existence, noted that pitza actually improves over several hours after it is cooked, aging to a point where the crust firms up, the sauce cures, and the cheese mellows. It is made round or square, red or white.

PIZZA

America's favorite one-dish meal used to be foreign food. Before the 1950s, **pizza** was a rarity in this country, found only in Italian neighborhoods at restaurants where the ambience, if any, was supplied by drippy candles stuck in wicker-clad Chianti bottles.

Pizza went mainstream after World War II. Sherwood "Shakey" Johnson opened a little place in Sacramento, California, that begat hundreds of Shakey's Pizza Parlors throughout the West, and Dan and Frank Carney of Wichita, Kansas, created Pizza Hut. No longer confined to cities' ethnic enclaves, pizzerias appeared in suburbs and small towns, and going out for pizza became one of the cheap-eats pleasures of the postwar years. It remained an odd enough meal in the 1950s that an early edition of *Mad* magazine ran hilarious instructions explaining how to eat it without dripping cheese in your lap, but as the baby boom entered its teens, pizza became nearly as familiar—and as fun—as **hot dogs** and **milk shakes.**

Pizza today can be anything you want it to be: junk food delivered by a local franchise, low-fat or low-carb, gluten-free or vegan, a cheese-gobbed

Superbowl snack or a dainty hors d'oeuvre adorned with baby vegetables, confits, and confitures.

Sameness of nationwide chains notwithstanding, the diversity of pizza styles in the United States is as striking as our nation's wildly varied definitions of **barbecue** or chili. Here's a roundup of the major venues.

CALIFORNIA

California deserves credit (or blame) for transforming pizza into boutique food. The renaissance began in the 1970s, when American gastronomes began to rediscover the pleasures of Mediterranean cuisine. Like extra-virgin olive oil and sun-dried tomatoes, pizza grew fashionable and acquired an aura of refinement. To the connoisseur, it was no longer just a mass-produced pie-in-a-cardboard-box heaped with rubbery mozzarella. Born-again pizza boasted heretofore unheard-of luxury. Its dough was made lovingly from scratch, sometimes with whole wheat flour and laced with herbs; and its toppings consisted of such deluxe groceries as shrimp, proscuitto di Parma, wild mushrooms, goat cheese, and caramelized garlic. In Hollywood, Spago's creator, Wolfgang Puck, first got famous by feeding movie stars unimaginably opulent pizzas, including an eight-incher topped with smoked salmon and three kinds of caviar that sold for a hundred dollars. Puck's salmon and crème fraîche toppings are still headliners, as is smoked duck sausage.

CHICAGO

Chicago pizza was born in 1941, when Ike Sewell and Ric Riccardo partnered up to opened a place called Pizzeria Uno, serving a **deep-dish pizza** inspired by **Neapolitan pizza** but unique to the United States. Since then, the Second City has become second to none in pizza personality. Here you can eat double-crusters, soufflé pizzas, **pizza pot pie,** and ultra-thin or extra-thick pies.

Chicago's signature pizza.
STEPHEN RUSHMORE

DETROIT

See **Square Pizza**

ITHACA, NEW YORK

Any hearty eater who attended Cornell University in Ithaca, New York, in the last forty years knows about **hot truck,** the mobile food wagon that invented French-bread pizzas in the early 1960s. As served from the campus truck starting every night at 11 p.m. (and round-the-clock at the associated Shortstop Deli), these fusions of pizza and submarine sandwich are piled with ingredients, then baked open-face until the bread is shatteringly crisp, the cheese bubbles, and the meats sizzle.

MARYLAND PIZZA

Introduced to the Mid-Atlantic region in the 1950s at Pizza Oven, Italian Inn, Gentleman Jim's, and Ledo (now a huge chain), Maryland pizza is medium thin with a crust that is flaky and oily, similar to **Greek pizza.** It is made with lots of cheese and extremely sweet tomato sauce as a large square or rectangle and cut into small slices, one thick-cut slice of pepperoni per piece. In the pizza forum at Roadfood.com, it was defended by Treetop Tom as "Not the greatest pizza you ever tasted, but sized and priced right to feed a dorm room full of hungry guys or your family on Friday night."

MEMPHIS

If you've eaten **barbecue spaghetti** and **barbecue salad** in and around Memphis, barbecue pizza won't likely come as a big surprise. At Coletta's Italian

Restaurant, a nice round pie with plenty of mozzarella is topped not with Italian sauce and sausage or pepperoni, but with heaps of barbecued pulled pork in a zesty cinnabar pit sauce. Weird as it may seem, it works wonderfully—and it is a fitting salute to the unrepressed personality of American pizza.

Barbecue pizza, Memphis, Tennessee.

NEW HAVEN

New Haven–style pizza is brittle-thin crust with a brawny edge, gilded with plenty of garlic and oil. The daddy of all Elm City pizzerias is Frank Pepe Pizzeria Napoletana in the old Italian neighborhood on Wooster Street, where Frank Pepe began selling "tomato pies" in the 1920s. Pepe's original pizzas were closer to what eaters today might call focaccia: broad flatbreads frosted with tomato and perhaps a few pinches of anchovy.

New Haven pizza.

NEW YORK

Across from its original location on Spring Street in New York City, Lombardi's introduced pizza to America in 1905. In the back of the cramped storefront, pies are cooked in a brick-floor, coal-fired oven that infuses the crust with smoky savor and buoys the edge in chewy puffs. New Yorkers also are fond of pizza-by-the-slice, street food you can eat while on the stroll. At Patsy's, uptown in Spanish Harlem, the street slice was defined seventy years ago. Customers stand

New York pizza.

around outside or lean against an open-air counter, wolfing down slices of simple, perfect pizza with a fragile crust that bends just enough so the slice can be neatly folded up one-handed, using middle finger and thumb at the edges, first finger holding down the vertex.

OLD FORGE, PENNSYLVANIA

See **Old Forge pizza**

SOUTHWEST

It may be stretching the definition of the dish to include Southern Arizona's Mexican pizzas in this entry, but they belong as an expression of regional character. Known as cheese crisps at Tucson's venerable El Charro (since 1923), these Sonoran-style pies are broad circular tortillas available in minimalist form with only cheese and a scattering of *cebillitos* (green onions) or dressed up with such regional favorites as green chiles, guacamole, refried beans, and house-made **carne seca** (air-dried beef).

ST. LOUIS

St. Louis–style pizza is as thin as a saltine cracker and just as crunchy. The pies are round but traditionally cut into small rectangles that can be lifted like an hors d'oeuvre. (The crust is too rigid to bend or fold.) In addition to the ultra-thin crust, which is unleavened, Gateway City pizzas are distinguished by the use of **Provel cheese,** which is a tangy mixture of provolone, Cheddar, and Swiss that is virtually unheard of elsewhere.

Ultra-thin-crust St. Louis pizza. CHRIS AYERS AND AMY BRIESCH

WEST VIRGINIA

Many people are surprised to learn that West Virginia has a rich, thriving pizza culture all its own, thanks to a population with a lot of Italian ancestors. (See also **pepperoni roll.**) Its unique style was created by Di Carlo's, a local chain that started in Wheeling in 1949. Square, relatively thick-crusted but not pan-cooked, it is flash-baked in the oven with only sauce atop the crust. The baker pulls it out and strews it with shredded sweet provolone and, if desired, pepperoni discs and peppers.

Di Carlo's of West Virginia applies cheese only after the cooked tomato pie comes out of the oven.

Although the crust's heat will melt much of the cheese as the pizza is carried from kitchen to table, the provolone remains more like a luxurious wrap than an intrinsic part of the pie.

PIZZA POT PIE

Chicago did not invent **pizza,** but it has invented more kinds of pizza than anywhere else. Starting with the **deep-dish pizza** devised by Ike Sewell at his Pizzeria Uno in 1943, Chicago pizza culture has expanded to include the *soufflé pizza* (whipped-up cheese on top), **stuffed pizza** (with a crust on top), *pan pizza* (like deep-dish, but with a thicker crust), *thin-crust pizza* (crisper than thin-crusted pizza anywhere else), and the awe-inspiring **pizza pot pie.** As codified by Chris Ayers and Amy Briesch in their Roadfood.com review of the Chicago Pizza and Oven Grinder Company, which invented it, ordering a pizza pot pie is simple, requiring four decisions:

1. Are you hungry (order a half pound) or super hungry (order one pound)?

2. Are you a traditionalist (order white crust) or on the whole-grain train (order wheat crust)?

3. Are you a carnivore (order the meat sauce) or unexplainably opposed to sausage made from prime Boston butts (order no meat sauce)?

4. Do you believe that fungi are meant to be eaten (order with whole, "doorknob-size" mushrooms) or best left in the forest (order minus the 'shrooms)?

The ingredients one chooses are put in a ceramic bowl and baked underneath a thick cap of Sicilian-style crust. The cooked dish is brought to the table, where a server flips it over and lifts off the ceramic dish, resulting in a pizza contained in a bowl of crust. As Chris and Amy put it, "What magically appears is a form that is cognitively consistent with the idea of what a pizza should be."

PIZZA TALK

Although **pizza** has become as American as **hamburgers,** many Italian words are still used in its making, serving, and eating. Here are some basics for any pizzaphile to know:

00 (double zero): The most finely ground flour, as soft as talcum powder, yielding an elegant pizza crust. This is what traditional **Neapolitan pizza** makers use.

Bianca (white): A *pizza bianca* is made without tomato sauce. It may not have any cheese either, resulting in just a flatbread with salt and herbs on top.

Buffalo mozzarella: Mozzarella di bufala is a moist, creamy cheese made from the milk of water buffaloes. It is a hot-ticket item on pizzas, and while it is prized for its delicate flavor, it tends to weep a lot of moisture when it cooks, softening the crust below.

Calzone: Pizza crust folded over to pocket ingredients (aka *stromboli, panzarotti*).

Chicago-style: Chicago has many other styles, including ultra-thin, but the deep-dish pizza, created here in the late 1940s, is its signature. See separate entries on **deep-dish pizza**, **stuffed pizza,** and **pizza pot pie.**

Cornicione: The technical Italian term for the collar or edge at the circumference of a Neapolitan pizza.

D.O.C.: Created in 1955, the Denominazione de Origine Controllata sets standards for many Italian food products, including buffalo mozzarella cheese.

EVOO: Extra-virgin olive oil, the cream of the crop. It has low acidity and a refined taste.

Focaccia: A flatbread, similar to a pizza, but with minimal (or no) toppings.

Grandma pizza: A pizza created in Elmont, New York, cooked in a rectangular pan with a medium-thick crust and minimal toppings. See separate entry on **Grandma pizza.**

Margherita: The classic margherita pizza is made of San Marzano tomatoes, extra-virgin olive oil, fresh basil, mozzarella, and Pecorino Romano. Nothing more, nothing less. It is personal-sized, 12–14 inches in diameter, and the wood-burning oven in which it cooks should be hot enough that it cooks through in approximately 90 seconds.

Marinara: Tomato sauce without meat. A classic Neapolitan topping, with or without cheese.

Neapolitan: Strictly speaking, a Neapolitan pizza is individually sized and cooked in a very hot wood-burning oven, but in America the term is used much more broadly to describe any circular, thin to medium-thin pizza with sauce and cheese and other toppings. See separate entry on **Neapolitan pizza.**

Party cut: A term popular throughout the Midwest and as far east as New Jersey. It refers to a pizza that is cut into squares rather than triangles. Both round and rectangular pizzas can be party cut. The seldom-heard antonym, referring to the triangular slice, is pie cut.

Peel: The long-handled spatula on which pizzaioli assemble a pizza. They then use it to slide the pizza deep into the oven, move it around on the oven floor, and retrieve it when it is done.

Pesto: A concentrated spruce-green paste made of basil, olive oil, garlic, and pine nuts. Frequently spread on pizza in lieu of tomato sauce.

Pizzaiolo: Pizza-maker. The plural is *pizzaioli.* The feminine is *pizzaiola* (which also is the name for a tomato sauce flavored with oregano).

Pumate: Sun-dried tomatoes, usually sold packed in olive oil. They have an intense flavor.

San Marzano tomatoes: Firm plum tomatoes grown in volcanic soil around Naples; especially good for pizza because they have few seed cavities and minimal sugar content.

Sicilian pizza: Thick-crusted, baked in a pan, and almost always rectangular rather than round. Traditional versions do not include cheese but are topped with herbs and seasonings, perhaps with a puttanesca paste. The quality of Sicilian pizza depends overwhelmingly on the dough. It must rise very slowly and the pan in which it cooks must be oiled enough that the crust gets crunchy at its edges but remains cream-soft within, maintaining proud yeast posture. Too dense, too much time elapsed after it is pulled from the oven, overweight toppings: All spell Sicilian disaster.

Tray: Throughout the Northeast and Midwest, rectangular pizzas with medium or thick crusts frequently are referred to not as *pies* but as *trays.*

V.P.N.: The initials stand for Verace Pizza Napoletana, a worldwide organization that trains pizza-makers and certifies that they are making pizza the traditional Neapolitan way.

PLOYE

Eaten in the remote north country of the upper St. John River Valley, a **ploye** (rhymes with toy) is a pancake made by pouring a circle of thin buckwheat batter onto a hot griddle, cooking it very briefly, and never flipping it. The underside gets crisp while the top stays soft and develops countless little holes that are porous enough to absorb substantial amounts of butter and maple syrup or to sop up the last of the gravy from a plate of pot roast. A well-made ploye looks like an especially elegant crumpet or a crepe. In Maine's Aroostook County, they are earthy fare and a symbol of cultural identity. They are thought of with great affection as the daily bread of lumberjacks and as ordinary people's sustenance, traditionally made by farm wives who had minimum resources to feed large families. Acadians use ployes as flatbread, serving stacks of them alongside supper or breakfast. Old-timers eat them spread with *cretons,* a coarse-ground pork hash sweetened with onions. Ployes are mostly the province of home cooks, but a handful of restaurants along the International Boundary make a point of honoring an Acadian culinary heritage that also includes rappie pie (potato casserole), ham-based **boiled dinner,** and the much-maligned but occasionally transcendent **poutine** (fried potatoes and cheese curds smothered with gravy).

A recently invented variation of the ploye is the *ployeboy,* currently available for only a few days in August when served by the American Legion at the annual Muskie Derby and Ploye Festival in Fort Kent at the end of Route 1 in northernmost Maine. Apparently ployeboys took shape during the 2008 Festival when the American Legion ran out of ingredients to make **doughboys** and used ployes instead, dipping a soft buckwheat pancake into the fry kettle just long enough for it to curl at the edges and turn crisp. Brushed with butter and then sprinkled with cinnamon and powdered sugar, the soft pancake is transformed into a wavy buckwheat sugar cookie. Each year, the Festival features ploye-eating contests and hosts the creation (and serving) of the world's largest ploye.

Aroostook County, Maine: A stack of ployes, waiting to be buttered or used as a mop for gravy.

PO' BOY

In the Delaware Valley, a distinction tends to be made between the *sub,* which is hot, and the *hoagie,* which is cold. A Louisiana **po' boy** can be either. In the extended American family of overstuffed sandwiches on lengths of horizontal-sliced bread, the po' boy probably boasts the most diverse variations. It can be roast beef or catfish, a cheeseburger or peppered wiener, ham and cheese or fried oysters and gravy **debris.** When ordering a po' boy of any configuration, the eater will be asked if he wants it dressed. That adds lettuce, tomato, mayonnaise, and, usually, pickles. Variants made with sausage pose another question: Regular mustard or Creole mustard?

Aside from a plethora of great ingredients, the po' boy's distinguishing feature is the bread on which it's made—about one-third lighter than a typical Northeast sub loaf, and with a crisp elegant crust. A large majority of New Orleans po' boy makers use loaves from Leidenheimer Bakery, which has been around since the late nineteenth century. An Acadian variation of the po' boy is sometimes called a *pirogue,* named after the shallow-bottom bayou canoe, and an obsolete nickname is *la mediatrice,* meaning "peace-maker," supposedly because it was the favorite sandwich for a wayward husband to bring back in an attempt to appease his wife. One account says the sandwich originated when it was offered by a French Quarter restaurateur to streetcar workers ("poor boys") during a 1929 strike. Another story is that the original po' boys were simply lengths of bread sopped with gravy, hence affordable by poor boys. Some po' boy shops still offer very inexpensive sandwiches of nothing but gravy and debris, lending some credence to the latter explanation.

New Orleaneans are wild for po' boys made of roast beef with lots of gravy.

POLISH BOY

212

The **Polish Boy** is a sandwich unique to the **barbecue** restaurants of Cleveland, Ohio. Its main ingredient is a massive length of crisp-cased, juice-spurting kielbasa. It is packed into a bun along with French fries and coleslaw, and the whole, huge cylinder of food is sopped with radiant barbecue sauce. You might think utensils would come in handy, but experienced customers easily do it by hand, rolling up sleeves, leaning forward to avoid drippage, and using sheaves of napkins.

POP-TARTS

Test your knowledge of convenience food: Of course you know that Kellogg's Pop-Tarts come two to a packet, but suppose you choose to eat only one. Admittedly, this is an unlikely scenario because, as comedian Paula Poundstone is fond of pointing out in her stand-up routine, after the packet is open, it seems illogical to leave half of it uneaten. But for the sake of argument, let us hypothesize that you are on a diet and you are forced to limit your intake to only one 200-calorie toaster pastry—which, according to the *Nutrition Information* area on the side of the box, is in fact a single serving. What do you call it?

If you said "a Pop-Tart," you are wrong. According to Kellogg, which conceptualized toaster pastries and introduced them to the world in 1964 (originally as Country Squares), even a single slab of the number-one heat-and-eat table tile is properly referred to as a Pop-Tart*s*. The *s* on the end not only confirms Paula Poundstone's craving to eat them in multiples; it also suggests the profusion of Pop-Tarts among America's daily rations.

Pop-Tarts aren't merely very popular; they have become a paramount symbol of corporate creativity—an ingenious method for harried eaters to ingest warm, complex foodstuff almost instantly and without exertion. Plucked from a foil packet in a cardboard box on an unrefrigerated pantry shelf, they need only a few minutes in a toaster to become something that resembles freshly baked food!

We asked Kellogg to tell us who exactly eats them, and their creator responded (and we quote): "Everyone in the country." A nice person in the department of Corporate Communications advised us that the age range of Pop-Tarts eaters was between two and thirty-five, but that most people who eat them are between six and seventeen. The bigger the family (3+ kids), the more likely it is that Pop-Tarts will be a regular staple. At one point, the *My Three Sons* television family were Pop-Tarts spokespeople.

Eighty percent of all Pop-Tarts are eaten warm; in fact, "warmth" is one of the top three reasons people like them ("taste" and "convenience" are the other two). Although nobody mentioned it in the Kellogg surveys to which we were privy, one of the truly remarkable qualities of Pop-Tarts is the way they feel: They are substantial pieces of food, denser and heftier than any pastry you would find in a bakery, and whether they are cold or toasted, fresh from the foil packet or abandoned on the kitchen counter days before, they are relentlessly crisp. A Pop-Tarts's shelf life (in the box) is six to nine months, depending on whether or not it is a fruited variety. No matter how you treat it, it always feels ready to eat; and it is so wieldy that most people don't bother putting it on a plate. The only thing capable of killing a Pop-Tarts is a microwave oven. People too impatient to wait the full two minutes required in a toaster oven wind up with a hideous clump of sodden, fissured dough engulfed by sticky globules of corn syrup, partially hydrogenated oils, dextrose, gelatin, and xanthan gum it once encased.

PORK ROLL

◇◇◇

Pork roll is frequently known by one of its brand names, Taylor Ham, which was created before the Civil War by New Jersey resident John Taylor. Until the government determined that Mr. Taylor's product did not meet the definition of ham, it was known as Taylor's Prepared Ham. Sliced thin and pan-fried, it frequently is used in sandwiches, but it is most popular as breakfast meat in lieu of higher-on-the-hog options such as bacon, sausage, or actual ham. Packed into a hard roll with egg and cheese (known in **diner** slang as a "triple bypass"), it fairly gushes fatty savor. A single slice supplies 26 percent of the fat recommended in a normal daily diet.

Pork roll remains a local passion, beloved with mischievous glee by home-sick Garden Staters. In a Roadfood.com discussion on the subject back in 2008, New Jersey resident Leethebard commented, "Pork roll is NOT Spam or Treet NOR is it like bologna. It has its own taste that needs to be tried . . . I had my breakfast Taylor pork roll, egg and cheese on a crisp Kaiser roll this morning: It starts the day!!!"

POT LIKKER

Pot likker is the spruce-green broth retrieved from the pot in which greens have been boiled. The greens—mustard, collard, turnip, dandelion—cook for hours, leeching vegetable goodness into the water (or, commonly, chicken broth) and giving it a tonic punch like no other soup.

It is customary for the greens to share the pot with a hambone or hunk of fatback, the pork adding a mighty measure of fatty animal savor to the vegetable leaves and to the liquid. But pork is not necessary, as evidenced by the pot likker and greens made at the Little Tea Shop in Memphis. Made without

any pig meat whatsoever (proprietor Suhair Lauck follows halal dietary laws), this soup is verdant, radiating the energy of a plant with leaves that have marinated for weeks in sunlight. The likker is served in a bowl filled with sultry dark greens, the once-tough leaves cooked so limp that you can easily separate a small clump of them with the side of a soup spoon and gather it up with plenty of the liquid. At Mary Mac's Tea Room in Atlanta, diners are instructed to temper the salty smack of their pot likker by crumbling a corn muffin across the surface, adding sweet, earthy heft.

Pot Likker

This meal in a bowl should be served with corn bread. Some dunk it; others crumble it onto the top of the pot likker.

> 3 pounds fresh turnip greens
> 4 cups water
> 1 tablespoon salt
> 1 teaspoon pepper
> ½ pound salt pork, cut into small cubes
> 2 cups chicken broth
> Hot sauce

1. Remove thick stems and *thoroughly* rinse the greens. Rinse them again twice (grit is a problem). Combine the water, salt, and pepper and bring it to boil. Add half the salt pork, and then the greens, mixing as they wilt. Cover the pot and simmer 1 full hour.

2. Fry the remaining salt pork over medium heat until crisp, but not burnt.

3. Thoroughly drain the cooked greens, saving all the liquid. Greens can either be chopped or left whole.

4. Combine the liquid in which the greens were cooked, the fried salt pork and drippings, the chicken broth, and a cup of the cooked greens in a saucepan. (Remaining greens can be refrigerated and served later.) Simmer 5 minutes, adding salt, pepper, and hot sauce to taste.

4–5 CUPS (6 SMALL BUT POWERFUL SERVINGS)

POTATO CHIPS

The first **potato chips** were cooked by Chef George Crumb at the Moon Lake Lodge in 1853 when, the culinary legend says, Cornelius Vanderbilt returned an order of French fries to the kitchen because he thought they were cut too thick. To spite Vanderbilt, Crumb sliced a potato wafer-thin—too thin to be spearable by a fork—and fried the discs. When he sent them into the dining room, instead of getting angry at the sight of see-through slender, brittle spuds, Vanderbilt was delighted. He threw down his fork and ate the fried chips of potato with his hands. A snack food was born, named Saratoga chips for the New York resort town in which the invention took place.

For a good while, they were known only among people in the Northeast, served at the home dinner table to accompany meat or fish and then by seafood restaurants as a companion for raw clams and oysters. It wasn't until the 1920s that they began getting popular in other regions; and by the end of the next decade, as James Beard later recalled, "the ghastly potato-chip-dip invention had . . . begun to spread across the country." After World War II, potato chips' popularity soared because they were so handy for suburban-style casual entertaining in rec rooms or on patios, at teen parties, and—most important of all—as the munchable best-suited for television-watching. Furthermore, the very shape of potato chips seemed to match the era's adoration of things with swoopy curves. *Populuxe,* Thomas Hines's imaginative exegesis of the golden age of American materialism, observed "The potato chip, with its free-form shape and double curving plane, recalled some of the high-design objects of the day—Danish coffee tables and American molded fiberglass and bent plywood chairs. Formally, it is a very short jump from the standard potato chip to the great double-curving furniture of Charles Eames and Eero Saarinen."

The great date in the ascent of the potato chip to supremacy among snack foods is 1954, when **California dip** was invented—a stroke of simple genius, requiring minimal preparation and no utensils for eating. However, California dip and the hundreds of other hot and cold dunks popularized as party food in the fifties tended to be weighty compounds. Ordinary chips frequently broke when plowed into them or, worse, on the way from serving dish to mouth. The solution was the corrugated chip, known by such brand names as Ridgies,

Ruffles, and Dipsy Doodles—all strong enough to dig through even claylike, day-old dip without cracking.

As Americans settled down at their televisions to watch Super Bowls and miniseries in the 1970s, many grew accustomed to bleached-white chips with scarcely a hint of potato flavor, enjoying them for their high salt and fat content. Following the lead of Pringles, a mass-produced chip of uniform size and shape that is sold

Potato chips are a snack food that has gotten better in recent years.

stacked in a can, chip purveyors marketed "potato snack chips" reconstituted from dried potatoes and potato starch, a process that eliminates the inconveniences of actually slicing and frying potatoes (real spuds stick together; they vary wildly in color depending on the sugar content, which changes from season to season).

Sales of bland-tasting, blemish-free chips have never faltered, but at the same time, potato chip connoisseurship has thrived, too. America's myriad regional brands continue to have devotees who treasure their real potato look (mottled, irregularly shaped), their distinctive feel (thicker, brittle, and more fragile), and their actual potato taste. Since the beginning of chip history, small companies have remained an important part of the landscape, supplying local taste with the likes of superspicy Voodoo chips from Zapp's in Cajun country and Luau Barbecue chips from Tim's of Seattle.

Potato chips' new age of excellence began in 1980, when Cape Cod began nationally marketing what it called *kettle-style chips:* sliced thicker than ordinary chips, crunchier, and with a real potato flavor. Kettle chips, which cost more than ordinary ones, are made by hand rather than by the ton on conveyor belts. The best of them, which probably taste something like the original Saratogas, are made in small batches, and the best of the best—the unbearably addictive ones—are still fried in lard and are still salty as hell.

POUTINE

One way to refer to yucky leftovers in colloquial Québécoise is to call them **poutine.** While seldom known by that name south of the International Boundary, non-leftovers poutine is a popular side dish in northernmost Aroostook County, Maine, where it also is known quite simply as *fry mix:* a plate of French fries covered with mozzarella cheese and dark, beefy gravy, the cheese melting into pools. Traditional Canadian poutine is made with **cheese curds** rather than mozzarella, and one story of its origin is that a customer at a cheese

Poutine is rarely called poutine south of the International Boundary. Most northern Maine restaurants bill it as mix or fry mix.

factory in Kingsey Falls asked chef Fernand Lachance to combine the curds and spuds, at which Lachance is said to have declared the combo a mess, aka *poutine.* Variations add sausage, bacon, ground beef, or marinara sauce, and for reasons yet to be known, the same dish is known in New Jersey as *disco fries.*

PROVEL CHEESE

A made-in-Wisconsin pasteurized processed cheese food product distributed primarily in and around St. Louis, **Provel cheese** is a mix of provolone, Cheddar, and Swiss. It can be used in Italianate casseroles and in hot sandwiches, but its most prominent role is on top of **pizzas.** Because it does not weep oil like fattier cheeses, it is an ideal component of the ultra-thin, unleavened-crust pizza St. Louisians prefer. In fact, it was invented in St. Louis in the 1940s when a grocery store in the Hill (the Italian neighborhood) worked with a cheese company to develop something for pizza that didn't stretch and drip like melted mozzarella.

Although made in Wisconsin, Provel cheese is most popular in St. Louis, where it is the standard pizza topper. CHRIS AYERS AND AMY BRIESCH

PUFFY TACO

The taco is a pillar of San Antonio cuisine, served for breakfast, lunch, supper, and snacks, in variations that range from bacon and eggs to *barbacoa* and beyond. No worthwhile taqueria buys its tortillas. Wheat and corn dough are rolled out and cooked on the spot and generally used to wrap the filling of choice within moments of getting lifted off a hot griddle. The puffy taco is made by eliminating the griddle and briefly tossing the uncooked tortilla (usually corn masa, but wheat works, too) into a hot oil bath, causing it to puff up like a **sopaipilla.** A restaurant called Henry's Puffy Tacos claims to

Nearly every taqueria in San Antonio offers puffy tacos as an alternative to those made with griddle-cooked tortillas.

have invented it in 1978, but it is likely that Henry's only named a dish that in fact has been around since at least the 1950s. Deftly made, a puffy taco seems more like air than dough, its crispness evanescent, its flavor deliciously elusive. If the tortilla spends too much time in oil, it can emerge grease-sopped and leaden. Although a simple procedure, the making of tortillas for tacos—especially for puffy tacos—requires a seasoned hand.

RAW FOOD MOVEMENT

The discovery of fire and its subsequent mastery was without doubt a good thing for the human race. It must have been a very happy moment when one of our precocious ancestors realized that a hunk of well-marbled mammoth flesh held over a fire sputtered and dripped fat and tasted especially delicious. Since then, the practice of cooking food is one of the things that has separated *Homo sapiens* from other beasts: We have pots and pans and propane to transform groceries into dinner.

Fie on that, says the **raw food movement,** which started about the same time Sylvester Graham and John Harvey Kellogg were touting big, regular bowel movements as the secret of good health. Raw foodists believe that any cooking whatsoever messes up anything edible. "Cooking foods makes them addictive," recently declared a customer at the Chicagoland restaurant Karyn's, where absolutely nothing is warmed beyond 115 degrees Fahrenheit. Proprietor Karyn Calabrese explained that the act of heating something destroys its enzymes and makes it toxic. Karyn's restaurant, which shares space with a holistic health center offering cellulite treatment, colon therapy, and ear coning (don't ask!), offers ravioli-like food that is actually turnips, pâté made from almonds, pasta that is zucchini, and crepes that are mashed cashews.

Among the proponents of rawism are celebrities Demi Moore, Laura Dern, Woody Harrelson, and Uma Thurman. While most raw foodists also are vegetarians, Mel Gibson represents the Paleolithic branch of the movement, adherents of which believe in eating maximum amounts of raw meat, just like our forebears did before they knew how to start a fire.

RED BEANS AND RICE

Because Creole beans demand a ham bone and ham was a popular Sunday meal in New Orleans, **red beans and rice** became a Monday tradition in homes and restaurants. Nearly every cafe kitchen without airs offers it, but few ever have been famous for it (other than the late, great Buster Holmes). It is, after all, a déclassé dish that relies on leftovers. Always humble, red beans and rice can be transcendent. When made right, each bean, saturated with the savor of pork, delivers silky richness that belies its leguminous virtue; the sausage that is *de rigueur* as a companion to rice and beans is deeply smoky and vividly spiced, its vibrancy balanced by the avoirdupois of rice. Red beans and rice is so soulfully satisfying that it has come to serve as an emblem of proletarian brio, virtue, and warmth. When New Orleans jazz pioneer Louis Armstrong wrote a letter, his complimentary close was "Red beans and ricely yours."

Hearty enough to be a main course, red beans and rice frequently is offered as a side dish.

RED BEER

There are plenty of beers brewed to be red, their blush and burly nature a result of the yeast and malted barley from which they are made. But in taverns of the Nez Perce country, from Moscow, Idaho, to Walla Walla, Washington, **red beer** means something different: beer mixed with tomato juice (or V-8 or Clamato). The exact proportions for a Snake River Bloody Mary range from an effervescent five-to-one, in which the tomato juice barely flavors the beer, to a half-and-half blend reminiscent of a juice-bar smoothie. The garnishes that come in Bloody Marys are anathema. They only get in the way. This is a beverage for gulping. It is drunk for breakfast, lunch, supper, and snacks. *Brunch* remains a seldom-heard term in red beer country.

RED BULL

Energy drinks have been around since the Scots started bottling Iron Brew at the beginning of the twentieth century (now marketed as Irn-Bru so consumers aren't led to believe that it actually is brewed). Gatorade, named for the University of Florida football team that drank it to play harder, has been on the market since the 1960s. But it was Jolt Cola, introduced in the mid-1980s with the slogan, "All the sugar and twice the caffeine," that opened the floodgates to the contemporary market of high-octane, nonalcoholic libations. There now are more than a hundred brands, grossing some $10 billion annually in the United States alone. The wide-awake, 900-pound gorilla among them is **Red Bull,** which accounts for nearly half of all energy drinks sold in America.

Red Bull, which originated in Austria, hit the States in 1987. A single can has less than a coffee cup's worth of caffeine, but it is turbocharged by taurine (inspiration for the beverage's bovine name), which originally was derived from bull bile but is now made synthetically. In addition to taurine, which the body needs to support the stress of vigorous exercise, it contains vitamins B6 and B12, niacin, and glucose, all adding up to a seismic kick in the head and heart. You won't get drunk sucking down four Red Bulls, but you will get seriously buzzed, sometimes to the point of panic. One study indicated that a single serving will put a normal person at the same risk of having a heart attack as someone with coronary disease, and in early 2009 a woman died after drinking four cans (plus, it must be noted, a quart of VK, which is vodka *plus* caffeine), but it is generally considered no more harmful (or helpful) to physical well-being than strong coffee. Actually, Red Bull is relatively mild compared to such energy drinks as Speed Freak Fruit Punch, Endorush Orange Fix, the briefly marketed Cocaine Energy Drink, and the strongest of all, Wired X505, of which each serving contains six coffees' worth of caffeine, quadruple the taurine in Red Bull, and approximately 1000 percent of the daily recommended dose of B vitamins.

Although it has been around for more than twenty years, Red Bull, in the svelte can that is slimmer than dowdy old soda pop, remains a happening beverage, especially among the young and the restless. Two-thirds of the people who regularly consume energy drinks are under thirty-five years old, most of those students, a segment of society that typically never gets enough sleep.

RED FLANNEL HASH

Hash used to be a dirty word, and to call a restaurant a *hash house* still has an unsavory connotation. That's because dubious eateries of yore used to make hash out of any old scraps that appeared in the kitchen, including mystery meat of unknown provenance. But the fact is that well-made hash is one of the great blue-plate meals of the American kitchen. It is especially typical of thrifty New England kitchens because it is a waste-not dish, made from leftovers. If it is made from yesterday's **boiled dinner**—and if that dinner was the classic configuration containing beets—it will be **red flannel hash,** so named because of beet juice's ability to turn all it touches a deep pink color reminiscent of comfortable flannel pajamas. Corned beef adds its own crimson hue, the two reds punctuated by pieces of potato and caramelized onion. Bacon frequently is added, especially if the corned beef is lean.

Red flannel hash is closely associated with New England, but we found this excellent example at Rick & Ann's Coffee Shop in Berkeley, California.

RED-EYE GRAVY

When **country ham** is served, **red-eye gravy** is its natural condiment. It is a salty, viscous liquid that is made by combining rendered fat attained when ham slices are fried with black coffee. It serves to moisten slices of fried ham or as a dunk for biscuits on the side. One tall tale says it got its name because when you look in the pitcher, the swirly spiral of ham drippin's resembles a blood-shot eye. While a well-set country table demands it, diners seeking maximum caloric intake will find *pepper cream gravy* more appropriate.

RED HOTS

Chicagoans call hot dogs **red hots.** Frankfurter historians believe the red hot as we know it was first configured in 1929 by Abe "Fluky" Drexler at the erst-while street bazaar on Maxwell Street. The Vienna Beef sausage company had been supplying sausages to vendors since the Columbian Exposition of 1893, but Drex-ler's genius was to bun the sausage and top it with so many condiments that it seemed more like a meal than a snack.

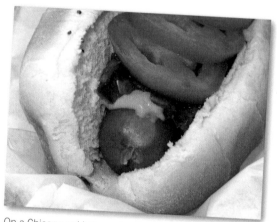

Today, nearly 2000 vendors sell red hots in Chicagoland, and the question of who serves the best is a source of never-ending debate. The curious thing is that most of Chicago's purveyors use the very same **hot dog**: Vienna brand all-beef. The differences are in how it is cooked, the variety and quality of the condiments, and the fresh-ness of the bun. The hot dog itself is no slouch: long and fairly slim, dense-textured

On a Chicago red hot, mustard and relish are fundamental. Tomato slices are common, as are pickle spears, which are not shown.

and with a garlic kick, packed tight in a natural casing. Most places steam it until taut enough that a first bite erupts with savory juices.

Other than New England, where the bun of choice is a split-top affair suitable for grilling crisp, and Tucson, where Mexican *bolillo* rolls are used to encase **Sonoran hot dogs,** Chicago boasts the nation's highest bun consciousness. A Windy City red hot comes nestled in a steamy-soft, gentle-flavored pocket of fleecy bread, preferably one from Rosen's bakery spangled with poppy seeds across its tan outsides. Although they run contrary to most bread-lovers' passion for crustiness and character, they are far more than just a handy mitt to hold the meat. Their gentleness is an absolutely necessary soft-flavor environment that abets full appreciation of the spicy red hot and its condiments.

A vocal coterie of fans believe that anything beyond mustard, relish, and hot peppers is overkill . . . and untrue to the soul of a red hot, which is, they contend, Bauhaus-simple. Nevertheless, conventional wisdom asserts that it's the constellation of condiments that elevate Chicago wieners to a higher plane. Indeed, no franks keep better bun company. Bright yellow mustard and radioactive-green piccalilli are the basics, but nearly every good red hot purveyor offers plenty more, so much more that the now dearly departed Gold Coast Dogs on State Street saw fit to display a technical drawing titled "Anatomy of a Gold Coast Hot Dog," which precisely diagramed all the vital components: the all-beef dog, the poppy-seeded bun, yellow mustard, green relish, sport peppers, raw onions, two full slices of tomato, a bun-length pickle spear, and a dusting of celery salt. Throughout the city, when you ask for a dog with the works, only the sport peppers are considered optional, and don't dare ask for ketchup. On a Chicago red hot, it is taboo, as much a heresy as mayo on a pastrami sandwich in New York.

REUBEN

Corned beef, sauerkraut, Swiss cheese, and Russian or **1000 Islands dressing** sandwiched in rye bread and grilled: That is a **Reuben** sandwich, which any New York foodie will tell you was created at Reuben's Delicatessen. The late Arnold Reuben (who is believed to have invented the double-decker sandwich and was the first New York restaurateur to name sandwiches for celebrities) said he first made it in 1914 as a late-night, clean-the-kitchen dish for a hungry actress who wanted an especially hearty sandwich.

Nebraskans have a completely different story of origin, which traces the sandwich to the Blackstone Hotel in the late 1920s, where Omaha butcher Reuben Kulakofsky came up with the idea and shared it with his poker buddy, Charles Schimmel, the hotel's owner. Schimmel started serving it for lunch in his dining room, known as the Plush Horse, and in the mid-1950s, Fern Snider, former Blackstone waitress, won the National Sandwich Idea Contest with the recipe.

No matter whether it was invented in New York or Nebraska, the Reuben now is nearly everywhere in the USA.

Variations of the Reuben include the Rachel, which substitutes pastrami for corned beef (and, sometimes, coleslaw for sauerkraut), and the Southern Reuben, in which **barbecue** sauce is substituted for Russian dressing.

RHODE ISLAND CHICKEN DINNER

All around Woonsocket, in the Blackstone Valley north of Providence, the nation's smallest state sports big restaurants that serve gigantic meals built around boundless bowls of roast chicken. Sides always include pasta and fried potatoes, a garlicky salad, and baskets of bread. For dessert: ice cream and coffee. Meals in **Rhode Island's chicken dinner** halls are dished out family-style, all-you-can-eat.

The state's habit of abundant weekly poultry feasts—an inland echo of its passion for multicourse **shore dinners**—took shape at the Bocce Club in the 1920s when the Pavoni family began serving dinner to friends who came to their house to play bocce. Today's biggest purveyor of chicken dinners, and one of the largest restaurants in the nation, is Wright's Farm, which actually began as the chicken farm where the Pavonis bought their birds. Every night it is open, Wright's Farm's seventy-five ovens send out over a ton of chicken to six cavernous dining rooms that can seat over 1200 people at one time.

RIBS

◇◇

Ribs are among the most beloved of barbecued meats, and the most diverse. They can be wet (slathered with sauce) or dry (packed with dry rub); they can be pork or beef (the latter huge, caveman-style) or even mutton; they might be slow-cooked in a classic **barbecue** pit or more quickly done over charcoal. Here are basic definitions of pork ribs:

Spare ribs on the grill at Curtis's Barbecue in Putney, Vermont.

BABY BACK RIBS

Also known as *loin back ribs*, baby backs are the easiest kind of rib to eat with the largest percentage of meat to bone. Slightly curved and fairly small—about three inches long—they are quite wieldy and hence a favorite in more polite restaurants, where big, sloppy bones would be uncouth. Baby backs come about a dozen to a rack.

RIBLESS RIBS

For those who are dentally challenged or simply don't want to expend the effort required to pull meat from bones, some restaurants offer *pork steak*, which is rib meat only. Jigg's Smoke House in Clinton, Oklahoma, offers a rib meat sandwich known as a *triple pigsickle*.

SPARE RIBS

Flatter and longer than baby back ribs, spare ribs have more bone than meat and what meat they do have is striated with more fat. That means that they are intrinsically more flavorful, especially when cooked low and slow enough for the fat to insinuate itself into the fibers of the meat.

ST. LOUIS RIBS

St. Louis ribs are spare ribs from which the tips have been cut away, yielding a rectangular slab that is flat and very easy to disassemble and eat, rib by rib.

TIPS

Tips are the least expensive item on barbecue restaurant menus, and compared to full ribs that offer long strips of meat, they demand significant worrying with teeth and tongue to retrieve all the good stuff. The work is rewarded by intense flavor and great textural variety.

Memphis Dry Ribs

One of the best-known ribberies in Memphis is the raucous, subterranean dining room named Charlie Vergo's Rendezvous. Vergos serves what are known as dry ribs—sauceless. You won't miss the sauce, because the ribs are encrusted with the flavor of a powerhouse dry rub. Used in abundance, the rub not only seasons the meat; it helps keep the juices in. Warning: Have plenty of ice tea and/or beer on hand to accompany dry rubbed ribs!

2 tablespoons brown sugar
2 tablespoons coarsely ground black pepper
1½ teaspoons ground white pepper
2 tablespoons paprika
1 tablespoon chili powder
1½ teaspoons crushed red pepper flakes
1 teaspoon garlic powder
1½ teaspoons salt
2 3-pound racks of St. Louis–style spare ribs

1. Combine all seasonings and rub them vigorously into the ribs. Wrap well or seal in a tight container several hours or overnight.

2. Set your smoker to 250°F and cook ribs about 6 hours.

3. If you do not have a smoker, start your outdoor charcoal grill. Place the charcoal grate at its lowest setting and the food rack at the highest setting. When the coals are white-hot, move them all to one side. Place the ribs on the cold side. If desired, add dampened hickory chips to the fire and close the lid, aligning the vent holes in its top to get maximum smoke flow across the meat. Add chips every hour or so and charcoal as needed to keep the fire smoldering.

4. You know the ribs are done when only moderate pressure begins to slide meat off the bone. If desired, use a cleaver to hack the racks into manageable lengths of 3–4 bones.

Memphis Wet Ribs

Sticky, sweet, peppery, porky, and finger-sucking delicious, wet ribs—glazed with sauce—are the star of barbecue pit. Be sure to serve them with rolls of paper towels and plenty of moist towelettes. Ordinary napkins, whether paper or linen, are useless.

½ cup light brown sugar
½ teaspoon salt
½ teaspoon garlic salt
¼ cup chili powder
2 teaspoons cracked black pepper
2 3-pound slabs St. Louis–style ribs

Glaze:
1 cup light brown sugar
¼ cup cider vinegar
½ cup barbecue sauce (your favorite)

1. Mix together all the seasonings. Pat spices evenly all over the ribs.

2. Start your smoker (set to 250°F) or fire up the backyard charcoal grill with the charcoal as low in the kettle as it will go and the meat rack as high as it will go.

3. When the coals are white-hot, push them all to one side of the grill and place the rib racks on the other side. Close the lid and adjust the vent holes so the coals just barely smolder. If they flame up, moisten them with a spray of water. If the fire is dying, add white-hot charcoals to keep it cooking for 6 hours. If desired, you can periodically add damp hickory chips to the charcoals for flavor.

4. If using a smoker, the time will be about the same, up to 6 hours.

5. While the ribs smoke, mix together the glaze ingredients. Apply glaze to ribs during the last 15–20 minutes of cooking. (Earlier than that and the glaze will singe.) The ribs are done when the meat will slide fairly easily off the bone.

RIPPER

In New Jersey's frankfurter patois, a **ripper** is a **hot dog** deep-fried long enough for its skin to tear. The best known purveyor of rippers—and likely the place where the nickname originated—is Rutt's Hut in Clifton, where ripper variations include a *cremator*, which is cooked long enough to shrivel and turn chewy, a *weller*, which also is well-done, but not to such an extreme, and an *in-and-outer*, which is hoisted from the boiling oil after only a short spell, thus remaining pink and plump. Rutt's Hut rippers are approximately 2-to-1 beef-to-pork and are offered with a proprietary relish that includes mustard, onions, carrots, and cabbage.

At left, a naked ripper. Right, a ripper topped with Rutt's Hut's proprietary relish.

RIVER HERRING

Since 2006 the National Oceanic and Atmospheric Administration has designated **river herring** a "species of concern." That means the population has declined steeply, and in North Carolina along the Roanoke River, where eating river herring has long been a tradition, fishing frequently is suspended. So even if it is the right time of the year—January through April, when they swim upstream to spawn—there is no guarantee of herring for supper.

Leslie Gardner, who, with his wife, Sally, runs one of the last remaining herring shacks, the Cypress Grill, in Jamesville, North Carolina, explained to us that herring were a local staple well into the middle of the twentieth century. "Fish you catch in the river taste nothing like ones from the ocean," he asserted. "By the time they get here, they are eating plankton from the river, and they taste better." He recalled that once it was not uncommon for fishermen to net 500,000 or more of the gleaming silver sardines in a single day. Today, the population of the Roanoke River, which is a prime breeding area, is reserved strictly for sport fishermen and cannot be sold commercially.

Those lucky enough to find a herring shack like the Cypress Grill at a time when herring are available should know that these delicate fish, sheathed in cornmeal and fried, have a nomenclature of their own. *Sunnyside up* means a quick fry, yielding a fish that is as rich as butter itself, especially when accompanied by fried-crisp packets of opulent roe. On the other hand, *cremated* herring is fried long enough that the meat, crust, and even the little bones are a single, savory mass as rich as a hunk of well-done bacon.

ROUND TABLE DINING

Round table dining is an old Southern boarding house ritual for which guests are seated at a circular table big enough for fifteen or twenty places. In the center is a lazy Susan nearly as big as the table, leaving enough room at the perimeter for plates, tea tumblers, and silverware. All the platters, bowls, casseroles, breadbaskets, pitchers, and condiment jars are set out on the lazy Susan. When you want something, spin it and grab.

What fun! It's practical, too: cuts down on the reaching, stretching, and "pass-it-to-me's" that obstruct ordinary boarding house meals. Whenever a serving tray on the lazy Susan gets close to empty, a member of the staff snatches it back to the kitchen and returns with a full one.

A few matters of etiquette and protocol need to be mastered to take full advantage of a round table meal. For instance, it is considered bad form to spin the table counterclockwise merely to nab something out of reach to your left. If the table is moving in one direction, you'll just have to wait until those candied yams come around again. (Don't worry; round tables travel *fast*!)

You will also have to figure out what to do if you have hefted the squash casserole off the lazy Susan so you can spoon some out, but the table has spun on, leaving you no free space in which to return the bowl. (You might try offering it to your neighbor, sticking him with the problem of waiting for an empty space to circle 'round.) As for how much it is polite and proper to eat, that was

On the wall in the dining room at the old Mendenhall Hotel in Mississippi, this sampler encouraged guests to reach for seconds.

explained by a needlepoint sampler on the wall of the late Mendenhall Hotel in Mendenhall, Mississippi, where round table dining was devised nearly a century ago. It read: EAT TIL IT OUCHES YOU.

SALAD BAR

Depending on where you are and which restaurant you're in, **salad bar** can mean anything from cold iceberg lettuce and bottled store-brand dressing to potluck Sunday supper of **hot dishes,** composed salads, and baroque Jell-Os. Historians trace the phenomenon to the mid-twentieth century and one of three possible sites of origin: The Cliffs, a Springfield, Massachusetts, restaurant that advertised a *salad bar buffet* as early as 1950; Chuck's Steak House, which began in Waikiki in 1959 and gave steak eaters the opportunity to fill a plate with salad fixin's and slice-it-yourself bread as their steak cooked; and R. J. Grunt's, the singles bar/restaurant that in 1971 became the cornerstone of Chicago's hugely successful Lettuce Entertain You Enterprises by offering a plethora of choices so substantial that a main course wasn't necessary.

Long before the term *salad bar* was coined, its spiritual ancestor, known as *seven sweets and seven sours,* had become a much appreciated feature of the groaning-board meals tourists expect when visiting Pennsylvania Dutch country. The name is not literal, for frequently there are more than merely seven

A selection from the Dutch Kitchen's salad bar.

bowls of sweet and/or tangy pre-served vegetables and fruits on the table to accompany such stalwart fare as roast ham or pot pie thick with dumplings sided by mashed potatoes, bread filling (aka stuffing), and corn pudding. The spread offers a variety of bright, brilliant flavors to provide rejuvenation for a palate confronting monumental heaps of protein and starch.

No region of the country has riffed more bountifully on the concept than the Midwestern heartland, where the salad bar principle is a reflection of the same hospitable spirit that animates church suppers: the more, the merrier. Lettuce, tomatoes, radishes, and other such rabbit food may not even appear on vast tables where customers graze along an array of such concoctions as green peas with Miracle Whip and shredded cheese, beef 'n' bean taco towers, pineapple/Cool Whip ambrosia, macaroni salad with pickle bits and crumbled hard-boiled eggs, carrot-raisin slaw, soups, breads, muffins, fruit cobbler, and butterscotch pudding.

It must be noted that epidemiologists consider salad bars the gastronomic equivalent of Chernobyl. While the danger of direct germ salvos is minimized by the evocatively named "sneeze guard" (the plastic panel that according to New York state law must be "mounted so as to intercept a direct line between the customer's mouth and the food display area"), some cootie conveyance is inevitable. A University of California study of salad bar behavior noted that 60 percent of customers commit at least one infraction of basic food safety, foremost among them:

- Spilling food out of the container

- Dipping fingers for sample licks

- Eating from plates while waiting in line

- Ducking heads underneath the sneeze guard for better access

SALT WATER TAFFY

No family-friendly seaside resort is without purveyors of **salt water taffy,** the bite-size pastel bonbon that evokes good times in waves and sunshine. Despite the name and its association with the ocean, it contains no salt water. According to Joseph Marini of Marini's candy store on the Santa Cruz, California, boardwalk, the confection was named in 1907, after a shoreline fire was extinguished using seawater pumped up from a fireboat. Finding his taffy spritzed, Joseph's great-grandfather, Victor Marini, staged a "salt water taffy" sale on the boardwalk . . . and the name stuck. "He used to tell kids that every morning he walked to the end of the wharf to fill five-gallon buckets of salt water to make the candy," Joseph remembers. "In fact, we use no salt at all in our taffy."

The East Coast story of conception goes back to 1880 and the Atlantic City boardwalk. Built above sea level to keep sand from creeping into hotel lobbies, the broad wooden walkway featured a taffy stand at St. James Place run by candy man David Bradley. One night, strong winds and a high tide sent ocean foam all over Bradley's supply of just-made taffy. Extremely grumpy that his stock had been dampened, he sarcastically corrected a little girl who stepped up the next morning and asked for taffy. "You mean *salt water taffy!*" he sneered. The child nodded yes; he sold her some; and later that day her boasts of buying salt water taffy were overheard by Bradley's mother. A bulb illuminated above Mom's head, and the next summer when Bradley opened his candy store, he printed signs that advertised a unique—or more precisely, a uniquely named—product.

SAUERKRAUT BALLS

We have been unable to find out anything about the genealogy of **sauerkraut balls,** which are a specialty of Ohio—Akron in particular. Clearly the basic ingredients of ground pork and sauerkraut reflect the strong Central and Eastern European culinary traditions that continue to infuse the northern part of the state, but there must be more than that to the story of their Buckeye identity or else you'd find them also in Milwaukee, Chicago, and the Texas Hill Country.

The LEXICON of REAL AMERICAN FOOD

They are an hors d'oeuvre. About the size of Ping-Pong balls, they are presented in most restaurants by the half dozen, usually with a frilled toothpick stuck in each one. They come sizzling hot, straight from the deep fryer, with a tough golden crust around the moist mélange of kraut and pork inside. The traditional condiment is a red cocktail sauce with some horseradish bite.

In 1996, readers of the *Akron Beacon-Journal* voted sauerkraut balls the city's official food. When the Akron Aeros played the Portland (Maine) Sea Dogs for the AA Eastern League baseball championship in 2006, Jim Cohen, the mayor of Portland, was prepared to send Akron's mayor, Don Plusquellic, a basket full of Maine lobsters if his team lost. But it was the Aeros who lost, and so Mayor Plusquellic sent Mayor Cohen sauerkraut balls.

Sauerkraut Balls

¾ cup finely chopped ham
¼ cup finely chopped onion
1 teaspoon minced parsley
1 tablespoon butter
⅓ cup flour, plus more for rolling
½ teaspoon dry mustard
⅓ cup milk
1 cup thoroughly drained cooked sauerkraut
2 eggs, lightly beaten
Dry unflavored bread crumbs
Cooking oil for frying

1. Mix ham, onion, and parsley and sauté them in butter until the onion is soft. Stir in flour and mustard. Add milk, stirring constantly until thick. Add sauerkraut.

2. Pulverize the mixture in a food processor or food grinder. Let mixture cool.

3. Preheat oil in a deep skillet or deep fryer to 360°F. Form the cooled mixture into spheres a little less than 1 inch in diameter. Roll each in flour, then dip it in eggs, then dip it in bread crumbs. Fry in hot fat until the balls are well-browned, about 3 minutes. Serve warm with cocktail sauce.

ABOUT 24 SAUERKRAUT BALLS

SAUGY

Rhode Island is a small state with a big culinary personality: unique dishes, funny names for dishes, and strange ways of serving familiar dishes. And not one, but two **hot dog** cultures of its own. The better-known one is **New York System** weenies, but any Ocean State tube steak devotee wants you to know also about **Saugys.** Actually a brand name (Saugy's), the word may be used as a synonym for *hot dog,* but a real Saugy dog is something special: a chubby reddish-pink frank in a natural casing that snaps dramatically each time it is bitten. Saugys are rarely, if ever, topped with the sort of spicy meat sauce used on New York Systems. Mustard, onions, and perhaps sauerkraut are the usual condiments, and the roll is a Yankee split-top. Saugys are sold in grocery stores and delis but seldom served in restaurants. The company, founded by Alphonse Saugy in 1869, went out of business in 2001 but reorganized and reopened the next year.

SAZERAC

Like Coca-Cola, the **Sazerac** began as medicine. Instead of cocaine, its healing agent was—and continues to be—alcohol. It was concocted in New Orleans in the 1830s by Antoine Peychaud, who ran a pharmacy and served his potion to customers who frowned on drinking (as well as on the taxes applied to adult beverages) but were perfectly happy to enjoy their medicine. In its earliest incarnation, the Sazerac (named for the French cognac it contained) included absinthe. After 1912, when absinthe was banned for driving people insane, Pernod or Herbsaint was substituted.

Peychaud served his drink in the sort of egg cup bartenders use to measure out jiggers of liquor. In French, the name for this cup is *coquetier* which, when pronounced while drunk, sounds something like *cocktail.* It is speculated that the Sazerac was in fact the first drink called a cocktail. It has been declared the official cocktail of New Orleans—the nation's only formally designated official cocktail—but after a legislative slugfest in 2008, lawmakers refused to make it the official cocktail of Louisiana. A state senator who voted against it worried, "Is there a possibility that we could be encouraging folks, who were not intending to drink, that it would be acceptable and they could become an alcoholic?"

SCHAUM TORTE

A traditional Austrian **schaum torte** is meringue topped with berries and whipped cream. There is nothing wrong with that, but in Wisconsin, when you see it on a menu, you should expect more. In lieu of whipped cream or in addition to it, the meringue may be topped with rich, eggy **frozen custard.** Or it may be transmogrified into what is locally known as a *cream torte:* a layer of graham cracker crumbs or gingersnap crumbs topped with a thick ribbon of cheesecake, the flavor of which cannot be described any more accurately than fresh heavy cream. Atop the dairy-rich block of edible alabaster will be a layer of blueberries or strawberries, giving the dessert a fruity twist.

SCONE

Although Utah's legislature has proclaimed Jell-O to be the state's official snack food, the **scone,** in our opinion, would be more appropriate. Not that Utahans don't eat a large amount of Jell-O, but so do folks in Maine, Kansas, and California. Nowhere else do people eat scones like those served in Utah.

Exactly why it is called a *scone* remains a mystery, since it is nothing like the dense Scottish quick bread that has become a familiar coffee companion in caffeine stations around the country. In fact, it most resembles (and is no doubt a descendant of) the **sopaipilla** of New Mexico and the **Navajo fry bread** found throughout the Southwest. A puffy, deep-fried pillow of sweet yeast dough that develops a slightly crisp skin around airy insides, a scone is served hot from the kettle, accompanied by a pitcher or squeeze bottle of honey. Utah's modern scone shops offer them dolloped with jelly and jam and even a la moded with ice cream.

SCRAMBLED DOG

Scrambled dog means two different but related things in southern Georgia. At most of the lunch counters that serve it, the scrambled dog is a bright red **hot dog** in a toasted bun topped with meat-and-bean chili that includes a full measure of chopped onions. A few places quite literally scramble the dog by cutting it into pieces and mixing it with the chili, condiments, oyster crackers, and slices of dill pickle. At Dinglewood Pharmacy in Columbus, scrambled dogs are presented in a shallow rectangular dish with a long-handled spoon sticking out from under everything. The spoon is essential, as no bun is included.

SCRAPPLE

Scrapple is a loaf of pork and cornmeal that is sliced and fried to a crisp, appearing as breakfast meat in the Mid-Atlantic states. Unlike bacon, sausage, and ham, which make nearly every pig-eating human very happy, scrapple is a love-it-or-hate-it proposition. Originally a Pennsylvania Dutch dish (called *ponhaus*), scrapple's lack of appeal stems mostly from its visceral essence. Its taste and aroma are clear evidence that it is not ham, sausage, or bacon; it is, as its name implies, pig scraps. Like such similar ignominia as fried testicles (**gonads**) and **livermush,** scrapple tends to inspire lofty hyperbole among its fans. The overbearing praise serves as a preemptive strike against nonbelievers who wail about its repulsiveness.

SHAVE ICE

Shave ice is a snow cone with class. Yes, it is ice and flavoring, but rather than being chopped and clumpy, shave ice is as fluffy as freshly fallen snow. Whereas the ice and syrup in a normal snow cone never quite blend, shave ice literally sops up its flavor and delivers such intensely compelling refreshment that brain freeze is a near-certain side effect.

With historical antecedents in Asia and in Hawaii, shave ice was originally a time-consuming product to make, requiring that the ice actually be shaved from a block with knives. That changed in 1934 when Ernest Hansen of New Orleans invented a machine that shaves ice. Five years later, he opened Hansen's Snow-Bliz, where homemade tropical syrups were applied to the ice in layers. Now run by Hansen's granddaughter, the little shop continues to set the gold standard, offering shave ice with such special flavors as cream of peach and cream of coffee, tart satsuma and limeade, as well as luxury toppings that include condensed milk, marshmallow, crushed pineapple, and whipped cream.

SHEBOYGAN BRAT

A *brat* (rhymes with "hot" and is short for *bratwurst*) can be made of almost any kind of meat and cooked almost any way, but to be a **Sheboygan brat,** it must be cooked over charcoal. Cooking over coals is so much a signature of this community north of Milwaukee that many Wisconsinites refer to anything cooked on a grill as Sheboygan-style food. The makin's of a Sheboygan brat usually are pork or pork and beef; chicken, venison, and turkey are alternatives. Despite differing ingredients, nearly all Sheboygan brats are served in a similar manner: as a pair in a hard roll with mustard, pickle, and onions and—another crucial element, reflecting their Dairy State roots—plenty of melted butter. It is OK for a brat enthusiast to add ketchup to the mix or delete the pickles or choose fried onions over raw ones, but unless one bellies up to the bar with an exculpatory note signed by a cardiologist, all Sheboygan hot meat sandwiches—brat, burger, or butterflied pork chop—are served dripping butter.

The rolls on which Sheboygan brats are served look like regular hard rolls, but they have a unique consistency that combines light weight and ruggedness. The surface of a brat roll is tough and chewy—essential for shoring in juices that sop its fluffy interior. All kinds of places serve brats, from convenience stores to linen-tablecloth restaurants, but their natural habitat is at the counter or in a booth of a corner tavern.

SHOOFLY PIE

Shoofly pie is a legacy of Amish cooks for whom electric-powered refrigerators are anathema. There are several explanations for the name of shoofly pie, the most unlikely being that its crumbly top vaguely resembles the texture of a cauliflower and *shoofly* is a corruption of the French word *choufleur,* meaning "cauliflower." More logically, consider that once it is baked, a shoofly pie should be set out to cool. Loaded with molasses and brown sugar, it is fly bait supreme. Somebody needs to shoo them away.

Coffee never had such a righteous companion as a wedge of shoofly pie.

There are two basic forms: wet-bottom shoofly pie, which is a huge-flavored, ooey-gooey confection as sweet as any pecan pie, and dry-bottom shoofly pie, which is more like a coffee cake, made from the same ingredients, but in proportions that are less sticky and more crumbly.

SHORE DINNER

The oldest feast in America is a **clambake**—clams and corn layered in seaweed over hot stones—a recipe the Pilgrims learned from the native Algonquin. Ensuing cooks added fish and sausage and lobster and **chowder** and **clam cakes** and **Indian pudding** and strawberry shortcake to the formula, creating the mighty, multicourse **shore dinner** that was a common summer banquet in Downeast eating halls

Lobster, potatoes, corn, steamers, and lots of melted butter: A nice shore dinner along the coast of Maine.

well into the twentieth century. Greatest among them was the Rocky Point Park Shore Dinner Hall of Warwick Neck, Rhode Island, which sat 4000 people at long, paper-topped tables and offered a choice of meals, either a smaller all-you-can-eat deal of clam cakes, chowder, and watermelon, or the complete dinner of lobster, chowder, clam cakes, steamers, baked fish, bread, boiled potatoes, corn, and warm Indian pudding. Rocky Point Park closed in 1995 and today, while many restaurants along the Northeast coast offer some kind of shore dinner, the big-bore Yankee banquet is, with rare exception, a thing of the past.

SHRIMP DE JONGHE

Firm peeled shrimp enveloped in a paste of bread crumbs laced with garlic, sherry, butter, and thyme are packed into a casserole dish and then baked until the crumbs bubble and the rim becomes a dark crust. **Shrimp De Jonghe** is strictly a Chicago dish, more popular among home cooks than in restaurants, where its old-fashioned casserole character puts it at odds with cutting-edge cookery.

It does go back at least a century, although its exact provenance is uncertain. Nancy Buckley, granddaughter of Pierre De Jonghe, believes it was Pierre who invented it after arriving in America from France for the Columbian Exposition in 1893. He and three brothers and three sisters opened a restaurant on Monroe Street downtown in 1899, and it was there the dish was created, either by Pierre himself or by Pierre and the restaurant's chef, Emil Zehr. The De Jonghe family sold the restaurant when Prohibition became law (with no wine for cooking, what was the point?), and it finally closed in the 1930s. Nevertheless, the evocatively aromatic dish lived on, and while it used to be available in many middle-class dining rooms throughout the city and suburbs, it now is more likely to be an off-the-menu special in white-tablecloth restaurants and steak houses.

Shrimp De Jonghe

All recipes for shrimp De Jonghe contain pretty much the same ingredients, the primary difference among them being how much garlic is used. One clove results in a chafing-dish meal reminiscent of ladies lunch. Six cloves make a macho casserole.

2 pounds jumbo shrimp, shelled and deveined
1½ sticks salted butter, softened
1 cup fine dry bread crumbs
⅓ cup minced fresh parsley leaves
½ cup dry sherry
1–6 cloves garlic, minced
1 teaspoon salt
Dash of cayenne pepper
Dash of paprika
Toast points (optional)

1. Add the shrimp to a kettle of salted boiling water and cook until barely pink, about 2 minutes. (Shrimp will not be cooked through.) Drain shrimp and cool.

2. Preheat the oven to 375°F. Butter a shallow casserole just large enough to hold all the shrimp in one layer.

3. Stir together the butter, bread crumbs, parsley, sherry, garlic, salt, cayenne pepper, and paprika.

4. Place the shrimp in the prepared casserole and spoon the bread crumb mixture evenly over them.

5. Bake until the crumbs are golden brown and sizzling, about 30 minutes.

6. Serve shrimp on toast points, if desired.

4–6 SERVINGS

SHRINE OF THE HOLY TORTILLA (OR, WAITER, WHAT'S THIS SAVIOR DOING IN MY BURRITO?)

Usually it's gross to find something unexpected in your food, but when the surprise is holy, it's a miracle. The best-known sighting in the last half century happened in October 1977, when Maria Rubio of Lake Arthur, New Mexico, gazed at the browned area on a tortilla she had heated in a skillet and saw Jesus. Family, neighbors, and friends were summoned to corroborate the kitchen vision, and Mrs. Rubio convinced a local priest to bless it. She subsequently created the **Shrine of the Holy Tortilla,** mounting the flatbread under glass in a shed behind her home. Tens of thousands of pilgrims journeyed to Mrs. Rubio's backyard exhibit to pray for the tortilla's blessings.

Mrs. Rubio did not turn her vision into cash, but the rapture of an edible advent is often complemented by financial good fortune. One of the most famous eBay auctions, in November 2004, was for a ten-year-old, partially eaten melted cheese sandwich that had come off the grill with an image of the Virgin Mary and, according to the auction listing, had brought its original owner a decade of good luck in casinos. The hammer price for the sandwich was $28,000; its seller soon also auctioned the pan in which it was cooked for $5999.99. (The buyer of both sandwich and pan was the online casino GoldenPalace.com, which also has been winning bidder in auctions for Britney Spears's egg salad sandwich and four toilets once owned by Jerry Garcia.)

Godly victuals are not confined to Christianity. After a Kazakhstani chicken laid an egg with Allah's name inscribed on its shell in 2006, the chicken farmer said he was convinced that the egg's sanctity would keep it from spoiling. But not all such apparitions are eternal. Being food, they rot. By the time we saw the legendary Jesus tortilla of New Mexico in the mid-1990s, Southwest sun and natural decay had transformed His three-by-three-inch face into an abstract pattern that not even Hermann Rorschach would recognize. And five years ago, when Maria Rubio's granddaughter brought the tortilla to school for show and tell, it dropped and smashed to pieces on the floor. The shrine was closed and the tortilla's remains were entombed in a drawer at Mrs. Rubio's home.

SLIDER

Formerly a disrespected black sheep in the hamburger family, the **slider** became trendy in the early twenty-first century. For a while, it was not unusual to find one-ounce hamburgers nestled in brioche microbuns served as a butlered hors d'oeuvre at cocktail parties and on menus in expensive taverns. A gourmet slider might taste good—what's not to like about a divot of grilled Kobe beef?—but the soul of a true slider is déclassé, and classic slider service is off an oily grill under fluorescent lights.

Fancy-pants sliders at a trendy bar. Onion rings are inappropriate with proletarian sliders, for which the only possible companion is a bag of potato chips.

Aficionados consider the Cozy Inn of Salina, Kansas, to be the ne plus ultra of the itty-bitty burger world. Opened in 1922, one year after White Castle debuted farther south in Wichita, this eat shack with its six-stool counter claims the high moral ground in terms of burger purity by refusing even to offer cheese. You could get one without pickles, but that would be a mistake, as the deuce of dills in the bun actually outweighs the meat and contributes significantly to the Cozy Inn magic. Grilled onions are mandatory; their smell is as much a component of the little sandwiches as meat itself. The slippery pucker of the pickles and onions teases maximum flavor from the elusive little patty. You can buy a single slider for well under a dollar, but nobody eats just one. They are consumed as trios and quartets.

SLINGER

Springfield, Illinois, has its **horseshoe,** and Rochester, New York, its **garbage plate**; St. Louis's devil-may-care meal of outrageous proportions is known as a **slinger.** Eaten for lunch or breakfast or as a predawn prophylactic for an oncoming hangover, its exact configuration varies, but a typical slinger would be two hamburger patties sided by fried potatoes, topped with a fried egg or two, completely blanketed with chili, then garnished with grated cheese and chopped raw onions.

St. Louis's venerable Goody-Goody Diner (60+ years in business) serves a very similar dish, known there as a Wilbur. Rather than being anchored by burgers, a Wilbur is more an omelet. It comes loaded with peppers, onions, tomatoes, and home-fried potatoes and blanketed with chili and then shredded cheese. It's the chili that makes the dish: a moderately spiced concoction laced with plenty of meat, also available plain in a bowl or as part of the magic Midwest duet known as **chili mac**: noodles topped with chili. Usually, chili mac comes garnished by a mass of shredded cheddar cheese . . . unless you order *chili mac a la mode,* which in St. Louis means a crown of two fried eggs.

SLOPPY JOE

Most Americans think of **sloppy joe** as ground beef in sweet tomato sauce served on a burger bun—a happy mess of a meal that Sloppy Joe's bar in Key West, Florida, claims to have introduced during Prohibition. Regional variations are known as *slushburgers* in the Great Plains, *yip-yips* along the Mississippi River near St. Louis, *gulash* in Minnesota, and **barbecue** throughout the heartland. In northern New Jersey, however, *sloppy joe* has a completely different meaning. It is the name for any deli sandwich (especially a double decker) that augments meat and/or cheese with a layer of coleslaw and Russian dressing. Limited slaw spillage is a measure of the sandwich maker's craft and the eater's poise.

SLOW FOOD

America is known for a fast-track culture in general and for fast food in particular. Still, increasing numbers of food-focused citizens have come to think of eating as a pleasure to be prolonged rather than a routine to be gotten done with; they are part of the **slow food movement.** First articulated in 1986 by Italian journalist Carlo Petrini, the worldwide phenomenon has formally dedicated itself to "mankind's inalienable right to pleasure through good eating." Slow Foodies celebrate local produce and regional foodways; they support small-scale growers and producers; and they advocate for "an adequate portion of sensual gourmandaise pleasures, to be taken with slow and prolonged enjoyment."

The culture of jiffy cookery notwithstanding, America's foodways are rich with traditions that are all about slowness. Consider such no-hurry feasts as the Downeast **clambake,** Wisconsin's **chicken booyah,** and the lazy culture of **barbecue,** which takes forever to cook, whether it's at a Carolina **pig pickin'** or from a Texas butcher's back room pit. Years ago, when asked what made his beef so tasty, the legendary Dallas pitmaster Sonny Bryan said, "There are no secrets. There is just time. Time and smoke." Bill Armbrecht of the Brick Pit in Mobile, Alabama, cooks pork shoulders 30 hours before meticulously hand-pulling the meat. At Clark's Outpost in the Red River town of Tioga, Nancy Ann Clark lets her briskets bask over low-smoldering green hickory and pecan wood for four full days.

As for slow savoring, observe the way people eat at Stroud's in Kansas City, where fried chicken is unhurriedly cooked in a skillet to brittle-edged perfection, and where it is devoured sensually from the first, audible crunch through crust to the final, toothsome worrying of every bone to get its last shreds of flavor. Or visit one of the Deep South restaurants that carries on the boarding house tradition of all-you-can-eat family-style meals composed of countless serving bowls of vegetable casseroles, biscuits and **corn bread, fried green tomatoes** and sliced fresh tomatoes still warm from the sun, and, of course, huge piles of catfish and **hushpuppies** or chicken and dumplings.

In recent years, as chefs have become celebrities and their restaurants cultural shrines, a new wrinkle has been added to the slow food movement—waiting in an interminable line for the privilege of ingesting the famous food. An hour, two hours, or even more is not an uncommon wait time at some urban hot-ticket eateries, although an evening spent hoping to be seated probably ought not to be included in the manifesto's definition of "prolonged enjoyment."

SMOOTHIE

When we began looking for American regional food in the 1970s, the **smoothie** was a California thing and a symbol of the elevated nutritional consciousness that sun-worshippers sought. Today it is nearly as common as Coke. The original smoothies, known also as *smoothees*—made possible by the introduction of the Waring "Miracle Mixer" blender in 1937—combined fruit and juice with ice to make a refreshing, healthful, easily consumable beverage. They remained a novelty until adopted by the mid-twentieth century counterculture, but the hippies' and health nuts' once righteous drink has gone the way of **granola** and so many counterculture icons. While maintaining a vaguely virtuous aura, it has become a big-dollar business in which some of the best-selling smoothies—laden with frozen yogurt and such other nutritionally correct junk as carob instead of chocolate and agave nectar instead of sugar—are as fattening as a Mickey D **milk shake.** Juice bars and smoothie stores no longer need to stock fruit; the product can be concocted using starter bases and mixes in the form of powder or syrup.

SNAIL SALAD

Snail salad at a seafood joint in Narragansett, Rhode Island.

What Italians throughout New England call *scungilli*, Rhode Islanders know as snails. And while scungilli salad is fairly rare, **snail salad** is ubiquitous in the Ocean State. It is on Italian menus, seafood menus, and chicken dinner hall menus, a spotlight hors d'oeuvre at waterside picnic shacks as well as on linen tablecloths in fine dining rooms. To understand the locals' passion, you must first realize that it is not a salad of garden snails. The creature in question is a sea snail, what south Floridians might recognize as conch—actually a very pretty mollusk in a

246

spiral shell. It is boiled, its meat extracted and sliced thin, and then mixed with olives, celery, onion, and spice and sopped in a marinade that is bright and usually quite garlicky. Snail salad almost always is served as an hors d'oeuvre to be shared by all at the table, family-style.

SNOOT

As you might guess by its name, a **snoot** is a nose; a pig's nose to be exact, listed formally on some of the **soul food barbecues** around St. Louis (its home) as a *snout*. But it is pronounced "snoot," and does not look like one. In fact, snoots are not whole pig proboscises on plates; the meat is shaved and cut into long ribbons, baked and deep-fried to become something like *cuchifritos*, served with barbecue sauce on a bun or as part of a platter. Many restaurants that make snoots also offer ears, but unlike snoots, ears look exactly like what they are, and rather than getting baked and fried to become something alluringly crunchy, they are boiled to a point of gelatinous wiggle.

Snoot Sauce

Rest assured: This classic Midwest-style barbecue sauce, inspired by that used to enhance the snoots at C&K Barbeque in St. Louis, tastes fine on ordinary cuts of pork such as tenderloin or ribs. It's also great on beef or chicken. Use it to baste the meat as it cooks, then serve a cupful on the side for dipping.

    4 cloves garlic, minced
    4 tablespoons butter
    1 tablespoon lemon juice
    ½ cup minced red onion
    2 cups cider vinegar
    2 cups tomato juice
    ½ cup dark brown sugar
    4 tablespoons Worcestershire sauce
    1 tablespoon soy sauce
    1–4 teaspoons Tabasco sauce (to taste)
    2 teaspoons salt
    1 teaspoon coarsely ground black pepper

1. In a heavy cast iron skillet, sauté the garlic in the butter until it is soft but not yet browned. Add the remaining ingredients and bring them to the lowest possible simmer, then lower the heat a notch or two. Cook uncovered 1 hour, stirring frequently and keeping the temperature just below a boil.

2. Serve warm. Store in refrigerator.

1 GENEROUS QUART

SONORAN HOT DOG

For many years Tucson's alone, the **Sonoran hot dog** has become familiar beyond the Southwest desert thanks to the proliferation of food trucks everywhere and to television food shows, where its flamboyance is a telegenic virtue. While a novitiate might mistake it for a novelty food from some state fair midway or a gimmick to attract the cameras, it is in fact an inspired recipe, and its roots go back to the mid-twentieth century. It is unclear whether it was invented by vendors on Tucson's south side or originally came from Hermosillo, the capital of the Mexican state of Sonora; either way, Tucson now is its home.

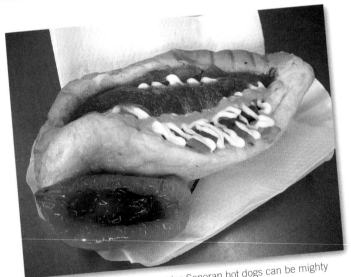

The guero pepper that accompanies Sonoran hot dogs can be mighty hot. Some places temper the heat by stuffing it with cheese and wrapping it with bacon.

It begins simply, as a slim, all-beef frankfurter. The frank gets wrapped in bacon and grilled in a trough alongside other bacon-sheathed **hot dogs,** whose shed grease makes the process very much like deep-frying. This causes bacon flavor to melt into the dog, leaving the outside patched with streaks of lean that provide marvelous chewy contrast to the frank they embrace. The condiment lineup is presupposed: a scattering of pinto beans underneath the hot dog and on top, chopped tomatoes, grilled or raw onions, a line of yellow mustard, a green ribbon of hot jalapeño sauce, and an artistic squiggle of mayonnaise. On the side of every Sonoran hot dog comes a roasted guero pepper, which looks like a pale jalapeño (*guero* = "blond") and can be every bit as hot. When you bite through the thick wall of this fruity pod and hit the capsicum-charged membrane within, the mercy of the bun can be welcome tongue relief.

Unlike the wan bun used for ordinary hot dogs, the roll in which a *"hot-dog estilo Sonora"* is planted is a supple, yeasty loaf fresh from one of the local Mexican bakeries. Known as a *bolillo* roll, it is cut to form a capacious pocket with closed ends that will hold all the ingredients—even a pair of dressed hot dogs, which is a common variation—and it is substantial enough not to disintegrate under its heavy load.

Other than at happy hour in the J-Bar grill of the Westin La Paloma resort, when the city's star chef, Janos Wilder, offers his J-Dawg (a high-end gloss on the concept using Chicago hot dogs topped with *poblano crema* in lieu of mayonnaise as well as chopped cactus pads), all Sonoran hot dogs are eaten outdoors and served from carts or trucks. Tucson abounds in vendors who park at street corners and in empty lots, arrange a few tables and chairs and a canopy for protection from the sun, and dish out hot dogs from late morning to late night.

SOPAIPILLA

From the most casual **diners** to bistros at fashion's cutting edge, if a New Mexico restaurant purports to serve native foods, **sopaipillas** will be part of its repertoire. They might not be listed on the menu, because they are taken for granted, usually occupying a basket that would elsewhere hold dinner rolls. Significantly lighter than the substantial discs known as **Navajo fry bread** in

Sopaipillas are served at breakfast, lunch, and dinner in New Mexico.

the Southwest, a sopaipilla is a buoyant pocket of dough puffed up by quick cooking in boiling lard, its surface slightly crisp, its interior heat-stretched to become more air than pastry. A sopaipilla must be served fresh and still warm. It is finger food, easy to tear and use for mopping **chile** from a plate of **carne adovada** or eggs from **huevos rancheros.** Its only condiment is honey, which can be drizzled on, bite by bite.

Clearly it is on the same family tree as the Utah **scone,** and it is arguably a distant relative of the **beignet** and of **fried dough.** But its exact lineage puzzles even the experts. A while ago, when we were dining at the venerable La Posta restaurant in Mesilla, we enjoyed a sopaipilla colloquy with Dr. Paul Bosland of New Mexico State University's Chile Pepper Institute, and proprietor Jerean Hutchinson, whose grandmother founded the restaurant in 1939, and neither could say with certainty which of the several cultural streams that flow into New Mexican cookery brought them or how they got named. "*Sopa* means 'pillow,' so *sopaipilla* is a 'little pillow,'" Dr. Bosland said. "But there is no word *sopaipilla* in Spanish." Ms. Hutchinson added, "I suspect they are Native American . . . and that maybe Spanish settlers took credit for them!"

Elaborations include stuffed sopaipillas (with chili, **carne seca,** or refried beans) and dessert sopaipillas topped with ice cream and fruit or sauce.

JANE and MICHAEL STERN

SOUL FOOD

America's oldest cuisine (aside from Native American), **soul food** is defined in dictionaries as what African Americans eat in the South or in Northern cities to which their Southern ancestors migrated. In fact, it is cherished by all sorts of eaters, all across the U.S.A. While some people generously apply the label to any ethnic comfort food, from Jewish matzoh ball soup to Italian Sunday gravy, the definitive soul food is what emerged out of the experience of slaves and their descendants from the Carolinas through the Mississippi Delta. Beginning three centuries ago as a "make-do" menu for which resourceful cooks transformed meager groceries and unwanted cuts of meat into something delicious, soul food has become an abundant branch of American cookery that reflects its humble origins in grand as well as modest meals.

No one knows exactly where and when the term originated, but the energy of modern soul food can be traced directly to the halcyon days of the mid-twentieth century Civil Rights movement. It was a time when so many African Americans made a point of prizing all things soulful, from natural haircuts to rhythm and blues. Soul food became a touchstone by which black people could remember who they were and where they came from, and to be proud of what has borne their families and community.

While it continues to provide an edible sense of identity for those whose mothers and great-great-grandmothers created it, soul food is too beguiling to be confined in a culinary ghetto. It specifically reflects the African-American experience, but it is also a microcosm for the way this nation's most emblematic foods have been created—not by exalted chefs of the Cordon Bleu, but by humble cooks applying unlimited ingenuity to limited resources. It was the slaves who tossed ham hocks disdained by their white masters in with simmering greens to create a porky **pot likker**; they made croquettes from leftover fish and **hushpuppies** from scraps of catfish dredging; and they used the otherwise discarded leafy parts of beets, turnips, and pokeweed to make savory seasoned greens.

Some of soul food's best contributions actually climbed their way up the food-status ladder long ago. When hog jowls were the only part of the pig Colonial African-American cooks could get hold of, they stuffed them with

251

highly spiced collards and mustard leaves—a combination of sweet pork and tonic vegetables so delicious that soon cooks of the wealthiest people applied the same principle to the most prized part of the pig, and in St. Mary's County, Maryland, **stuffed ham** was born. Today, no Easter table in the region is complete without it, and it is equally enjoyed by people of all colors.

It is impossible to neatly separate Southern food and soul food, but one big thing that defines soul food is the influence of the cooks' West African heritage. Yams, peppers, rice, peanuts, watermelon, sesame seeds, and all sorts of legumes are ingredients brought to American shores along with the knowledge of how to make the most of them. African flavors are particularly strong along the coast of South Carolina and Georgia, where sea-island dwellers were so isolated from the mainland that they developed their own African-American culture, including a whole catalog of recipes and the musical dialect called Gullah.

While certain soul food dishes may be an acquired taste—**chitlins,** for example—much of the culinary canon is comfort food for anyone. Baked chicken with dressing, pork chops with stewed apples, mac 'n' cheese, and sweet potato pie are menu standards with broad appeal. Even for those who have little or no actual connection with its history, soul food can provide good nurture for the soul as well as nourishment for the body.

SOUR CREAM RAISIN PIE

Once a staple of self-published cookbooks throughout the heartland, **sour cream raisin pie** is now found almost exclusively at restaurants in Midwest dairy country—Wisconsin and Minnesota, primarily, with occasional sightings in Iowa and Illinois. It is a powerhouse pie that balances a tangy sweet custard filling spiked with sour cream and raisins in a flaky crust and an ethereal cloud of airy meringue on top. Proportions vary. Some SCR pies are all filling with just a halo of meringue on top; others are mostly meringue with only an edge of sour cream filling. Some are so packed with raisins that the sour cream custard seems like little more than an afterthought. While it is, of course, dessert—especially right and good after a meal of pork chops—in the Midwest it is a common afternoon snack, and it is not uncommon to find truck stops serving it for breakfast. At some of the best cafes, customers know to reserve a piece before they sit down at a table because the whole pie could be sold before lunch is over.

SPIEDIES

Many cuisines have their own take on skewered meat, from Indonesian satay to Greek shish kebab to American **corn dogs.** Binghamton, New York, has the **spiedie.** Historians of upstate eating have detected a version of Italian *spiedinis* served in Binghamton for the first time in 1937 by an immigrant named Augustino Iacovelli, but for decades now, America's own spiedie has been defined by a Binghamton bar called Sharkey's. Cut from what proprietor Larry Sharak describes as pork sirloin, each cube of charcoal-cooked meat is thoroughly moist but not drippingly so, its fibers saturated with the tang of a garlic marinade in which it soaks before being cooked on a grate behind the bar.

The presentation is elementary: The meat on the skewer rests on a slice of plain white bread which rests on a small paper plate. That's all there is to it. The bread is not interesting, but you need it as a mitt to hold the meat. The custom is to grab the slice in one hand and use it to slide a few hunks of lamb or pork off the metal rod, thus creating an instant sandwich. The bread's blandness is a foil for the meat's zest in the same way supermarket white bread is *de rigueur* with spicy Southern **barbecue.** Condiments are irrelevant.

Spiedies
- ¾ cup olive oil
- ½ cup red wine
- ½ cup red wine vinegar
- 4 cloves garlic, finely minced
- 1 teaspoon pepper
- 1 teaspoon thyme
- ½ teaspoon allspice
- 2 fresh mint leaves, crushed
- 1 bunch fresh parsley, finely chopped
- 2 pounds lean lamb, cut into 1-inch cubes

1. Combine all the marinade ingredients and pour over lamb. Toss to coat all the meat, and cover and refrigerate for a full 24 hours. Rearrange the meat occasionally so it all soaks evenly.

2. Thread the lamb chunks on metal skewers and cook over hot coals about 8 minutes altogether, turning them so they cook evenly.

3. Serve meat on skewers, accompanied by French or Italian bread sliced thin enough to use as mitts for holding chunks of meat.

4–6 SERVINGS

SPONGE CANDY

Among chocolate obsessions in the city of Buffalo, none is so fervent as that for **sponge candy.** Sugar is cooked to a high temperature with water and corn syrup, then furiously whipped as baking soda slowly is added to create a giant brittle spongelike bubble. Covered overnight, it rises like a cake, the sugar's clout honed to an elusive caramel as its body turns brittle-crisp. The chewy exterior of the sponge is cut away, leaving only the lightest, most fragile inside, which is cut into blocks a little bigger than a cubic inch each, which are in turn thickly robed in milk chocolate or dark chocolate. The experience of eating a piece of sponge candy is unique. Teeth sink through a thick coat of chocolate then hit a spun-sugar center that is at first crisp and brittle, but immediately evaporates into nothing more than ghostly verge-of-burnt sugar flavor that haloes the chocolate.

Buffalo chocolatiers are expert in spinning sugar to near weightlessness and enrobing it in profound chocolate.

Regional cognates for sponge candy, as it is known from Syracuse to Erie, include Wisconsin **fairy food,** Oregon seafoam, and Missouri molasses puffs.

SPOONBREAD

◇◇◇

Spoonbread is too tender to be sliced with a knife, and it looks nothing like a loaf of bread. It is served in a baking dish and portioned out with a spoon. It is a mid-South side dish made with milk or buttermilk and cornmeal, reminiscent of lightweight polenta or a fairly heavy soufflé more than of bread. The center may be nearly as moist as custard, while the top and edges tend toward crisp. It is pretty much a rarity in the twenty-first century South, except in restaurants that make a point of honoring culinary history. Spoonbread goes back to Colonial times and possibly earlier, to a Native American porridge called *suppone.* It is said that George Washington was its biggest fan.

SQUARE PIZZA

◇◇◇

Square pizzas may indeed be square, but not every **pizza** that happens to be square qualifies as *square pizza,* which is a style unique to Detroit. In fact, large Motor City pizzas, known as eight-squares (because that's how many portions you get), are rectangular. Small ones, cut into four slices, are baked square and cut into quarters. This distinctive style was created by Gus Guerra at a tavern named Buddy's at the end of World War II. Now grown into a successful local chain, the joint began during the 1930s as a *blind pig* (a place that serves drinks without a license and after hours), but it went legit when the war was over. To attract customers, Guerra created his own version of Sicilian pizza. It is baked in a pan and the crust is substantial enough to provide crunch and chew all the way from the center to the edges. Of the two sizes available—four-square and eight-square—the smaller one is preferred by many connoisseurs because each slice delivers two super-chewy borders embossed with luscious amounts of caramelized cheese.

ST. PAUL

Among St. Louis's curious culinary specialties, which include **gooey butter cake** and fried brain sandwiches, none is as enigmatic as the **St. Paul.** You will find the St. Paul on menus in nearly every take-out chop suey parlor in town, of which the city has a bounty. No Gateway City food authority or cultural historian owns up to knowing anything about its origins or the inscrutable logic of its name, which one assumes is a reference to the city in Minnesota or possibly to the Apostle. One apocryphal story holds that it was a St. Louis chef originally from St. Paul who invented the dish to attract non-Chinese sandwich-eaters to his restaurant.

If its genealogy is unclear, its architecture is certain: a patty of egg foo young is cooked to the customer's specifications with diced pork, ham, chicken, beef, shrimp, or just vegetables, placed between two pieces of soft white bread, and dressed with lettuce, tomato, pickle, and mayonnaise. A slice of American cheese is optional.

STEAMED CHEESEBURGER

Ted's of Meriden, Connecticut, has been a steamed cheeseburger destination since 1959.

Known to locals as a steamer, the **steamed cheeseburger** was invented at a place called Jack's Lunch of Middletown, Connecticut, in the 1920s. Steamed food was becoming a popular nostrum (countering the evils of frying), but as successful as Jack's steamers were on Main Street, they never went viral like **Buffalo wings,** Chicago **deep-dish pizza,** or Tucson **chimichangas.** The steamed cheeseburger remained a local phenomenon. Even today, in Connecticut cities as close as Hartford and New Haven, most people never have heard of it.

A special steam cabinet is used to cook individual portions of ground beef and blocks of Vermont cheddar cheese, the latter transformed by steam into a pearlescent mass just viscous enough to seep into every crevice of the meat below, but not so runny that it escapes the sandwich. The soft hamburger (no crust on a steamer) and cheese are layered in a hard roll along with lettuce, tomato, pickle, and onion. A steamed cheeseburger might be accompanied by steamed-cheese-topped potatoes and even followed by steamed-cheese-topped apple pie.

STONE CRAB

Claws are the only part of the **stone crab** worth eating. They are regal, so swank and expensive that Damon Runyon once joked that they were sold by the carat. Their meat resembles steamed lobster—sweet, pearlescent, and full of juice, especially when served at a balmy temperature that coaxes out maximum marine flavor and with creamy mustard sauce for dipping. Unlike most animals' limbs, stone crab claws grow back if they are removed. It used to be that only a single claw was harvested from each stone crab pulled out of the water, but studies have shown that if both claws are removed, both will grow back when the crab is returned to the sea. Stone crab season runs from October through May.

The most famous place to eat them is the unambiguously named Joe's Stone Crab of Miami Beach, a culinary landmark opened by Joe Weiss in 1918. At the time, the place was simply named Joe's Restaurant and stone crabs weren't even on the menu. They were, at best, a novelty, and Weiss believed few customers would want to eat them. But once he was convinced to offer them, he soon realized that they could be his trademark. Joe's is still run by his progeny, and it is a reminder of when Miami Beach was the epitome of fancy-dress glamour.

STREAK O' LEAN

It's surprising that bacon's recent surge in popularity hasn't lifted **streak o' lean** out of obscurity, for the old Dixie farmhouse dish is superbacon. Bacon squared. The ultimate. Being bacon with extra fat (containing only a streak of lean) and cut extra thick, it has little or no redeeming value among nutrition prigs, but for those who enjoy sizzled pork belly that verges on chunks rather than strips, it is edible nirvana. The handful of restaurants that do serve it (all in the Deep South) fry streak o' lean so that its crisp exterior encases melty fat. On the side, you want biscuits and pepper cream gravy.

STUFFED HAM

Everybody knows about the Chesapeake Bay's exemplary soft-shell crabs, spiced boiled shrimp, and **crab cakes,** but few outsiders have heard of **stuffed ham.** "They are ham-ignorant in Baltimore," a local chef once bluntly told us. But to the residents of St. Mary's County, stuffed ham is at the core of their culinary identity. It is a mainstay of church suppers and firemen's balls from Thanksgiving to Christmas and into spring, and many restaurants serve it in the cool-weather months, at least intermittently. Its seasonal appearance dates

back to the days of the autumn hog slaughter, when plantation slaves were given the hog's head, which they made more appealing by stuffing it with such late-crop produce as kale, turnip tops, wild watercress, or collards and mustard greens. The harmony of pork and greens was so good that the concept went up the food-status ladder from head to ham. Stuffed ham generally is served cold, in slices that resemble piggy braciole with alternating ribbons of meat and filling. A roadside tavern in Charlotte Hall called St. Mary's Landing has it on the menu year-round, for breakfast, lunch, and supper.

Those greens are tart and spicy—a welcome balance for sweet ham.

STUFFED PIZZA

A branch of Chicago **deep-dish pizza** cookery, the **stuffed pizza** is a huge, savory pie with a crust on top as well as on the bottom. It first appeared on the scene in the 1970s at Nancy's pizza, which claims to have created it based on the proprietor's mother's Old World recipe for Easter pie. Made in a deep-sided metal pan with a fairly thin, biscuity crust that measures over two inches tall around the circumference, it is filled with tomatoes, cheese, and ingredients that range from familiar sausage, pepperoni, spinach, and broccoli to chicken cacciatore or garlic shrimp. The ingredients are topped with another layer of dough. The top crust is brushed with tomato sauce and perhaps sprinkled with grated cheese, then baked. One twelve-inch pie easily feeds four.

STUFFIE

The easiest place to come across a **stuffie** is Rhode Island, where it is featured on seafood menus high and low, although we have found a few along the shore in southern Massachusetts and eastern Connecticut. An invention of necessity—what do you do with a quahog clam, whose meat is delicious but is too tough to eat whole?—it mixes finely chopped clams into seasoned bread stuffing, a combo returned to the clam shell and baked. Stuffies may also contain the spicy linguiça sausage so popular in Portuguese-settled regions of New England. Indeed, the menu at Flo's Clam Shack in Middletown, Rhode Island ("Home of the fiery stuffed quahog"), advertises that its stuffies are made "from an ancient Portuguese recipe."

SUGAR ON SNOW

It's an old farmhouse tradition: During maple sugaring season in the spring, warm syrup is drizzled onto freshly fallen snow, where it hardens and forms a chewy-crisp candy as crazy looking as the work of a drunken spider. Known also as *frogs* or *leather aprons*, **sugar on snow** is so intensely mapley that it is sometimes eaten with dill pickles, which help revive an exhausted sweet tooth, as well as with apple cider donuts, corn fritters, or common crackers. It is impractical for restaurant service, but it sometimes is available at sugarhouses in New England in the spring.

The ad hoc confection became inspiration for a candy branded Chocolate Lace, for which filaments of caramel resembling sugar on snow are dipped in pans of melted bittersweet chocolate. The chocolate hardens and creates a gossamer confection of two completely different sorts of sweetness that are dramatic complements for each other. Chocolate Lace is a proprietary product; for information, www.hauserchocolates.com.

SUGAR PIE

Cream, butter, and sugar are the essential ingredients of **sugar pie,** also known as *sugar cream pie* as well as *Indiana farm pie* because most of it is made and eaten in the Hoosier State. A favorite of the Amish who settled Indiana as well as Ohio, it is a product of scarcity: No fruits are required and even eggs are not needed (although sometimes they may be added) to create the characteristic fragile jiggle by which the pie is known. Farmland *bec fins* are said to like sugar pie best in the spring when Jersey cows are on new, green grass and their milk is especially rich. Brown sugar or maple syrup frequently is used, vanilla extract will flavor it, and a dusting of nutmeg is common, but any further customization goes against the pie's elemental nature.

SUPERMARKETS

Before there were supermarkets, buying groceries was a one-on-one affair: A customer handed the grocery list to a clerk, who went into a back storage area to retrieve the goods. Shoppers had scant opportunity to select one apple over another or even to inspect the beef steaks they would get for supper. They were subject to the whims of the fishmonger or fruit seller and the favoritism of an autocratic butcher. The death knell of such full-service grocery shopping sounded in Memphis, Tennessee, on September 6, 1916, when Clarence Saunders opened the first Piggly Wiggly store. Saunders moved the stock room to the front of the sales area and, calling the configuration a "self-serving store," invited customers to enter through a turnstile (a device Saunders was the first to use in retail sales), walk among the aisles, and select their own goods. A new way to shop was born.

At first, meats and produce were not part of the inventory, which was strictly nonperishables. Despite *Time* magazine's concern that Saunders's new system provided "latitude to shoplifters," it was an immediate success. For the customer, it meant the end of waiting in line to be helped. Store owners were thrilled to have a dozen or more people shopping at one time. Self-serving stores, also known as *cafeteria groceries,* were a shot in the arm for the retail food business, suddenly introducing the opportunity to create enticing displays of merchandise that encouraged impulse buying.

Within five years there were over a thousand Piggly Wigglies in twenty-nine states, but it wasn't until August 4, 1930, that the supermarket earned its moniker. As the Great Depression weighed upon consumers, Mike Cullen suggested to his boss at Kroger grocery stores that he consider opening really large self-serving markets in low-rent locations, offering cut-rate products in order to attract budget-conscious customers. Kroger wasn't interested, so Cullen quit. He found an abandoned garage in Jamaica, Long Island, stocked it with groceries, and placed newspaper ads touting King Kullen Market as "The World's Greatest Price Wrecker." Many items were sold at cost. Cullen was the first to recognize the potential symbiosis of cars and supermarkets (which blossomed with the growth of suburbia); he offered a parking lot, thus encouraging customers to purchase carloads of bargain groceries. The store's selection was of unprecedented scope, including not only meat, vegetables, and canned, boxed, and frozen food, but also soaps, small appliances, and pharmaceuticals. It was the first true supermarket, as well as a harbinger of big box stores and warehouse clubs.

Grocery shopping was once again revolutionized in 1937, when an Oklahoma City grocer named Sylvan Nathan Goldman, inspired by the design of a folding chair, patented a carrier that would hold two full-size carry baskets and rolled easily through the aisles. Although customers did not instantly warm to the idea—most thought it seemed too much like a baby carriage—the "No Basket Carrying Plan" he introduced at his Humpty Dumpty chain encouraged customers to gather weeks' worth of food in one swoop. (Beneficiary of royalties on every shopping cart sold until the patents expired, Goldman also invented the still-prevalent "Nest Kart" with a child seat at the push bars, folding back for easy storage. He also invented airport luggage carts.)

The cavernous, convenient supermarket now is as common around the globe as television, but for a long while it was considered uniquely American. Forward-looking citizens eager to escape their forebears' way of life in urban ethnic neighborhoods or small towns saw the old way of shopping—butcher to baker to greengrocer—as a burdensome remnant of times gone by. All that effort and personal contact were signs of the era's bête noire—being old-fashioned. As late as 1955, the *Silver Jubilee Super Market Cook Book* singled out the supermarket as nothing less than a beacon of national pride, "a symbol of America's attainment of a high standard of living through democracy, so looked upon as one of the great institutions of the world." The implication was that shoppers in less fortunate nations still bought their food like serfs, hat in hand, hoping Lord Grocer would treat them well. Here in America, everything was laid out: meat and produce prewrapped and ready to be freely inspected and chosen by the customer with no intervening authority.

It has long been a national tradition for counterculture values to seep into mainstream culture, a tide that flowed vigorously into late-twentieth-century food preferences. Peasant bread displaced once-aristocratic white bread as a status symbol; Ben & Jerry's cloyingly folksy ice cream kicked snooty brands' butts; former alternative fare such as **granola** and yogurt proliferated on supermarket shelves, reveling in their ostensible unrefinement. Concurrently, huge corporate supermarket chains prospered by positioning themselves as the alternative to huge corporate supermarket chains. In 2007, Whole Foods, which began as Saferway alternative grocery in Austin, Texas, in 1978, paid nearly $600 million to acquire Wild Oats, which began as the Crystal Market alternative grocery in Boulder, Colorado, in 1987. Such determinedly enlightened enterprises sell health-food products that once were the domain of smelly seed-and-sprout shops; they feature shelves devoted to dietary supplements and to books and pamphlets about composting and organic farming; they offer on-the-spot massages and nutrition clinics and, at the Whole Foods in West Hollywood, a "Lifestyle Store" that sells organic bedding to make one's home "a haven from impurities" and "hip clothing from U2's Bono for consumers with a conscience."

SUSTAINABLE

It is not possible to pinpoint precisely when the adjective **sustainable** joined the ranks of *fair trade, local,* and *natural* as modifiers that signal virtuous food. A decade into the twenty-first century, it has become nearly as common in culinary palaver as the word *organic*—and, like *organic*, in danger of emasculation due to overuse. To wit: In 2010 the Sustainable Supply Steering Committee of McDonald's Corporation announced, "McDonald's vision for sustainable supply is a supply chain that profitably yields high-quality, safe products without supply interruption while leveraging our leadership position to create a net benefit by improving ethical, environmental, and economic outcomes."

A major milestone on sustainable's rise to the big time came in 2001 when chef Alice Waters and a group of students and faculty founded the Yale Sustainable Food Project in New Haven, the mission statement of which declared, "The world's most pressing questions regarding health, culture, the environment, education and the global economy cannot be adequately addressed without considering the food we eat and the way we produce it." Dining halls on the Yale campus have set a goal of serving 45 percent sustainable food by 2013; students who major in Environmental Studies can concentrate in Sustainable Agriculture.

While there is no cut and dried measure of the term (as there is for *organic*), to dub food sustainable means that eating it will not eventually kill it off. Furthermore, the word suggests that creation and consumption of the food enrich the earth rather than deplete it. Sustainable's favorite things include small-scale production rather than agribusiness, the use of manure instead of chemical fertilizer, humane treatment of animals while they are raised and slaughtered, and happy farmers with an equitable stake in their product (aka *fair trade*), as opposed to downtrodden migrants. Conventional wisdom assumes that just as sustainable food enhances the well-being of the planet, it also is good for the health of individuals who eat it.

SWEET TEA

Sweet tea—iced, of course—is *eau de vie* throughout the South. It quenches thirst, replenishes verve and vitality, tamps down tongue fires created by **hot chicken** and **barbecue** and stimulates the appetite for more. It is best drunk from a tall, wide-mouth glass with clear fresh ice cubes or heaps of crushed ice. Lots and lots of ice, always lots of ice. And, of course, a big pitcher for refills, as needed. If you wish, you can be fancy and squeeze a little lemon in it or add a sprig of mint, but really, any addition is gilding the lily. Sweet tea should be perfect just the way it is served—no garnish necessary.

According to Louis Van Dyke, proprietor of the Blue Willow Inn of Social Circle, Georgia (where sweet tea is called "the champagne of the South"), "Grandmothers and mothers of the old South serve sweetened iced tea at every meal. In the old South, children were never allowed to drink iced tea until they were twelve years old. They drank milk, water, or lemonade. Soft drinks were never allowed at the dinner table."

Sweet Tea

One important rule for making sweet tea, according to Louis Van Dyke of the Blue Willow Inn, where this recipe comes from, is to use regular supermarket tea, not fancy gourmet tea. Another rule is to make it sweeter than you think it should be. Indeed, the motto at the Blue Willow is to serve tea "strong and just a little too sweet."

    1 gallon water
    4–5 family-size tea bags (each one is enough for a quart of tea)
    3 cups sugar, at least
    Lemon slices to garnish (optional)
    Sprig of mint (optional)

Bring the water to a boil in a 1½ gallon saucepan. Turn off the heat and add the tea bags. Cover and steep 12–15 minutes. For stronger tea, let it steep longer, up to 20 minutes. Add the sugar, stirring vigorously until dissolved. Allow tea to cool and pour over ice. Garnish with lemon and mint, if using.

16 CUPS, ENOUGH FOR 4–6 DINERS

TAMALE

The **tamale**—corn masa, meat, and spice packed into a husk and steamed—is popular everywhere there are Mexican restaurants, but it has a special resonance in the Mississippi Delta and in the American Southwest.

In the Delta, from Memphis down to Vicksburg, tamales are sold by men and women, black and white, from street carts, off back porches, and in eateries of every kind. They come either ready to eat or tied up with string by threes and packed into coffee cans that can hold three dozen. There is no clear genealogy that explains the ubiquity of a Mexican dish in cotton country, other than the surmise that workers from Mexico who came to pick cotton inspired African Americans to give the pork and corn dish their own unique twist. Some accounts hearken back to a visiting cook from the Texas-Mexico border who instilled the passion in local eaters. Pat Davis, grandson of the founder of Abe's Bar-B-Q in Clarksdale, Mississippi, told us, "No doubt Granddaddy got it from someone in town," reminding us that Abe had come to the United States from Lebanon, where tamales aren't a big part of the culinary mix. Why Abe thought they would sell well in his pork parlor is a head-scratcher. "There were no Mexican restaurants here then," Pat says. "And as far as I know, not many Mexicans." Even tamale cooks who have no idea why they are the area's signature dish agree that hot tamales are a tradition that stretches back in time as far as the blues.

Tamales accompanied by chili are a popular hors d'oeuvre at Doe's Eat Place in the Mississippi Delta.

In the Southwest, where the tamale directly reflects Mexican cuisine, it is much more than nutritional sustenance. It is supreme comfort food; and the making of tamales is a bonding experience for families and communities. Carlotta Flores, the culinary pillar of Tucson's El Charro (which her grandmother founded in 1922), told us, "I recall the comfort of tamales at times of bereavement, at times of joy, at times of closeness with others. This ancient food holds memories good and sad—but most of all it contains our family identity."

At Christmas, El Charro hosts its own version of the time-honored *tamalada*, a tamale party, at which expert cooks demonstrate to people how to make the simple but exacting dish. The varieties they make are far flung, from *tamales de chile Colorado* (the classic red tamale) to the yuletide sweet bean tamale made with raisins, brown sugar, and cinnamon, to pumpkin-cranberry tamales, even tofu tamales. Carlotta has identified fifty different kinds of tamale, the two basic kinds being the regular tamale made in a dried corn husk that must be softened in warm water before shaping, and the **green corn tamale** of late summer and early fall (corn season) that is made in fresh, soft husks that impart an earthier flavor to the masa inside.

In Mexican-American households, tamales are as much a part of Christmas as cookies are in other cultures. It is traditional for families to gather on December 24 to make and eat tamales together. The best way to learn to make a tamale is to watch someone do it (hence El Charro's demonstrations every Christmas), because while it is a simple process, it requires a significant amount of work. As Carlotta says, it is "not something to attempt if there is anything else you would rather be doing." She does offer these basic tips to lead the tamale maker on the right path:

Never cook tamales in an aluminum pot or steam them under aluminum foil. If your pot does not have a good lid and you must use aluminum foil, first place white freezer paper over the tamales, then layer on the foil to form a seal on the steamer. If the tamales are ever close to aluminum, you will taste it!

If making green corn tamales, use the corn the day it is ground. Fresh corn does not retain its sweet flavor longer than a day.

While red tamales may be frozen without harm, green tamales change for the worse in the freezer and take on "a hint of sourness."

Rhoda Adams of Lake Village, Arkansas, attributes her tamale-making expertise to guidance from the Lord.

Red tamales reheat well in the microwave oven, wrapped in damp paper towels.

If making red tamales, the meat mixture can be prepared a day or two in advance, thus cutting down on the workload of tamale-making day.

Consider the tamale a breakfast food. Leave the steamed *tamal* in its husk and heat it in the oven until the husk turns crisp. Open the husk and top the hot steamy corn with a fried egg.

TAMALE PIE

The familiar **tamale** is cornmeal batter laced with ground meat, cheese, and/ or chile, wrapped in a husk (or parchment) and then steamed until the ingredients attain soft harmony. A **tamale pie** uses the same ingredients; instead of

being wrapped, they are mixed or layered and baked in a casserole. While most iterations are humble dishes meant to feed maximum family members at minimum expense, the tamale pie also can be as elegant as a soufflé. So it is at Tucson's inspired Cafe Poca Cosa, where tamale pie is on the menu every night as the vegetarian special. Chef Susanna Davila whips her corn batter up with enough cream to make it like custard, then festoons it with toppings that range from sweet mango chutney to savory marinara sauce.

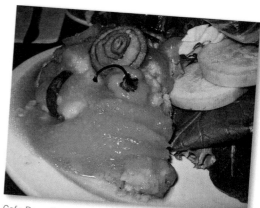

Cafe Poca Cosa of Tucson offers a different kind of tamale pie each day. This one includes a swirl of mango and peppers.

TANG

Introduced by General Foods in 1959 as a breakfast beverage made by mixing water with a spoonful of what the manufacturer called "aromatic, orangy-tasting powder," **Tang** was touted as convenient, nutritious (loaded with vitamins A and C, as well as tricalcium phosphate), pleasant-smelling ("like oranges, but with a flavor all its own"), long-lasting in its jar on the shelf, and

Tang is convenient, nutritious, and pleasant-smelling.

most wonderful of all, *modern*. To serve Tang for breakfast instead of orange juice was to say you were riding high on the wave of progress; history would not leave you behind with all the fuddy duddies who still struggled to squeeze juice from oranges the way generations of unlucky homemakers had done before them.

At the time, General Foods was predicting a dazzling future menu of scientifically reconstituted foodstuffs. "Picture an instant, king-sized steak—made of beef-flavored corn cereal—sizzling in the breakfast skillet," General Foods' *Monsanto Magazine* rhapsodized, going on to describe Tang as the logical next step after instant coffee in the march of progress from the laborious past to the effortless future.

Tang made the leap from convenience food to pop culture in 1965, when it was conspicuously drunk by astronauts on board Gemini flights. But in the 1970s, as the terms *fresh* and *natural* displaced *modern* and *convenient* as foods' highest benediction, Tang quickly lost its cachet, going from an emblem of the future to a quaint, even silly, reminder of what we used to think was groovy. The nerdy Loopner family of television's *Saturday Night Live* drank Tang by the pitcherful.

TENDERLOIN

Tenderloin refers to a cut of pig or cow that is the tenderest. It can be prepared in all sorts of ways, but in the lower Midwest, the word refers to a bunned sandwich for which a slice of pork is pounded thin, breaded, and fried to a crisp. Through much of Iowa, Illinois, and Indiana, tenderloins (sometimes called *breaded pork tenderloins* or simply *BPTs*), stir opinion and argument no less fervid than that inspired by **green chile cheeseburgers** in New Mexico and **crab cakes** around the Chesapeake Bay.

A wide and handsome tenderloin from Nick's Kitchen in Huntington, Indiana.

Girth is a big issue, some cutlets pounded out so wide that the sandwich is literally impossible to hold by its tiny bun. But thinner isn't always better. A super-thin tenderloin runs the risk of frying dry. Excellence is built upon a fine balance: There should be a vast amount of crisp, crunchy crust, but the ribbon of pork within needs to be thick enough to remain juicy. Too thick, however, and a tenderloin loses its elegance. Traditionally, tenderloins are garnished with mustard and pickle chips, with the option of lettuce and tomato.

The tenderloin originated in Huntington, Indiana, where, in 1904, Nick Frienstein started selling breaded pork cutlets from a street cart. Four years later, he opened a restaurant called Nick's Kitchen. The method of pork preparation was changed one winter, shortly after Nick moved to the cafe, when his brother Jake suffered such severe frostbite that he lost the fingers off his hands. Jake, whose job it was to bread the slices of pork, found that his stumps made good tools for pounding the meat to make it tender. Since then, all tenderloins are either beaten tender (with a wooden hammer) or run through a mechanical tenderizer (or both). Considering this genesis story, the motto of Nick's Kitchen, which boasts of tenderloins that are nearly too wide to handle, is ironic: "Bet You Need Both Hands."

Tenderloin

Frying tenderloins for BPTs (breaded pork tenderloin sandwiches) is like frying chicken. All recipes share common elements, but everyone who does it has a twist, ranging from how the flour coating is seasoned to what the cooked meat ought to be drained on (paper towels? brown paper bags?). This recipe comes from the kitchen of a family friend who grew up on a central Indiana farm in the 1950s and who makes tenderloins today whenever he feels homesick for the sandwiches of childhood.

> 4 1-inch-thick slices from a boneless, center-cut loin of pork
> 1 cup flour
> 1 teaspoon salt
> ½ teaspoon pepper
> 2 eggs mixed with ¼ cup milk
> Yellow cornmeal
> Oil for frying
> 4 hamburger buns
> Lettuce, tomato, mustard, and pickle, as condiments

1. Trim the fat from each slice of pork. Place each one between two pieces of lightly oiled parchment or wax paper. Using a mallet, pound vigorously until the slice is 6–8 inches across.

2. Mix the flour, salt, and pepper. Dip each slice of pork in the egg-milk mixture, then in the seasoned flour. Pat both sides with yellow cornmeal.

3. Heat ½ inch of oil in a skillet to 365°F. Slip in one tenderloin and fry 2–3 minutes. Flip and fry until golden brown. Drain on a paper towel. Continue until all tenderloins are done.

4. Serve on buns, with condiments of choice.

4 SANDWICHES

TEQUILA DRINKER'S GUIDE

Here is the correct right way to drink tequila: Open the bottle, pour some into a glass, and swallow it.

We risk being obvious only because so many more elaborate methods have been invented for drinking tequila, and for getting drunk on it. The most popular one, known as the *Mexican itch,* is to bracket hammered-back shots of it by licking salt off the base of one's thumb and squeezing a wedge of lime between one's teeth—a slavering ritual that makes the drinker sound like a bulldog sucking a mouthful of Jell-O. It also is frequently slugged back neat with a bottle of beer: a *bordertown boilermaker.* For a *slammer,* the liquor is combined in a glass with champagne, tonic, or soda, banged on the table a couple of times until it fizzes, then gulped in one greedy, effervescent swallow. It seems fair to say that in none of these examples is the act of tequila-drinking an expression of connoisseurship or gentility: the point is to ingest the stuff fast and get drunk.

Tequila doesn't necessarily deserve its rowdy reputation. Like fine Kentucky bourbon, it is distilled with care and precision. The best, made from the heart of the agave plant, is aged in smoke-flavored, wax-lined barrels until it is as suave as good cognac. However, such smooth tequila is fairly rare, and most drink-'til-you-drop brands are about as tasty—and as effective—as chloroform. Tequila has always had a certain outlaw swagger about it in the United States, conjuring up images of dusty cantinas where cowboys pass out on the floor, shoot holes in the ceiling, or fall in love with a pretty señorita (or all three, in reverse order).

The most fearsome tequila is *mezcal con gusano,* known as *mescal,* which is made without the polish of double-distilling and aging and with the added attraction of a dead maguey worm (that's the "con gusano" part, and it is actually a caterpillar) submerged in the bottom of the bottle. The worm, which feeds on the agave plant, was originally packaged in mescal as proof that there was enough alcohol in the booze to preserve it. It is widely believed to induce hallucinations, or at least to make whoever drains the bottle's dregs into an ornery son of a buck. In fact, the worm is considered by protozoa connoisseurs to be so excellent that mescal is sometimes drunk like tequila, by the shot with chaws of lime, but with heaps of crushed, mummified worms on the side to lick in lieu of salt.

Tequila's bellicose reputation has mellowed in recent years, thanks mostly to the popularity of frozen margaritas, which have helped establish its image as a fun libation for civilized middle-class people. Whipped into a frothy confectionery cooler the color of folding money and about as sweet as a green river, tequila nowadays needn't seem any more dangerous than sloe gin.

TEXAS WEINER

A **Texas weiner** (*e–i*, not *i–e*) is a modest-size **hot dog** cooked in oil until ready to burst and bunned with sweetly seasoned meat sauce (and usually onions and mustard). It was configured in Paterson, New Jersey, about a hundred years ago by John Patrellis, who apprenticed at his father's hot dog stand at the city's Manhattan Hotel. Paterson and environs now have a bounty of shops that sell Texas weiners, which are a broad class of the deep-fried phylum of the frankfurter kingdom, along with **Newark hot dogs** and **rippers.** Buns are soft and somewhat shorter than the rugged-skinned dog, which is small enough

that few people order only one. The Lone Star name was invented by Mr. Patrellis because he thought the slightly hot, beanless beef topping was like Texas chili. (It is not; nor will you find anything like a Texas weiner in Texas.) French fries blanketed with gravy are a traditional accompaniment.

Texas weiner chefs in Port Chester, New York, split and grill their tube steaks.

Variations of the Texas weiner are found in southeastern New York and western Connecticut, where they are known as *Texas hots*. In these places the hot dogs are split and grilled and served in buns toasted on the griddle.

TEX-MEX LEX

A handful of helpful menu terms in Spanish, pigeon Spanish, Mexican, Cal-Mexican, and Tex-Mexican.

Ajo: Garlic
Carne seca: Air-dried beef (a Tucson specialty)
Carne verde: Beef with green chile
Cebolla verde: Green onion, usually grilled in Arizona
Chile colorado: Red chile
Chile con carne: Beef with red chile

Chimichanga: A deep-fried burrito

Chorizo: Spicy pork sausage

Fajitas: Grilled beef (or chicken), served sizzling with vegetables and tortillas

Flauta: "Flute" (a tortilla rolled around beef or chicken)

Frijoles refritos: Refried beans

Gordita: A cornmeal pocket filled with meat and/or cheese, grilled

Huevos rancheros: Eggs with salsa, always accompanied by tortilla and *frijoles refritos*

Menudo: Tripe soup (a hangover cure)

Mole poblano: A rich sauce of chile, chocolate, and spices (many variations)

Tostada: A crisp-fried corn tortilla, topped with cheese or guacamole

Quesadilla: Tortillas layered with cheese and heated

SOME COMMON FILLINGS FOR TACOS

Al carbon: charcoal-grilled beef or pork

Al pastor: roast pork

Carne asada: roasted beef

Carnitas: small pieces of pork (in California) or beef (farther east)

Frijoles enteros: whole beans

Hongos: mushrooms

Lengua: tongue

Picadillo: seasoned ground beef

Pollo: chicken

THEME RESTAURANT

Just as amusement parks have different rides, **theme restaurants** have different menus, but diners enter knowing what to expect. At the House of Blues, would-be **soul food** is served in a building with corrugated metal walls. Outback offers meat and potatoes with an Australian accent. At Medieval Times, "serving wenches" bring the victuals as rowdy banqueters cheer jousting knights. At these people-pleasing places, customers leave with sated appetites as well as bags full of souvenir hats, T-shirts, and key rings to recall their happy experience.

While formulaic foodtainment seems like a post-Disney pop culture notion, it actually goes back to the Moorish and rococo cafeterias of the 1920s and Depression-era Hollywood, when profligate celebrities ignored hard times at merry movie colony restaurants with jungle and pirate decor. One called the Pirate's Den featured mock floggings. At a hideaway called Don the Beachcomber, meals were served in palm-lined rooms, with water sprinkled on tin roofs to simulate tropical downpours. Inspired by Don's success, "Trader Vic" Bergeron of Oakland conceived a virtual-reality Polynesian paradise in 1937 and transformed his raffish beer parlor, then called Hinky Dink's, into the original Trader Vic's. To this day, at Trader Vic's in Asia, Europe, the Middle East, and North America, you can still eat flaming pu-pu platters and drink extravagant rum potations to the beat of far-off tom-toms in escapist dining rooms of wicker, totem poles, and scowling tiki masks.

Restaurant Associates added epicurean ambition to the notion of a theme restaurant in the 1950s in such high-tone New York dining rooms as the Forum of the Twelve Caesars and Tower Suite. At the former, customers were made to feel like emperors, ordering orgiastic meals from a menu with Latin subtitles, drinking wine from goblets proffered by waiters dressed as Phoenician guards. A review in *Gourmet* magazine found it "hard to believe that there has ever been such completely perfect service anywhere—even in the palaces of the Caesars themselves." Unlike today's democratic theme restaurants, the Forum was a high-rollers' haven, as was Restaurant Associates' Tower Suite, in which the gimmick was penthouse dining: One was attended by a "personal" servant who introduced himself by name at the beginning of the meal—a flourish that eventually trickled down to annoy millions of diners in all sorts of restaurants.

The modern era of theme restaurants aimed at average palates and modest pocketbooks started in 1971. That is the year a good-times eatery called R.J. Grunt's opened in Chicago. Grunt's had no single theme, but it was a jolly place, its menu riddled with puns, its audacious **salad bar** the progenitor of all huge salad bars. Proprietor Rich Melman's company, named Lettuce Entertain You, went on to open several personality-plus restaurants in Chicago, including Ed Debevic's, which was christened for an imaginary blue-collar proprietor. That year was also when the first Hard Rock Café opened, in London, offering hamburgers and loud music to homesick Americans and curious Europeans. When Hard Rock came to New York in 1984, it added memorabilia to the formula, soon boasting that it was the world's foremost rock-n-roll museum. Plastered with truckloads of stuff that once belonged to heart-throbs and hit-makers, and with a repertoire of nonstop tunes blasting through the chaos, Hard Rock became the defining theme restaurant of the late twentieth century, with branches nearly everywhere there were tourists. But of course the nexus of theme restaurants is Las Vegas, where everything, including the food, is meant to put customers into a state of dreamy fantasy. It could be argued that even the innumerable celebrity-chef eateries in Las Vegas reflect the theme restaurant concept, the theme in these cases being fine dining, with a menu and ambience meant to replicate the original experience that is somewhere else.

1000 ISLANDS DRESSING

It is easy to believe that **1000 Islands dressing** was named for its looks. At least as much as a chicken's leg could be a drumstick or a pastry-wrapped frankfurter evoke a pig in a blanket, the creamy, pickle-dotted stuff puts one in mind of myriad atolls in a smooth pink sea.

The dressing was named not for its appearance, but its birthplace, a stretch of the St. Lawrence River known as the Thousand Islands. Among the few competing stories that explain its origin, the most logical is that it was christened by actress and cookbook writer May Irwin, who went upstate to fish for black bass and northern pike a century ago. The outing featured a twilight meal hosted by wilderness guide George LaLonde, at which he served a salad made with a dressing concocted by his wife, Sofia. Miss Irwin brought the recipe back to New York and presented it to George Boldt, owner of the Waldorf Astoria Hotel, as "1000 Islands dressing." Boldt was so impressed that he put it on the menu just as Miss Irwin had enjoyed it—atop a tossed salad with a garnish of chopped hard-boiled egg. With maitre d' Oscar Tschirsky as its booster, Sofia LaLonde's picnic-style salad dressing became a Park Avenue counterpart of Creole remoulade and an emblem of fine hotel-room dining.

The hotel at which May Irwin stayed in Clayton, New York, then known as the Herald Hotel, is now the 1000 Islands Inn. Naturally the inn serves 1000 Islands dressing on its salads in the dining room, and it is still a base camp for charter boats and angling expeditions during which guests fish the St.

Lawrence River, then enjoy their catch, pan-fried over an open fire, with eggs, bacon, and potatoes. The inn annually puts up five thousand bottles of original-recipe dressing. They bear labels boasting that it is "the only salad dressing ever named for a region of the United States."

THROWED ROLLS

When Agnes and Earl Lambert opened Lambert's cafe in Sikeston, Missouri, in 1942, they were so short-handed on the floor that rather than carry bread baskets to the eight tables in their tiny dining room, they tossed still-warm rolls one by one from the kitchen door directly to customers. Their little eatery has since grown huge, with branches in Ozark, Missouri, and Foley, Alabama, but the self-proclaimed "Home of the **Throwed Roll**" continues the outlandish food delivery system, waiters calling "heads up!" as they heave buns into the dining room, then warning, "Careful, now," as they ladle out rivers of sorghum honey for roll-dipping.

TOASTED RAVIOLI

A misnomer, **toasted ravioli** in fact are deep-fried. Pasta pillows, filled with a spicy hash of meat, cheese, and vegetables, are dredged in seasoned bread crumbs and boiled in oil until the outside turns crunchy. They are served with a red sauce that can range from Italian marinara to the sort of cocktail sauce you'd expect with shrimp. The custom is to eat them by hand, dipping a ravioli in the sauce before having a bite.

Once a signature dish of the Italian restaurants of "The Hill" neighborhood in St. Louis, T-ravs have spread across the country to menus of taverns (where, like **Buffalo wings,** they are such a good drink companion) and all kinds of Italian restaurants, even Olive Garden. While there are vague antecedents in Sicilian cookery (where the filling is sweet), American folklore says they were invented at a restaurant called Angelo's (now Charlie Gitto's) after World War II, when chef Gina Oldani accidentally dropped ravioli into a pan of bread crumbs and decided to fry them rather than boil them.

TOMATO PIE

In pizzerias all around southern New Jersey it is common to hear talk of **tomato pies.** A style of **pizza** built upon a thin crust with a chewy edge that is occasionally blistered black, the tomato pie is fundamentally Neapolitan-American, but it is distinguished by the fact that cheese and any desired toppings are applied before the tomatoes.

Tomatoes, not sauce! At De Lorenzo's of Trenton and Robbinsville, they are hand-crushed and radiant with flavor. Cheese-free pies on which tomatoes star go back to the earliest days of American pizzerias, when pizza was poor man's food and mozzarella was a luxury. A completely different configuration is found in the American South, where the term *tomato pie* can refer to a casserole of long-cooked tomatoes topped with cheesy bread crumbs.

Frank Pepe Pizzeria Napoletana in New Haven, Connecticut, still boasts of tomato pies even though its repertoire has gone far beyond that.

TOPOPO SALAD

Near Mexico City is a 18,000-foot tall volcano called Popocatépetl, which has at least two reasons to be a footnote in North American history. The first is that when Che Guevara and Fidel Castro were plotting the overthrow of the Cuban government, Che desperately tried to overcome his asthma by climbing it. Castro's autobiography reports, "He made a heroic effort, although he never managed to reach that summit." Aside from causing Che to wheeze, Popocatépetl's other claim to fame is that it was the inspiration for the **topopo salad,** a star attraction on Mexican restaurants throughout Tucson and, rarely, beyond.

Topopo salads were popular in South Tucson long before trendy chefs thought of vertical food.

The story at the august El Charro in Tucson is that founder Monica Flinn was so impressed when she saw Popocatépetl that she designed a salad to look like it and named it using an old Indian word for volcano. Height is the common denominator of each topopo salad, no matter what its specific ingredients. Atop a crisp tostada, lettuce and vegetables are dressed and formed into a great conical mound, up to a foot tall, with columns of cheese, carrots, and celery running up the side. Mealworthy versions also include **carne seca,** roast chicken or shrimp, and garnishes include tomato, olives, avocado, and festive colored peppers.

TRAVELIN' MAN

The Roadfood.com screen name of Steve Koenigsberg, **travelin' man,** has become a commonly used verb among seekers of regional American food. It dates back to 2008, when Mr. Koenigsberg took a road trip between Christmas and New Year's with an itinerary of good restaurants at which he wanted to eat. But because of the holidays, an inordinate number of them were closed. To be *travelin' manned* is to arrive at a much-anticipated roadfood destination only to find the door locked.

RAY TURNER

The eel never had so staunch an admirer as **Ray Turner.** Yes, it's hideously slimy and it has an ugly face. But is it delicious? Is it nutritious? "It is good groceries!" Ray proclaims. His account of the lifestyle of the snake-shaped fish is inspirational.

"Your androgynous species, like the salmon," he scoffs, "they travel by rote back to where they were spawned. The eel migrates to where the water tastes best. It has an acute olfactory system with two sets of nostrils and can smell a few parts per million when it wants to look for brackish water. The male likes hanging back along the coast further south, but the female, she

Eel man of the Delaware River.

likes fresh water. She will stay here and grow for years—do you know you can read the age of an eel, just like a tree, by counting the rings on the stones in its head? After maybe twelve years she will reach sexual maturity, and when the drive hits to go down to the Sargasso Sea, look out, here she comes."

When she comes, Ray is ready and waiting. He has been an eeler on the Delaware River for over a quarter century, and he speaks of the migration with joy. "Once the weir is built in July, we'll catch maybe one or two a day from those who live in these waters," he says. "In August and September it will grow to double digits. Then one night in September, when the moon is full and there has been a good rain, we will start to see the large black females. It is about to happen." As he describes it, the spotting of the first big females in the weir is as awesome as seeing a couple of longhorns in a bedded herd rise to their feet—the signal of an impending slithery stampede. In the first good night he will trap over one thousand eels, which is about half of the whole season's catch.

Ray learned to love eels as a boy. Before World War II, his father used to catch them downriver from the smokehouse at Eel Weir Hollow, and before that, he says, "The codgers around here will tell you that their grandfathers used to do it. It's is an old, old art. Native Americans that lived along this river did it, that's for sure. Imagine a tribe enduring a long winter, realizing that there are tons of eels going downstream in the fall. What a great opportunity to enhance the larder! Do you know that scientists have radioactively carbon-dated an eel weir site that goes back 5900 years? It may be the oldest man-made structure on this continent."

The thought of a surviving prehistoric weir is spellbinding because building a sturdy one is an eeler's primary challenge. Each year starting in July, Ray goes into the river to construct a stone conduit some three hundred feet long, and he uses timber to erect a ramped trap that will funnel big parts of the migrating school into his eel rack. Although his full white beard and the backwoods setting of his smokehouse make him look like a Western Catskills King Neptune, this water man was trained as a civil engineer, and he relishes telling about the joists, studs, and lattice work that go into the wood structure, and how, by triangulating the pressure, he erects a rack impervious to high water torrents. "If you don't have a good rack, you can blow it and lose everything," he cautions. "That is why I devote so much attention to building it right in the summer. Once they start coming, you must have confidence in your weir."

Much as he delights in catching mature females on their way south, he disapproves of nabbing eels earlier in their life cycle as they float north with the currents. Eating the young ones, known to epicures as glass eels, is bad for the health of the species, he maintains. With avuncular affection for the little critters, he asks, "Do you know that when an eel is born, it looks like a willow leaf? It's that fragile. Aristotle believed that an eel grew from a single horse hair dropped in the water. So little is known about them, it's a shame."

What really chaps Ray Turner's hide is unfounded aversion to the *Anguilla rostrata.* "It is a cross the eel must bear," he says. "People think of it as a snake, which it is not. I guarantee you will find eel good to eat, if only you can get over the *eew!* factor."

TURTLE

Confectionery shops and ice cream parlors of the Midwest are no longer the only places where the **turtle** is king. Originally created by See's Candy of San Francisco and for a long time a passion mostly in the heartland, the turtle now is everywhere people have a sweet tooth. Its defining elements of chocolate, caramel, and toasted pecans are combined not only as a candy, but as cheesecake, layer cake, ice cream, and pie. The name Turtles is a trademark, owned by DeMet's Candy Company, but that hasn't stopped confectioners coast to coast from creating their own species, some of which do resemble an actual turtle, albeit one hiding from the world with its head and flippers drawn in underneath its shell (which can be either milk or dark chocolate or, in gourmet candy stores, white chocolate).

No single element of the turtle is essential for a candy to claim terrapin identity. Pecans may be replaced by cashews (which, when sticking out from the chocolate, are actually more flipperlike), macadamias, or almonds. Boston's Upstairs on the Square uses brown sugar praline instead of caramel, resulting in a turtle that is shockingly sweet. Turtle Alley of Gloucester, Massachusetts, infuses turtles with chipotle peppers and does a dazzling riff on the subject by including dried sour cherries and apricots. We even have seen naked turtles, which are globs of caramel and nuts with no chocolate shell.

A perfect turtle sundae, complete with crisp, salty, toasted nuts, as served at Condrell's in Buffalo, New York.

TWINKIES

The world's most famous snack cake was named after a shoe. In 1930, during the Great Depression, Jimmy Dewar, manager of Chicago's Continental Bakery, was looking for a way to use the company's "Little Short Cake Finger" pans year-round instead of only during strawberry season. On a trip to St. Louis, Mr. Dewar saw a billboard advertising Twinkle Toe Shoes. No one remembers if the gigantic shoes were depicted filled with feet or empty, but the vision inspired Mr. Dewar. "I came up with the idea of injecting the little cakes with a filling," he recalled, and he named his invention **Twinkies.** Once the recipe was perfected, Mr. Dewar ate three a day for half a century. "I have twelve great-grandchildren, all of them eating Twinkies," he boasted in 1981, shortly before he died at the age of 88.

The original filling was banana crème, but during the 1940s that was replaced by vanilla. Twinkies were the favorite petit four of 1950s TV marionette Howdy Doody, as well as of Doodyville cowhand Twinkie the Kid. Archie Bunker demanded them in his lunch box on *All in the Family*. Twinkies became so significant a part of American life that they took the blame for driving former San Francisco city supervisor Dan White insane. After he murdered Mayor George Moscone and Supervisor Harvey Milk in 1978, White's lawyers successfully used what jurisprudence now knows as *the Twinkie defense* to convince a jury that their client was suffering "diminished mental capacity" because he ate a diet of Twinkies and candy bars. White got off on a lesser charge and subsequently committed suicide. "Nobody knows what's going on inside of me," he said, neither blaming nor exonerating Twinkies for his condition.

ANTHONY AND GAIL UGLESICH

It is no small feat to achieve legendary status in the food-savvy city of New Orleans, but during a multidecade tenure at their eponymous lunch-only eatery, **Anthony and Gail Uglesich** did just that. As they explored and expanded New Orleans cuisine, gleefully inventing such glories as Shrimp Uggie and Muddy Water Trout, as well as honing Creole tradition, the family restaurant became a shrine to which devoted eaters thronged from everywhere. You seldom knew exactly what you'd find on the menu, but there was little doubt it would be shockingly good. And you could count on Gail and Anthony's charismatic presence behind the counter and among the dozen scattered tables, ever eager to share their culinary enthusiasm with friends and newcomers. They loved to tell you exactly which fish were running best that week (and about the dish they created with them) and what the produce market offered Gail that morning before dawn. Their talent, devotion, and endearing personalities made Uglesich's restaurant a roadfood classic: the informal eat-shack energized by a passion for perfection.

Anthony and Gail Uglesich behind the counter of their restaurant.

WALLEYE

◇◇

It is a fish—a freshwater perch named because of its large, light-reflecting eye—but at the western side of the Great Lakes, **walleye** is an obsession, both among fishermen and eaters. Roadfood.com contributor Davydd wrote, "No bar or pub in Minnesota serving food dare not have the walleye sandwich on its menu." Indeed, it is the state fish of Minnesota (as well as of South Dakota), famously moist and squeaky-clean when pan-fried or grilled, served as a dinner entree or in a sandwich on a torpedo roll or burger bun. Minneapolis's Hell's Kitchen restaurant is known for its walleye BLT; at the Tavern on Grand in St. Paul, which advertises itself as "Minnesota's State Restaurant Serving Minnesota's State Fish," the menu includes walleye cakes, walleye bites, walleye sandwiches, walleye shore lunches, and a surf 'n' turf supper of walleye and sirloin.

WEIGHT WATCHERS

◇◇

In 1961, when Jean Nidetch was a 200+ pound bowling alley babysitter in a size 44 dress, she went on a diet supervised by the New York City Department of Health Obesity Clinic. But Mrs. Nidetch cheated. She couldn't stop eating Mallomars, two packages per night. She was so embarrassed by her transgression that she didn't admit it to the clinic. Instead, one afternoon she called six overweight friends and invited them to her Long Island apartment, where she told them about her diet and, more important, unburdened herself about the forbidden Mallomars. With great relief, the women shared their own diet-busting sins. One confessed she hid peanuts behind asparagus cans in the cupboard; another snuck down to the refrigerator after her husband fell asleep. "All overweight people have this tremendous desire to talk," Mrs. Nidetch observed.

Each of the women took home a copy of the diet, and the next week, when they met again, they brought more fat friends who listened eagerly to stories that showed they were not alone in their dieting frustrations. The group grew. They chipped in and bought a medical scale for weekly weigh-ins. Soon there were forty of them, and as word spread across Long Island, Mrs. Nidetch found herself speaking to strangers who had been inspired by her group to get together to form their own. In May 1963, she created **Weight Watchers** and began charging two dollars to attend a meeting. Before the term "support group" had been coined, members were sharing anxieties about forbidden Entenmann's and revealing the secret hiding places for their emergency stash of Chunkys.

Calling it "Alcoholics Anonymous for the overweight," *Business Week* marveled in 1967 about the many ways Weight Watchers was making money, which soon included a cookbook, packaged nonfat milk and low-calorie sugar, food scales, whole frozen meals, and summer camps for obese girls. Two years later, *Look* magazine wrote about "Weight Watcher weddings, where reduced brides and grooms thank her [Nidetch] for making it possible" and said that people were clamoring for franchises around the world, "including undernourished India." In 1979, Nidetch and her business partner, Albert Lippert, sold Weight Watchers to Heinz for $100 million. Today, with three-quarters of all American women and half of American men believing they are too fat, Weight Watchers has a membership of 1.5 million people and annual sales of $1.4 billion.

WEST INDIES SALAD

We have met three old-time chefs from Mobile, Alabama, each of whom claims to have invented what has become one of the city's hallmark seafood dishes, **West Indies salad.** The most convincing story is that of long-time restaurateur Bill Bayley, a bigger-than-life gent never without a fat stogie clamped in his mouth, who also is credited with inventing fried crab claws in the early 1960s. "If you ain't et West Indies salad, you ain't et Mobile," the late Mr. Bayley once told us, his story of its origin going back to when he was a cook on a ship docked in the Cayman Islands shortly after World War II. One day he found himself with a bunch of lobsters but not much to go with them. So he mixed up what he did have—oil, vinegar, salt, pepper, and a chopped sweet onion—and marinated the cooked and cooled lobster meat in it. It was good. A few years later, when he opened a restaurant in Mobile, he wanted to include it

on his menu. But lobsters were scarce and expensive. So he substituted meat from the Gulf's abundant crab population. A great dish was born and is now available in seafood restaurants all around the Mobile Bay. At once rich and piquant, West Indies salad is served cool by the bowl—frequently family-style for the whole table, accompanied by saltine crackers. It usually is an appetizer, but it is often eaten in double portions as an entree.

West Indies Salad

1 pound fresh lump crabmeat, picked clean
⅔ cup chopped sweet onion
¼ cup light salad oil
⅓ cup cider vinegar
½ teaspoon pepper
½ teaspoon salt
½ cup crushed ice
Paprika
Chopped parsley
Saltine crackers

1. Make alternating layers of crabmeat and onion in a 1- to 2-quart canning jar. Combine the oil, vinegar, pepper, and salt, and pour it over the crabmeat. Top the crabmeat with the crushed ice. Cover the jar and refrigerate 24 hours.

2. Serve dusted with paprika and garnished with parsley, accompanied by saltines.

4–6 APPETIZER PORTIONS

WHITE CLAM PIZZA

White clam pizza was first made in New Haven in the mid-twentieth century. While its exact origin is uncertain, one frequently repeated story is that a clam vendor in an alley off Wooster Street near Frank Pepe Pizzeria Napoletana convinced Pepe that the two of them should pool their resources. Raw littlenecks on the half-shell already were on Pepe's menu as a prepizza hors d'oeuvre. Pepe used them on a pie with neither tomatoes nor mozzarella cheese—just the freshly-opened clams, minced garlic, a dusting of sharp Pecorino cheese and a sprinkle of herbs. The elegant medley is really more a flatbread than a **pizza,** its crust ultra-thin with a rugged underside from grains of semolina on the oven floor, its circumference puffed up in a golden circle that offers profound resilience in every bite.

Elaborations proliferate in Connecticut and beyond. A clam casino pizza adds bacon to the topping; when fresh clams are not available, some local pizzerias offer shrimp in their place; and while purists scoff at the idea, mozzarella cheese may be added, transforming an elegant pizza into one that is profligate.

White Clam Pizza

Dough

1 package dry yeast
1 teaspoon sugar
1 cup warm water
2–2¾ cups all-purpose flour
2 teaspoons salt
Cornmeal

1. Dissolve the yeast and sugar in ¼ cup of the warm water. Add the remaining ¾ cup water to 2 cups of flour. Add salt and when the yeast is proofed, add it, too. Stir together and turn out onto a floured board. Let the dough rest while you clean and oil the bowl.

2. Knead the dough vigorously for a full 15 minutes, adding flour if necessary to create a silky dough. Return it to the bowl, cover with two tight layers of plastic wrap, and let it rise in a warm place until doubled in size, 2–3 hours.

3. Punch down the dough and flatten it on a lightly floured board. Pounding with the heel of your hand and lifting the dough to stretch it, carefully and methodically work the dough into a round about 15 inches in diameter. Sprinkle a baker's peel with cornmeal, and put the dough on it. Cover the dough and let it rest.

4. Place your pizza stone in the oven (on the bottommost shelf) and preheat the oven to 500°F while you open the clams and gather other toppings.

Topping

3–6 large cloves garlic (to taste)
¼ cup olive oil
2 dozen littleneck clams
1 teaspoon oregano
2 tablespoons grated Romano cheese

1. While the dough is rising, mince the garlic and let it steep in the olive oil. After the dough has rested 10 minutes, brush on the oil and garlic, leaving a half-inch of untouched diameter. Open the clams and spread them around the pie with a dash of their own juice. Sprinkle on the oregano and cheese.

2. Slide the pizza off the baker's peel onto the preheated pizza stone. Lower the oven heat to 450°F and bake 15 minutes, or until the crust is medium brown. Remove, cut into triangles or squares, and serve immediately.

SERVES 2 AS A MEAL; 4 AS HORS D'OEUVRE

288

WHITE HOT

Although it resembles a weiss-wurst, the beloved **white hot** of upstate New York plays the role of a **hot dog,** served in a bun and frequently topped with chili. Originally devised by a Rochester butcher shop in the 1920s as an alternative to **red hots,** made with uncured (hence white) pork and veal (and even sometimes also beef), the white hot is today mostly (if not all)

Upstate New Yorkers refer to their beloved white hots as porkers. Need we mention that they are not kosher?

pork, earning it the local nickname *porker.* The Buffalo Bills of the National Football League have deemed the white hot their official hot dog.

WHOOPIE PIE

Individually wrapped in plastic or cellophane and sold at seafood shacks and in grocery stores for a dollar or two, a **whoopie pie** is two tender disks of dark chocolate cake with a layer of sugary white crème (not cream) or Marshmallow Fluff in between—like a large, soft Oreo cookie. It has become known throughout much of the United States, but for many years it was a local specialty of both the Downeast coast and Pennsylvania Dutch country—each of which is credited with its origin.

The New England story is that it was introduced in 1927 by the

A whoopie pie in its rightful place: On a picnic table along the Downeast shore on a sunny summer day.

Berwick Cake Company (which, two years before, had created the Devil Dog). At the time, Eddie Cantor was starring in a musical play in Boston called "Whoopie." During the performance, chocolate pies were tossed into the audience as Cantor sang the hit song "Making Whoopie." It is unclear whether the cake or the song was named first and inspired the other.

The alternative account of whoopie pie's genesis is that when Amish women served them to their husbands or children, the recipients were so delighted that they shouted "Whoopie!" Before the exclamation became its name, the pastry was called a *hucklebuck* (a term that has since been applied to the sexual congress known as Position of the Wife of Indra of the *Kama Sutra* and in 1949 was the title of a Chubby Checker song that contained the lyrics, "Wiggle like a snake, wobble like a duck / That's what you do when you do the Hucklebuck").

WONDER BREAD

Since the nineteenth century, when millers began extracting the germ from wheat to make grinding more efficient and bleaching flour white to make it prettier, bread has been the flashpoint for food fights among the gastronomically self-righteous. No brand is more symbolic than Wonder, the whitest of them all. Early proponents of this commercial loaf decried all the time home cooks wasted baking their own bread, which probably turned out coarse and heavy—too much like peasant fodder for people eager to elevate their tables to middle-class respectability. A 1934 booklet called *Vitality Demands Energy* (published by General Mills) took up the cause of white bread by crediting it with nothing less than America's survival. "An abundant supply of bread has meant a well nourished, satisfied people, the bulwark against revolt," it said, reminding readers what had happened in countries (Russia?) where the bread was black: "Weakened nations have succumbed."

But as far back as 1871, Reverend Henry Ward Beecher condemned white bread as soulless, writing, "What had been the staff of life for countless ages [has] become a weak crutch." Anti–white bread people never lost their skepticism about mass-produced bread, an attitude that won new converts as health food evolved from fringe faddism to a socially acceptable lifestyle choice.

Modern-day philosophical descendants of Beecher believe that virtually all white food (white rice, mashed potatoes, white sugar, white asparagus, even milk) is suspicious if not outright toxic. Conversely, dark food (brown rice, honey, bran) is honest and good. Waverly Root and Richard de Rochemont, worrying about the debasement of the American palate, concluded their 1981 screed *Eating in America* by saying "the poor will continue to buy the inflated white loaf," but that "some young households will get around the problem by baking their own bread, with a few of them grinding their own wheat and grains in little kitchen mills."

Even Wonder Bread has bowed to popular wisdom, now offering not only "Classic White," but also "Smartwhite" (less sodium), "Light White" (more fiber, fewer calories), and "Wonder Made with Whole Grain," not to mention a line of actual Whole Wheat Wonders. One amazing historical fact to consider is that the original Wonder Bread, introduced in 1920, was sold *unsliced*. Can you imagine what an unsliced loaf of Wonder Bread must have felt like? Perhaps like a balloon? Probably so, because the name "Wonder" came about when a bakery executive was watching a balloon race, and the balloons reminded him of the bread. Because they also filled him with wonder, he put the two thoughts together and realized he had a name for the company's new product. The package was almost the same as it is today, covered by pictures of balloons, which gave Wonder the nickname by which old-time housewives still know it, "Balloon Bread."

In 1930, Wonder became the first national brand to be sold in already-sliced loaves—a move that increased bread consumption in general and made Wonder number one. During World War II, the government determined that bread-slicing was a waste of national effort, leading to the still-heard expression "the greatest thing since sliced bread."

YA-KA-MEIN

Ya-ka-mein, dubbed Old Sober for its power to cure a bout of drunkenness, is known to some small degree by adventurous African-American eaters. But to Caucasians, it is pretty much invisible. As one listener of our report about it on radio's *The Splendid Table* noted, *yak* is found in "establishments located

Nutritional virtue in the form of ya-ka-mein, as made by Linda Green, the Ya Ka Mein Lady of New Orleans.

in areas many suburbanites would not venture. High-end Chinese restaurants look down on yak. They have labeled it black-people-food and refuse to serve it." New Orleans is nothing but welcoming, so it is no great surprise that a wider range of eaters know it there.

Occasionally served in a restaurant, but more commonly from a food truck in a Styrofoam bowl, ya-ka-mein is an exemplary melting pot dish. While it does have a vaguely Asian flavor, thanks to soy sauce, it is no more Chinese than is chop suey. Its origin has been credited to either African-American Korean war veterans who brought the idea back home or to railroad construction crew cooks trying to please both Chinese and black workers. Recipes vary, but the essential formula is spaghetti noodles in spicy broth topped with shredded beef, green onions, and half a hard-boiled egg: like Oodles of Noodles, but good.

INDEX

Italicized page numbers indicate illustrations.

Adams, Rhoda, *266*
alcoholic beverages
    ditch, whiskey, 91
    mint juleps, 180
    red beer, 221
    Sazerac, 235–36
    tequila, 270–71
Ali, Ben (Ben's Chili Bowl), 134, *134*
American chop suey (recipe), *1*, 1–2
andouille, 2
apizza, 3, *3*
apple(s)
    apple pan dowdy, 4
    Huguenot torte, 153
    Jewish apple cake, 158–59, *159*
artichokes, 96

baby back ribs, 226
Baker, Robert, 75
bakery pizza, 4, *4*
banh mi, 5
barbecue. *See also* ribs
    brownies (burnt ends), *29*, 29–30
    chipped, 55, *55*
    dips, 90
    dry rubs for, 97
    fried bologna, 111
    Kentucky mutton, 10–11
    Mr. Brown and Miss White, 181, *181*
    notable chefs of, 7–8, 32, *32*
    overview and history, *5*, 5–8, *6*, *7*, *8*
    pig pickin's, 200
    pulled pork, 8–9, *9*
    salad (recipe), 14
    Santa Maria, 12–13
    sauces, 247–48
    spaghetti (recipe), 15, *15*

Texas beef, 11–12
    whole hog, 9–10
Barberton chicken, 15–16
bean dogs, 16, *16*
beans
    bean dogs, 16, *16*
    butter, 34, *34*
    lima bean supper, 166, *166*
    red, and rice, 220, *220*
Beard, James, *17*, 17–18
Beaufort stew, 117, *117*
beef. *See also* burgers; corned beef
    American chop suey, *1*, 1–2
    breaded steak, 27–28
    cheese steak, 39–40
    chicken-fried steak, 43–44
    chili con carne, 49–52, *51*, *52*
    chili mac (recipe), 53–54, *54*
    chimichangas, 55
    chipped (barbecue), 55, *55*
    Cincinnati chili, 53, 59–61, *61*
    city chicken, 62
    debris, 84, *84*
    downstate chowder, 94
    dry links, 97
    flautas, 108, *108*
    French dip, 110–11
    fried bologna, 111
    garbage plate, 119, *119*
    half smoke, 134
    hanky pankies, 137
    hot, 143–44
    hot dish, 146
    hot links, 149–50, *150*
    Italian, 157, *157*
    jibaritos, 159
    joes, 160, *160*

loosemeats, *168*, 168–69
menudo, 173, *173*
pasties, 194
Sheboygan brats, 238
tenderloin, 268–70, *269*
Texas, 11–12
Texas chili, 50–51, *51*
Topeka chili, 52, *52*
on weck, *19*, 19–20
ya-ka-mein, 291–92, *292*
beer, red, 221
beignet, 20, *20*
Benedictine cheese, 21
bierocks, 21
Biloxi bacon, 22
biscochitos, 22
biscuits
cat head, 38
culinary experts of, 100, *100*
blind pig, 255
boiled dinners, 22–23, *23*
boiled peanuts, 23, *23*
bologna, fried, 111
boned and buttered perch, 24, *24*
boomerang Formica, 24–25, *25*
Boston cream pie, 26
boudin, 26–27
breaded pork tenderloins (recipe), 268, 270
breaded steak (recipe), 27–28
breads. *See also* pastries
cat head biscuits, 38
corn bread, 72–73, *73*
kummelweck, 19
muffalettas, 182, *182*
Navajo fry bread (recipe), 183–85, *184*
sopaipillas, 249–50, *250*
sourdough starters, 139
Wonder Bread, 290–91
broasting, 28–29
brownies (burnt ends), *29*, 29–30
Brunswick stew (recipe), *30*, 30–31
Bryant, Arthur, 7–8, 32, *32*
Buffalo wings, 33, *33*

burgers
butter, 35, *35*
cabbage, 21
green chile cheeseburgers (recipe), *130*, 130–31
hamburgers, 135–36, *136*
juicy Lucy, 162
onion-fried, 191
sliders, 243, *243*
slingers, 243–44
sloppers, 130
sloppy joes, 244
slush, 244
steamed cheeseburgers, *256*, 256–57
yip-yips, 244
burgoo, 34, *34*
butter beans, 34, *34*
butter burgers, 35, *35*

cabbage burger, 21
cakes
crumb, 81, *81*
gateau sirop, 119
gooey butter (recipe), 123–24
hummingbird, 153, *153*
Jewish apple, 158–59, *159*
whoopie pie, *289*, 289–90
California dip, 36, 216
California pizza, 203
candies
Charlie Chaplin, 38, *38*
Chocolate Lace, 259–60
coal candy, 64
fairy food, 101
Pez, 197–98
salt water taffy, 233
sponge candy, 254, *254*
turtles, 281, *281*
carne adovada, 36, *36*
carne seca, 37
cashew chicken, Springfield-style, 37
cat head biscuits, 38
Cesana, Renzo, 72

Charlie Chaplin, 38, *38*

cheese. *See also* cheeseburgers

    Benedictine, 21

    Cheez Whiz, 40–41

    curds, 39

    hot, sandwiches, 145, *145*

    nachos, 183

    pimiento, 201, *201*

    Provel, 218, *218*

    steak, 39

cheeseburgers

    green chile (recipe), *130*, 130–31

    juicy Lucy, 162

    steamed, *256*, 256–57

Cheez Whiz, 40–41

chess pie, 41–42

Chicago mix, 42

Chicago pizza, 203, *203*

chicken

    Barberton, 15–16

    booyah, 42

    broasting, 28–29

    Brunswick stew (recipe), *30*, 30–31

    Buffalo wings, 33, *33*

    cashew, Springfield-style, 37

    chimichangas, 55

    Cornell (recipe), *75*, 75–76, *76*

    downstate chowder, 94

    étouffée, 101, *101*

    fajitas, 102

    flautas, 108, *108*

    hot chicken, *145*, 145–46

    maque choux, 170

    nuggets, 75

    pasties, 194

    restaurant-lined roads specializing in, 43

    Rhode Island's chicken dinner, 225

    Sheboygan brats, 238

    topopo salad, 277–78, *278*

    Vesuvio (recipe), 44–45, *45*

Chicken Dinner Road, 43

chicken-fried steak, 43–44

Chicken Vesuvio (recipe), 44–45, *45*

Child, Julia, 46–47

chile(s)

    green, cheeseburger, *130*, 130–31

    overview, 48–49, *49*

chile rellenos, 53

chili dogs

    Coney Islands, 70, *70*

    Dixie (slaw) dogs, 91–92

    Michigan, 174–75, *175*

    scrambled dogs, 237

chilis

    Cincinnati, 53, 59

    Cincinnati five-way (recipe), 60–61, *61*

    con carne, 49–52, *51, 52*

    Green Bay, 129

    mac (recipe), 53–54, *54*

    mac a la mode, 53

    overview and history, 49–50

    Texas (recipe), 50–51, *51*

    Topeka (recipe), 52, *52*

chimichangas, 55

chipped (barbecue), 55, *55*

chitlins, 55–56

chitterlings, 56

chocolate

    Boston cream pie, 26

    Charlie Chaplin, 38, *38*

    Chocolate Lace, 259–60

    egg creams, 99, *99*

    fairy food (angel candy), 101

    gold brick sauce, 122

    sponge candy, 254, *254*

    turtles, 281, *281*

chop suey, American (recipe), *1*, 1–2

chowders

    clam/seafood (recipe), *56*, 56–58, *57, 58*

    conch, 69

    downstate (southern Illinois), 94

    farmhouse, 56

chow mein sandwiches, 59

Cincinnati chili, 53, 59

Cincinnati five-way chili (recipe),

    60–61, *61*

295

cioppino, 61
city chicken, 62
clam(s)
    cake, 63, *63*
    casino pizza, 287
    chowder, *56*, 56–58, *57*, *58*
    clambake, 62, *63*
    fried, *112*, 112–13
    fritters, 62
    shore dinners, *239*, 239–40
    stuffies, 259
coal candy, 64
cobblers
    Huguenot torte, 153
cochon de lait, 64
coffee
    milk, 64–65
    milk shakes (frappe), 65, 178
    terminology for, 66–67
coffee houses, 65
coffee shops, 65–66, *66*
Coleman, Joe, 68, *68*
conch
    chowder, 69
    snail salads, *246*, 246–47
concrete, 69
Coney Islands, 70, *70*
congealed salads, 71, *71*
Continental, The (television show), 72
corn bread/cakes, 72–73, *73*
corn dogs, 74, *74*
corned beef
    boiled dinners, 22–23, *23*
    red flannel hash, 222, *222*
    Reuben sandwiches, 224
Cornell Chicken (recipe), *75*, 75–76, *76*
cornmeal
    corn bread/cakes, 72–73, *73*
    corn dogs, 74, *74*
    hushpuppies, 154, *154*
    Indian pudding, 154–55, *155*
    jonnycakes, 162, *162*
    livermush, 166

scrapple, 237
    spoonbread, 255
country ham, 76–77, *77*
crab(s)
    cakes, 77–78, *78*
    étouffée, 101, *101*
    feasts, 78–79
    stone, 257
    West Indies salad (recipe), 285–86, *286*
cracklin's, 79, *79*
crawfish
    boil, 80, *80*
    étouffée, 101, *101*
    maque choux, 170
    pie, 172, *172*
crumb cake, 81, *81*
Cuban sandwiches, 82, *82*
Cuisinart, 82–83
custard, frozen
    basic, 118, *118*
    concrete, 69
    schaum tortes, 236

date shake, 83–84
debris, 84, *84*
deep-dish pizza, 85, *85*
deli terminology, 86
desserts. *See also* cakes; candies; ice cream;
    pastries; pies
    apple pan dowdy, 4
    biscochitos, 22
    concrete, 69
    frozen custard, 118, *118*
    Grape-Nuts pudding, 127
    Huguenot torte, 153
    Indian pudding, 154–55, *155*
    schaum torte, 236
    shave ice, 237–38
    sugar on snow, 259–60
    Twinkies, 282
Detroit (square) pizza, 255
devonshire, 86
diners, history and terminology, 87, 87–90

dips
  barbecue, 90
  California, 36, 216
dirty rice, 91, *91*
ditch, 91
Dixie dogs, 91–92
doggie bags, 92–93
dooryard fruit, 93
doughboys, 94, *94*
downstate chowder, 94
dressing, 1000 Islands, 275–76
drinks. *See also* alcoholic beverages; coffee;
  shakes
  egg creams, 99, *99*
  energy (Red Bull), 221–22
  horchata, 142
  Hubba (Texas) water, 152, *152*
  Italian ice, 157
  loganberry juice, 167–68, *168*
  Moxie, 181, *181*
  smoothies, 246
  sweet tea (recipe), 263–64, *264*
  Tang, 267–68, *268*
drive-ins, 95–97, *155*, 155–56
dry links, 97
dry rubs, 97
Duarte, Ron, 98, *98*

eels, 279–80
egg(s)
  hangtown fry, 137
  hoppel poppel, 141, *141*
  huevos rancheros, 152–53, *153*
  joes, 160, *160*
  matzoh brei, 170
  migas, 177–78, *178*
  and sausage pasties, 194
  sliders, 243–44
  Wilbur, 244
egg creams, 99, *99*
Ellison, Carol Fay, 100, *100*
energy drinks, 221–22
étouffée, 101, *101*

fairy food, 101
fajitas, 102
farmhouse chowder, 56
filberts, 102–3
fish. *See also seafood; specific types of shellfish*
  boned and buttered perch, 24, *24*
  hot, 149, *149*
  river herring, 229–30
  sandwiches, 68
  smoked mullet (Biloxi bacon), 22
  stew, 61
  tacos (recipe), 105–6, *106*
  walleye, 284
fish boils, *103*, 103–4
fish fries, 104–5, *105*
five-cup salad (recipe), 107
flannel cakes, 108
flautas, 108, *108*
Flinn, Monica, 109
fluffernutter, 110
Formica, boomerang, 24–25, *25*
frappe, 65, 178
French dip, 110–11
fried bologna, 111
fried dough (recipe), 113–14
fried green tomatoes, 115
fried pie, *115*, 115–16
Fritos pie, 116, *116*
Frogmore stew, 117, *117*
frozen custard. *See* custard, frozen
fruit
  dooryard, 93
  five-cup salad (recipe), 107
  smoothies, 246
fry sauce, 118

garbage plate, 119, *119*
gateau sirop, 119
Gerber sandwiches, 120
Ghetto fries, 120, *120*
giardiniera (recipe), 121, *121*
goetta, 122, *122*
gold brick sauce, 122

gonads, 123

goober peas, 23

gooey butter cake (recipe), 123–24

gorditas, 125, *125*

Grandma pizza, 125, *125*

granola, *126*, 126–27

Grape-Nuts ice cream (recipe), 128

Grape-Nuts pudding, 127

gravy, red-eye, 223

Greek pizza, 128–29, *129*

Green Bay chili, 129

green chile cheeseburgers (recipe), *130*, 130–31

green corn tamales, 131–32

grilled pizza, 132, *132*

grinders, 140

grits, creamy, 81, *81*

gulash, 244

gumbo, 132–33, *133*

half smoke, 134, *134*

halushka, 135

ham

    country, *76*, 76–77, *77*

    Cuban sandwiches, 82, *82*

    jambalaya, 158

    stuffed, 258, *258*

hamburgers, 135–36, *136. See also* burgers

hangtown fry, 137

hanky pankies, 137

Harvey, Fred (Harvey Houses), 136

hash, red flannel, 222, *222*

Hathaway's Coffee Shop, *66*

hazelnuts, 102–3

Herman, 139

heroes, 139–40, *140*

herring, river, 229–30

hoagies, 140, *140*

Hog Island sandwiches, 140

holy trinity, 141

hoppel poppel, 141, *141*

hoppin' john, 142

horchata, 142, *142*

horseshoes, 143, *143*

hot beef, 143–44

hot brown, 144, *144*

hot cheese sandwiches, 145, *145*

hot chicken, *145*, 145–46

hot dish, 146

hot dogs

    bean dogs, 16, *16*

    Coney Islands, 70, *70*

    corn dogs, 74, *74*

    Dixie (slaw) dogs, 91–92

    garbage plate, 119, *119*

    half smoke, 134, *134*

    Michigan, 174–75, *175*

    Newark (Italian), 187, *187*

    New York System and sauce (recipe), *188*, 188–89

    overview and history, *147*, 147–49, *148*

    red hots, *223*, 223–24

    rippers, 229, *229*

    Saugys, 235

    scrambled dogs, 237

    Sonoran, *248*, 248–49

    Texas weiners, 272, *272*

    turkey, 75

    white hots (porkers), 289, *289*

hot fish, 149, *149*

hot links, 149–50, *150*

hot truck (food delivery vehicle), 150, *150*

hot truck (sandwich, pizza), 150–53

Hubba water, 152, *152*

huevos rancheros, 152–53, *153*

Huguenot torte, 153

hummingbird cake, 153, *153*

hushpuppies, 154, *154*

ice cream

    gold brick sauce for, 122

    Grape-Nuts (recipe), 128

    turtle sundaes, 281, *281*

Indiana farm pie, 260

Indian pudding, 154–55, *155*

In-N-Out drive-ins, *155*, 155–56

Iowa pork chop, 156–57
Italian beef, 157, *157*
Italian hot dogs, 188–89, *189*
Italian ice, 157
Italian special, 140
Ithaca, New York, pizza, 204

jalapeño poppers, 53
jambalaya, 158
Jell-O salads, 71, 71
Jewish apple cake, 158–59, *159*
jibaritos, 159
joes, 160, *160*, 244
Johnson, John, 161, *161*
jonnycakes, 162, *162*
juicy Lucy, 162
jumbo slice, 163

Kentucky mutton barbecue, 10–11
Key lime pie, 163–64
klobasnikis, 165
Koenigsberg, Steve, 278
kolaches, 164–65, *165*
kringles, 165, *165*
kummelweck, 19

lamb
    spiedies (recipe), *253*, 253–54
lima bean suppers, 166, *166*
livermush, 166
liver puddin', 166
lobster
    chitterlings, 56
    (salad) roll, 167, *167*
    shore dinners, *239*, 239–40
loganberry juice, 167–68, *168*
loosemeats, *168*, 168–69
Lowcountry boil, 117, *117*

malasadas, 169, *169*
malts, 169–70
mangoes, 93
Manhattan chowder, 57

maple syrup
    sugar on snow, 259–60
maque choux, 170
margherita pizza, 208
marshmallows and Marshmallow Fluff
    Charlie Chaplin, 38, *38*
    fluffernutter, 110
    whoopie pie, 28–290, *289*
Maryland pizza, 204
matzoh brei, 170
meat and three, 171, *171*
meat pies, 172, *172*
medianoche, 173
mediatrice, la, 211
Memphis dry ribs (recipe), 227–28, *228*
Memphis pizza, 204, 204
Memphis wet ribs (recipe), 228, *228*
menudo, 173, *173*
metts (mettwursts), 174, *174*
Mexican itch, 271
Mexican pizza, 37
Mexican restaurants, 109
mezcal con gusano, 271
Michigan, 174–75, *175*
microwave ovens, 176–77
migas, 177–78, *178*
milk. *See also* shakes
    coffee, 64–65
    egg creams, 99, *99*
millionaire pie, 179, *179*
Minorcan chowder, 179
mint juleps, 180
morning buns, 180, *180*
Moxie, 181, *181*
Mr. Brown and Miss White, 181, *181*
muffalettas, 182, *182*
mullet, smoked, 22
mushrooms and butterflies, 182
mutton
    burgoo, 34, *34*
    Kentucky mutton barbecue, 10–11

nachos, 183

Navajo fry bread and taco (recipe), 183–85, *184*
Neapolitan pizza, 185–86, *186*
Newark hot dogs, 187, *187*
New England chowder, 57
New Haven pizza, 205, *205*
New York pizza, 205, *205*
New York System, *188*, 188–89
New York System sauce (recipe), 189
nonna pizza, 125, *125*
Norfolk-style seafood, 189
nuts
    boiled peanuts, 23, *23*
    hazelnuts (filberts), 102–3

Okie Sirloin, 111
olallieberry pie, 190
Old Forge pizza, 190
onion-fried burgers, 191
Oregon chowder, 57, *57*
oyster(s)
    Foch, 193
    hangtown fry, 137
    loaves, 191, *191*
    pan roasts, 193
    roasts, 192
    skillets, 192–93

pancakes
    cornmeal (jonnycakes), 162, *162*
    flannel cakes, 108
    ployes, 210, *210*
pan pizza, 207
pan roasts, 193
pasta
    barbecue spaghetti (recipe), 14–15, *15*
    chili mac (recipe), 53–54, *54*
    Cincinnati chili, 59
    Cincinnati five-way chili (recipe), 60–61, *61*
    toasted raviolis, 276
    ya-ka-mein, 291–92, *292*
pasties, 194, *194*

pastries
    beignet, 20, *20*
    doughboys, 94, *94*
    fried dough (recipe), 113–14
    kolaches and klobasnikis, 164–65, *165*
    kringles, 165, *165*
    malasadas, 169, *169*
    matzoh brei, 170
    morning buns, 180, *180*
    Navajo fry bread (recipe), 183–85, *184*
    ployes/ployeboys, 210, *210*
    Pop-Tarts, 212–13
    scones, 236
    sopaipillas, *249*, 249–50
    spoonbread, 255
peanut(s)
    boiled, 23, *23*
    soup, 194, *194*, 196
peanut butter
    fluffernutter, 110
    fried dough with, 113–14
Pepe, Frank, 195, *195*
pepperoni rolls, *196*, 196–97
perch, boned and buttered, 24, *24*
Pez, 197–98
pickle-sickles, 198–99
pico de gallo, 199, *199*
pies (savory)
    Fritos, 116, *116*
    meat, 172, *172*
    pizza pot, 207
    tamale, 267, *267*
    tomato, 277, *277*
pies (sweet)
    Boston cream, 26
    chess, 41–42
    fried, *115*, 115–16
    Key lime, 163–64
    millionaire and billionaire, 179, *179*
    olallieberry, 190
    shoofly, 239
    sour cream raisin, 252–53
    sugar (Indian farm, sugar cream), 260

pig pickin's, 200
pig sandwiches, *200*, 200–201
pigs in blankets, 165
pimiento cheese, 201, *201*
pirogue, 211
pitza, 202
pizza
    apizza, 3, *3*
    bakery, 4
    California, 203
    Chicago, 203, *203*
    clam casino, 287
    deep-dish, 85, *85*
    Detroit (square), 255
    goetta-topped, 122
    Grandma (nonna), 125, *125*
    Greek, 128–29, *129*
    grilled, 132, *132*
    hot truck sep pep (recipe), 151–53
    Ithaca, New York, 204
    jumbo slice, 163
    margherita, 208
    Maryland, 204
    Memphis, 204, *204*
    Mexican, 37
    Neapolitan, 185–86, *186*
    New Haven, 205, *205*
    New York, 205, *205*
    Old Forge, 190, *190*
    overview and history, 195, 202–3
    pan, 207
    Polish, 190
    pot pie, 85, 207
    soufflé, 85, 207
    Southwest, 206
    St. Louis, 206, *206*
    stuffed, 85, 207, 258–59
    terminology for, 208–9
    thin-crust, 207
    tomato pies, 277, *277*
    West Virginia, 206, 206
    white clam (recipe), *287*, 287–88
ployes/ployeboys, 210, *210*

po' boys, 211, *211*
Polish boy, 212
Polish pizza, 190, *190*
pony shoes, 143
poor man's ham/pâté, 166
popcorn
    Chicago mix, 42
    mushrooms and butterflies, 182
Pop-Tarts, 212–13
pork. *See also* hot dogs
    andouille sausage, 2
    banh mi, 5
    bean dog, 16, *16*
    Biloxi bacon, 22
    boudin sausage, 26–27
    brownies (burnt ends), *29*, 29–30
    carne adovada, 36, *36*
    carne seca, 37
    chitlins, 55–56
    city chicken, 62
    cochon de lait, 64
    Coney Islands (chili dogs), 70, *70*
    country ham, *76*, 76–77, *77*
    cracklin's, 79, *79*
    Cuban sandwiches, 82, *82*
    fried bologna, 111
    garbage plate, 119, *119*
    Gerber sandwich, 120
    goetta, 122, *122*
    hoppin' john, 142
    hot links, 149–50, *150*
    Iowa pork chop, 156–57
    jambalaya, 158
    lima bean supper, 166, *166*
    livermush, 166
    medianoche, 173
    metts, 174
    Mr. Brown and Miss White, 181, *181*
    pasties, 194
    pepperoni rolls, *196*, 196–97
    pig pickin's, 200
    pig sandwiches, *200*, 200–201
    pot likker (recipe), *214*, 214–15

pulled, barbecue, 8–9, *9*
red beans and rice, 220, *220*
rolls, 213–14
scrapple, 237
Sheboygan brats, 238
spiedies (recipe), *253*, 253–54
streak o' lean, 257–58
stuffed ham, 258, *258*
tenderloin (recipe), 268–70, *269*
whole hog barbecue, 9–10
porker, 289, *289*
porter steak, 226
Porubsky, Charlie (Porubsky's Grocery), 52, *52*
potato(es)
chips, 216–17, *217*
Ghetto fries, 120, *120*
hoppel poppel, 141, *141*
horseshoes, 143, *143*
poutine, 218, *218*
pot likker (recipe), *214*, 214–15
poutine, 218, *218*
Provel cheese, 218, *218*
pudding
Grape-Nuts, 127
Indian, 155–56, *156*
puffy tacos, 219, *219*
pulled pork barbecue, 8–9

Racioppi, James, 189, *189*
raw food movement, 219–20
red beans and rice, 220, *220*
red beer, 221
Red Bull, 221–22
red-eye gravy, 223
red flannel hash, 222, *222*
red hots, *223*, 223–24
Reuben sandwiches, 224
Rhode Island chicken dinners, 225
Rhode Island chowder, 57
ribs
baby back, 226
Memphis dry (recipe), *227*, 227–28

Memphis wet (recipe), 228, *228*
overview, 226
ribless, 226
spare, *226*, 227
St. Louis, 227
tips, 227
rice
dirty, 91, *91*
red beans and, 220, *220*
rippers, 229, *229*
river herring, 229–30
round table dining, 230–31
Rubio, Maria, 242
Rubio, Ralph, 105–6
rubs, dry, 97

salad bars, 231–32, *232*
salads
barbecue (recipe), *13*, 13–14
congealed, 71, *71*
five-cup (recipe), 107
snail, *246*, 246–47
topopo, 277–78, *278*
West Indies (recipe), 285–86, *286*
Sally's Apizza, 3
salsas
pico de gallo, 199, *199*
salt water taffy, 233
sandwiches. *See also* burgers; hot dogs
banh mi, 5
beef on weck, *19*, 19–20
breaded steak (recipe), 27–28
cheese steak, 39–40
chow mein, 59
Coney Islands, 70, *70*
Cuban, 82, *82*
devonshire, 86
fish, 68
fluffernutter, 110
French dip, 110–11
Gerber, 120
giardiniera for beef (recipe), 121, *121*
gorditas, 125, *125*

grinders, 140
hero, 139–40, *140*
hoagie, 140, *140*
hot brown, 86, 144, *144*
hot cheese, 145, *145*
hot truck pizza, 150–53
Italian beef, 157, *157*
jibaritos, 159
lobster roll, 167, *167*
loosemeats, *168*, 168–69
medianoche, 173
mediatrice, la, 211
oyster loaf, 191, *191*
oysters Foch, 193
pig, *200*, 200–201
pimiento cheese, 201, *201*
pirogue, 211
po' boys, 211, *211*
Polish boy, 212
Reuben, 224
Sheboygan brats, 238
sloppy joes, 244
spiedies (recipe), *253*, 253–54
St. Paul, 256
submarine (sub), 140
torpedo, 139
triple pigsickle, 226
wedges, 140
zep, 139
Santa Maria barbecue, 12–13
sauce(s)
    fry, 118
    gold brick, 122
    New York System (recipe), 189
    snoot (recipe), 247–48
sauerkraut balls (recipe), 233–34, *234*
Saugys, 235
sausage(s)
    andouille, 2
    boudin, 26–27
    gumbo, 132–33, *133*
    hanky pankies, 137
    hoppin' john, 142
    hot beef (dry links), 97
    hot links, 149–50, *150*
    jambalaya, 158
    kolaches, 164–65, *165*
    maque choux, 170
    metts, 174
    stuffies, 259
Sazerac, 235–36
schaum torte, 236
scones, 236
scrambled dogs, 237
scrapple, 237
seafood. *See also fish; specific types of
    shellfish*
    chowder, *56*, 56–58, *57*, *58*
    gumbo, 132–33, *133*
    Norfolk-style, 189
    shore dinner, *239*, 239–40
shakes
    coffee (frappe), 65
    date, 83–84
    malted milk, 169–70
    milk, 178
shave ice, 237–38
Sheboygan brats, 238
shoofly pie, 239, *239*
shore dinners, *239*, 239–40
shrimp
    étouffée, 101, *101*
    fajitas, 102
    Frogmore (Beaufort, Lowcountry boil)
        stew, 117, *117*
    maque choux, 170
    Shrimp De Jonghe (recipe), 240–41
    topopo salad, 277–78, *278*
Shrimp De Jonghe (recipe), 240–41
Shrine of the Holy Tortilla, 242
slammers, 271
slaw dogs, 91–92
sliders, 243, *243*
slingers, 243–44
sloppers, 130
sloppy joes, 160, *160*, 244

slow food movement, 244–45
slushburgers, 244
smoothies, 246
snacks
    boiled peanuts, 23, *23*
    boudin, 26–27
    California dip, 36
    Chicago mix, 42
    cracklin's, 79, *79*
    doughboys, 94, *94*
    fried dough (recipe), 113–14
    granola, *126*, 126–27
    mushrooms and butterflies, 182
    pickle-sickles, 198–99
    potato chips, 216–17, *217*
snail salads, *246*, 246–47
snoot, 247
snoot sauce (recipe), 247–48
Sonoran hot dogs, *248*, 248–49
sopaipillas, 249–50, *250*
soufflé pizza, 207
soul food, 251–52
soups. *See also* chilis; chowders; stews
    menudo, 173, *173*
    peanut (Tuskegee), 194, *194*, 196
    pot likker (recipe), *214*, 214–15
sour cream raisin pie, 252–53
sourdough starters, 139
sour oranges, 93
southern Illinois chowder, 94
Southern New England chowder, 57
Southern New England clear broth clam
    chowder (recipe), 58, *58*
Southwest pizza, 206
spaghetti, barbecue (recipe), 14–15, *15*
spare ribs, *226*, 227
spiedies (recipe), *253*, 253–54
sponge candy, 254, *254*
spoonbread, 255
square pizza, 255
St. Louis pizza, 206, *206*
St. Louis ribs, 227
St. Paul, 256

steak
    breaded (recipe), *27*–28
    cheese, 39–40
    chicken-fried, 43–44
    porter, 226
steamed cheeseburgers, *256*, 256–57
stews. *See also* chilis; chowders
    Brunswick (recipe), *30*, 30–31
    burgoo, 34, *34*
    chicken booyah, 42
    fish (cioppino), 61
    Frogmore or Beaufort (Lowcountry
        boil), 117, *117*
    gumbo, 132–33, *133*
    jambalaya, 158
stone crab, 257
streak o' lean, 257–58
stuffed ham, 258, *258*
stuffed pizza, 258–59
stuffies, 259
submarine (sub) sandwiches, 140
sugar on snow, 259–60
sugar (cream) pie, 260
supermarkets, 260–62
sustainable, 262–63
sweet tea (recipe), 263–64, *264*

tacos
    fillings terminology, 272
    fish (recipe), 105–6, *106*
    Navajo (recipe), *184*, 184–85
    puffy, 219, *219*
taffy, salt water, 233
tamale(s)
    green corn, 131–32
    overview and history, *265*, 265–67, *266*
    pie, 267, *267*
Tang, 267–68, *268*
tea, sweet (recipe), 263–64, *264*
television shows, 17–18, 46–47, 72
tenderloin (recipe), 268–70, *269*
tequila, 270–71
testicles, fried, 123

Texas beef barbecue, 11–12
Texas chili (recipe), 50–51, *51*
Texas water, 152, *152*
Texas weiners, 272, *272*
Tex-Mex terminology, 272–73
theme restaurants, 273–75
1000 Islands dressing, 275–76
throwed rolls, 276
tips, rib, 227
toasted raviolis (T ravs), 276
tomato(es)
    fried green, 115
    pie, 277, *277*
Topeka chili (recipe), 52, *52*
topopo salads, 277–76, *278*
tortes, schaum, 236
travelin' man, 278
T ravs, 276
triple pigsickle, 226
turkey
    devonshire, 86
    hot brown, 144, *144*
    hot dogs, 75
    Sheboygan brats, 238
Turner, Ray, *279*, 279–80
turtles, 281, *281*
Tuskegee soup, 194, *194*, 196

Twinkies, 282

Uglesich, Anthony and Gail, 283, *283*
Uglesich, John, 283

velvet, 178
visions, religious, 242

walleye, 284
wedges, 140
Weight Watchers, 284–85
West Indies salad (recipe), 285–86, *286*
West Virginia pizza, 206, *206*
whiskey ditch, 91
white clam pizza (recipe), *287*, 287–88
white hots, 289, *289*
whole hog barbecue, 9–10
whoopie pie, *289*, 289–90
Wilbur, 244
Wonder Bread, 290–91
Worcester Dining Car Company Diner, 87

ya-ka-mein, 291–92, *292*
yip-yips, 244

zep, 139

ABOUT THE AUTHORS

Jane and Michael Stern write books about travel, food, and popular culture. They are best known for their *Roadfood* books, website, and magazine columns, in which they seek out restaurants serving American regional specialties. They appear weekly on Lynne Rossetto Kasper's public radio program *The Splendid Table,* are contributing editors at *Saveur* magazine, and maintain the website Roadfood.com. They have won three James Beard Foundation Awards and the James Beard Perrier-Jouet Award for lifetime achievement. The Sterns' books on American popular culture include *Elvis World* (1987) and *The Encyclopedia of Bad Taste* (1990). Their memoir, *Two for the Road: Our Love Affair With American Food,* was published in 2006. They live in Connecticut. Visit them at www.roadfood.com.